Karl Barth,
a Theological Legacy

Karl Barth,
a Theological Legacy

Eberhard Jüngel

Translated
by Garrett E. Paul

The Westminster Press
Philadelphia

English translation © 1986 The Westminster Press

The material from which this translation was made was published in *Barth-Studien,* by Eberhard Jüngel. © 1982 by Benziger Verlag, Zürich-Köln, and Gütersloher Verlagshaus Gerd Mohn, Gütersloh.

Book design by Gene Harris

First American Edition

Published by The Westminster Press®
Philadelphia, Pennsylvania

PRINTED IN THE UNITED STATES OF AMERICA

9 8 7 6 5 4 3 2

Quotations from Karl Barth, *Church Dogmatics*, are copyright © T. & T. Clark, Edinburgh, and are used by permission.

Quotations from James M. Robinson, ed., *The Beginnings of Dialectic Theology* (translated from Jürgen Moltmann, ed., *Anfänge der dialektischen Theologie*), are used by permission of Chr. Kaiser Verlag, Munich, and Theologischer Verlag, Zurich.

For Adalbert Bohle
on his
sixtieth birthday

Library of Congress Cataloging-in-Publication Data

Jüngel, Eberhard.
    Karl Barth, a theological legacy.

    Translation of selections from: Barth-Studien.
    Bibliography: p.
    1. Barth, Karl, 1886–1968. I. Title.
BX4827.B3J782513 1986   230'.044'0924   86-7793
ISBN 0-664-24031-3 (pbk.)

Contents

Translator's Preface

Translators' prefaces usually include observations on the difficulty of the task of translation, often coupled with an insistence that one who has not attempted the task cannot really appreciate how challenging it is, and urging that those who can should consult the original. The reader who turns to this preface expecting similar comments will not be disappointed. Translation *is* a difficult task, and those who can *should* consult the original, especially for important or obscure passages.

I have striven for a rendering that is accurate, lucid, and readable, all without departing from the style of the author more than necessary. Where these goals have come into conflict, accuracy has won out. I have also tried to be consistent in using the same English words for key German terms, and in following established translations of Barth's technical terminology. I have used nonsexist language wherever possible so far as consistent with accuracy. Existing English translations of works cited by Jüngel have been used whenever possible (sometimes with minor stylistic changes). Revisions of existing translations are indicated in the notes by the word "revised." When a completely new translation has been deemed necessary, it is indicated by the words "my translation."

Readers of this book will find thorough scholarship and painstaking argument. Eberhard Jüngel has applied the same hermeneutic to his study of Barth that Barth (see pp. 75–76 below) applied to Paul: "I must press forward to the point where insofar as possible I confront the riddle of the *subject matter . . .* , where I can almost forget that I am not the author, where I have almost understood him so well that I let him speak in my name, and can myself speak in his name." Jüngel, in a refreshing departure from some of the current fashions in interpretation, repeatedly returns to Barth's *intention.* The result is a strong and persuasive restatement of major themes in Barth's theology: the otherness of God, the humanity of God, gospel and law.

The essay titled "Barth's Life and Work" is a most helpful contribution to our understanding of Barth. It is particularly valuable for the attention it devotes to the later Barth. Jüngel's extensive treatment of

Barth's anthropology throughout this book will also contribute much to our understanding of this sometimes neglected aspect of Barth's thought. In "Gospel and Law," Jüngel enters the debate between Barth and the Luther scholars who took him to task for his development of this theme. It becomes apparent that here too Barth was more a disciple of Calvin than of Luther, although he departed from both. It may safely be predicted that the Lutherans will remain unconvinced by Jüngel's essay, but also that it will continue to fuel the debate.

A particular target for Jüngel's criticism is Friedrich-Wilhelm Marquardt, who, like Jüngel, served Barth as an assistant for one of the volumes of the *Church Dogmatics*. Marquardt draws Jüngel's fire in the Introduction and in "Barth's Life and Work," and the entire essay on "Barth's Theological Beginnings" is largely a rejoinder to Marquardt's controversial book *Theologie und Sozialismus. Das Beispiel Karl Barths* * [Theology and Socialism: The Example of Karl Barth]. Thus, when Jüngel observes (p. 91 below) that Karl Barth's beginnings [*initia*] have already become the subject of controversy, he is certainly referring to Marquardt's argument (p. 86 of his book) that the *initium* of Karl Barth's theology was his encounter with social struggle and socialist praxis while he was a pastor in Safenwil.

Marquardt's book was originally an inaugural dissertation submitted to the faculty of the *Kirchliche Hochschule* in Berlin, where it was rejected. The rejection engendered the controversy to which Jüngel refers, during which Helmut Gollwitzer, himself a well-known Barth scholar, resigned from that faculty. The thesis was later accepted by the Free University of Berlin, where Marquardt is now an Assistant Professor. In his book, Marquardt protests against the abstract treatment, free of political commitment, that has characterized Barth scholarship until now. He argues that Barth's theology is inherently socialist and that it presupposes a socialist praxis. Thus Marquardt concludes that, for Barth, " 'God' can no longer be thought apart from revolution" (p. 159); that praxis takes the place of ontology in Barth's thought (pp. 321–326); and that "Barth came to his concept of God by way of social experiences, socialistically interpreted, and it must be interpreted accordingly" (p. 333). Jüngel's insistence (pp. 101ff. below) that Barth thoroughly depoliticized the concept of revolution in the second edition of his commentary on Romans, and his conclusion that for Barth "the political is surely a predicate of theology" and not the other way around, are both directed against Marquardt's position. By no means does Jüngel wish to paint a portrait of an unpolitical or nonsocialist Barth; but he does seek to show that Barth's theology is the key to understanding his politics,

---

*Munich: Chr. Kaiser Verlag; Mainz: Matthias-Grünewald Verlag, 1972.

not the reverse. Marquardt's book has not been translated, but his essay "Socialism in the Theology of Karl Barth" is available in English.*

It is my happy duty to thank several persons who have helped me with this translation. My wife, Betsy, has given me cheerful support throughout this project, and our sons, Christoph and Hans, have usually accepted the more frequent than usual absence of their father. Lisa Dahill, a former student at Gustavus Adolphus College, furnished a most helpful draft translation of the essay "Barth's Theological Beginnings," which I subsequently revised. Janine Genelin of the Secretarial Center at Gustavus Adolphus College endured confusing manuscripts as well as countless revisions and retypings, furnishing thoroughly professional copies in return. The staff of the Folke Bernadotte Memorial Library was most helpful in obtaining many books and articles I found it necessary to consult. Jack Clark, Will Freiert, and the late Sven Langsjoen, colleagues at Gustavus Adolphus College, and Theodore Hiebert, now of Harvard University, provided helpful advice. The editorial staff at the Westminster Press provided most of the translations of Latin and Greek terms and phrases used in the original.

GARRETT E. PAUL

St. Peter, Minnesota
July 15, 1986

---

*Friedrich-Wilhelm Marquardt, "Socialism in the Theology of Karl Barth," in George Hunsinger, ed., *Karl Barth and Radical Politics* (Philadelphia: Westminster Press, 1976), pp. 47–76. Along with the essays in this book one may consult the uncomplimentary review of *Theologie und Sozialismus* by H. Hartwell, *Scottish Journal of Theology* 28 (1975), pp. 63–72.

Introduction

A great man condemns the world to explain him. It was Hegel who said this, and his own life is evidence of the truth of his remark. His observation holds true for others who are great as well.

Karl Barth, although he rejected the application of the category "great" to noteworthy theologians, was himself a great man, and he compels others to explain him. I doubt, however, that we are really "condemned" to explain him. It could just as well be said that a person is "condemned" to being explained. At any rate, the study and discussion of Barth's writings has always been, for me, an occasion for joy. Their truth claims are always one-sided, but never one-dimensional. The theological insight expressed in these writings draws wholly and completely on the mystery of the Word of God and yet penetrates deeply into the secular world. And so, for the reader of these texts, spiritual and worldly understanding increase in the same measure.

The essays on Karl Barth assembled for this volume have arisen from these literary encounters. They reflect upon the seductive potential which—in both the beneficial and the perilous senses—lies hidden in the theology of this great man, and which is part of his greatness. The critical conclusions that grow out of such encounters are part of the specifically dogmatic task and, to that extent, are a different matter altogether. Nevertheless, the direction in which my criticism of Barth's theology tends will not remain hidden from the attentive reader. It will immediately become clear that this criticism proceeds in a manner entirely different from the customary earlier objections.

The writings of Karl Barth were seductive from the beginning. They have remained so. One reason for this is the extraordinarily expressive power of their language, which characteristically distinguishes it from the language of scholarly discourse. Barth's writings are also anything but one-dimensional in content. They impress; they attract and repel; they seduce both their defenders and their detractors. And this is something different from the creation of a school—although he has not been spared that as well. Precisely because the writings from the pen of Karl

Barth are not one-dimensional and thus also to that extent are seductive and impressive, they demand something more than to be read with approval (or rejection) and then to be cited as attractive (or repulsive). They demand to be studied.

The study of Barth certainly cannot be done with the intention of reducing the impressive language of his writings to the one-dimensionality of what passes for scholarly expression. To study Barth means, surely, to read his writings with something other in view than the simple alternative of acceptance or rejection. But this "something other" cannot mean that the reader should excuse himself from real participation in the concerns which those writings seek to raise. Thus it is quite in order that the theology of Barth continues to provoke fierce agreement and passionate rejection—while, significantly, it does this in constantly changing contexts. To study something is not to neutralize it.

But it is surely essential that the study of Barth's writings not become one-dimensional, to say nothing of sectarian, whether with a narrow-minded yes or with an equally narrow-minded no. Barth studies must be protected from the formation—today in one way and tomorrow in another—of parties of defenders and detractors.

Not the least task in the study of Barth, therefore, is to highlight the inner connection of Barth's language with his "subject matter," i.e., with the new discovery of the Word of God as gospel and judgment, so that the dialogue with and about the great theologian's views can become both more relaxed and more intensive.

Indeed, the understanding that both the form and the content of expression in Barth's work form an inner unity, and that his language changes along with changes in theological outlook, rules out any substitution of the mere repetition of Barth's style for the careful study his insights require.

Without a doubt, Barth's theology had style, great style. That was true for the first edition of *The Epistle to the Romans,* which "opened the way [for him] into the heaven of academics,"[1] and it was even more so for the second edition and for the lectures and essays that followed it. These early writings spoke not only with the expressionist language of their time but also with a vigorous recklessness that emphasized the new, the new which permeated Barth's thought and which, through his writings, would gain a hearing from theologians and the church. One should not be misled by the famous closing words of the foreword to the first edition of the commentary on Romans, that this book has "time to—wait."[2] From the start it surged ahead, for time itself could wait no longer. What Hegel had said about his own time and work more than a hundred years before was also true in its own way for Barth's time: "Ours is a birthtime and a period of transition into a new era. Spirit has broken with the world it has hitherto inhabited and imagined [and is] dissolving bit by bit the structure of the previous world, whose tottering state is only hinted at by isolated symptoms. The frivolity and boredom which unsettle the established order, the vague foreboding of something unknown, these are the heralds of change. The gradual crumbling that left unaltered the face of the whole is cut short by a bolt of lightning, which, in a single flash, illuminates the features of the new world."[3] Barth's *Epistle to the Romans* was such a bolt of lightning, rendering visible a new theological world. "The mighty voice of Paul was new to me: and if to me, no doubt to many others."[4] Barth's written style correspondingly broke with that of his theological predecessors in such a way that it led Adolf von Harnack to the ironic observation that Paul and Luther "and even my colleague Barth" were for him "primarily not subjects, but objects of scientific theology."[5]

For his part, the older Barth, looking back—not without irony—on Harnack's assertion, read it as a kind of prophecy which by then had actually begun "to be fulfilled word for word,"[6] insofar as his theology had in the intervening years become the object of a small library of studies.

During those years his theology had actually made history and, moreover, had been thoroughly reconstructed many times. The mature fruit of this process was the *Church Dogmatics,* which itself frequently started anew from the beginning. Barth emphasized most strongly that no one who really wished to understand him should become fixed on the so-called dialectical phase of his theology but should proceed to the substantive dogmatic exposition. He certainly remained true to the "departure for new shores" of those earlier days, but he was not content with the gesture of departure; he also wanted to arrive at the new shores. But that meant a commitment to the elaboration of the new, which involved another, more far-reaching transformation in style. He himself deplored the lack (once again to use Hegel's words) of "a breadth and depth of content in the newly emerging shape"; and he deplored, if not "even more," certainly no less, the lack of "the articulation of form" through which alone a claim for the binding character of the new theological knowledge could be made. "Without such articulation, Science lacks universal intelligibility and gives the appearance of being the esoteric possession of a few individuals."[7] Barth's path from *The Epistle to the Romans* to the *Church Dogmatics,* with all its carefully considered self-corrections and turnabouts, was consistent. From the enthusiastic (with negative or positive undertones), apostrophizing, prophetic, and powerful expression of the early writings, to the smoothly flowing forms of thought and speech in the vast (all too vast!) *Church Dogmatics,* the metamorphosis was direct and consistent. It is reminiscent of the inner consistency with which Schleiermacher traveled his path from the *Speeches on Religion* to *The Christian Faith.* The description of the momentous changes wrought by Barth's thought in terms of the history of a self-consistent change in literary style should be one of the most interesting tasks for Barth scholarship. This is a task that has received only scant attention, apart from that of Hans Urs von Balthasar, who in this respect, as in so many others, constitutes a laudable exception.

This is probably related to the fact that Barth scholarship—and here I include everything that passes for Barth scholarship—is particularly concerned to reduce the extraordinary wealth of his theology to a few meager structural principles, so that his theology may be totally circumscribed and then commended or refuted.[8] In this respect, it is astonishing what has happened, especially since Barth's death. Perhaps I may be indulged if I confess that I am quite perplexed by not a few of the publications that come to mind in this connection.

I marvel at the "reconstructions of the construction" of Barth's theology, which in Germany come primarily from Munich. They see through Barth's theology and pronounce it to be simply a genuine product of the spirit of its time, even though it was directed against that spirit. In this connection I should also like to expose, as an offense against good taste, the thesis that Barth's theology had a fascist structure. Surely theology can stand as a critic of its time only insofar as it is a child of its time. But in light of the work of Karl Barth this should not even be an issue.

I truly envy the imagination of the socialist interpretation of Barth (which in Germany comes primarily from West Berlin) and its practical-sounding yet preposterous theorems. In this connection I should like to continue to make a distinction between the artifice of word association and the strenuous task of interpretation and, in case of doubt, to prefer historical and logical argumentation to any sort of undisciplined explanation. Surely there is something like an "institutionally reflective form" to theological concepts—but this should not, above all in light of the theology of Karl Barth, even be an issue.

It still seems to me that in both cases an abstraction is allowed to eclipse Barth's dogmatic line of argument, and a thinker desires to be judged by his arguments! Barth's express warning *"Latet periculum in generalibus"* ["Danger lurks in generalities"] has been all too easily ignored by such interpretations, to their own detriment. Therefore, neither my admitted admiration (what systematician would not all too gladly also be the dialectician who understands an author better than the author himself!) nor my obvious envy (what theologian does not want to become "practical" as quickly as possible!) deter me from the classic European style of taking the text at its word, as we once used to say. The Barth studies submitted in this volume attempt to do this.[9]

This is a collection of lectures and essays, some of which have appeared previously. Insofar as Barth himself had read them, they met with his approval—broken only occasionally by certain disagreements. The survey titled "Barth's Life and Work" is an expanded version of what appeared in shorter form as an article in the [Krause-Müller] *Theologische Realenzyklopädie.* The brief essay "The Royal Man" grew out of the first seminar I conducted on Barth's theology. The studies on "Barth's Theological Beginnings" and "Gospel and Law" appear here for the first time. The first essay begins the book with reflections on the occasion of the death of Karl Barth. The entire book, to which my colleagues Dr. Hans-Anton Drewes and two theological students, Matthias Wünsche and Jörg-Michael Bohnet, gave valuable help, should serve to complement my treatise *Gottes Sein ist im Werden.* Like that little book, these Barth studies also have no other goal than, through painstaking interpretation, to attest to the theological fruitfulness of a thinker who knew always to begin at the *beginning,* the beginning which faith knows by the name *Jesus Christ.*

I recall with thanks the two theological teachers who induced me (certainly in very different ways) to make an intensive study of Karl Barth, and who to that extent may be held responsible for these Barth studies: Ernst Fuchs and Heinrich Vogel.

This same debt is also owed by many former students of the theology of freedom, who have become students not of a "school" but of the Holy Scriptures. This volume is inscribed with a dedication to a colleague in the Faculty of Medicine who, in his own way, demonstrates the truth of a concept that Barth borrowed from the early Protestant fathers: "that every Christian, as such, . . . is also a *theologian*" and, indeed, "can and must be a *good* theologian."[10]

EBERHARD JÜNGEL

Tübingen, December 10, 1981

Karl Barth:
A Tribute at His Death[1]

Karl Barth lived intensively. Until the very end he was alive in every inch of his rugged spirit and weakened flesh. His life was filled with an uncommon presence of mind which was in no way antagonistic to the presence of the body. The Pauline wish to depart was alien to him. When a serious illness forced him to face his own death, he gave it the same sideways glance[2] that he had given theologically to the powers of darkness. The light which shines in the darkness interested him more than the darkness. He thought it more important to dwell on the riches of the eternal God than on the somber dominion of death. Karl Barth lived with enthusiasm.

His most personable vitality, his incomparably vital personality in word and deed, will be missed by many, friends and opponents alike. His absence is already evident. Who was this man who commands the world's attention once again, now in his death? What made his life noteworthy?

Was he the last true theologian? Did he open new theological doors? Does an epoch in the history of theology come to a close with his death? Was it only a tentative beginning of a future for theological existence which began with him? He reached for the heights in his thinking, speaking, and acting, for the sake of a humankind which cries out to God from the depths, depths far deeper than usually recognized. But did his reach exceed his grasp? Will his gigantic output be of any help to a humanity which cries no longer to God, but simply cries to itself and consoles itself? Or did he think so highly of the God who stoops down, and did he therefore speak so confidently and act so uncompromisingly, because being hard beset taught him not only to pray, but also to think, speak, and act in that way? Everything depends on, and everything must return to, the small, feeble sigh in which we say to God, "Ah, yes!" Barth spoke of this while he was working on one part of a volume of his *Church Dogmatics*—a part which numbered 1,011 pages.[3] Did this "Ah, yes" animate his life? Who was Karl Barth?

Beyond a doubt he was a great man. But "great" is surely not a theological term. The Gospels speak with irony about those who would be great in the Kingdom of Heaven. And, in fact, all human greatness remains ambiguous, ironic, and ambivalent as long as it is thought to have no origin other than itself. The greatness of a great person becomes clear only when we recognize that that person became great through the greatness of something else. One must recognize in such a life an element of passivity, a kind of dispassionate passion, no matter how active that life may be. It is for this that we look when we ask what made Karl Barth into the great man he surely was.

To inquire into the source of Barth's greatness is to inquire into his history. From this point at the end of his life, we must look back with his eyes into that history, into his works, and, above all, into what befell him. Only in this way will we be able to say who he was. Of course, "no one can share with another the peculiar way that he looks back on his past life."[4] It was Goethe who said that; thus a great man warned against such audacity. And his warning is not to be contradicted by the belief in the equality of all before God. We must take the warning seriously as we reflect on such an extraordinarily rich life. It is proper also for Christians to allow a great person among themselves to be great—and to be himself.

When he was advanced in years, Karl Barth looked back thankfully on his long life. For him, however, thankfulness was indistinguishable from trenchant self-criticism: not criticism here and thankfulness there, but simultaneously and utterly both together. That was the peculiar way of looking back on his past life that no one can share with him. Right up to the last theological discussions, he asked himself and others where his work was not balanced and where he may have neglected something decisive. And this was not done in vague generalities, but as part of the most specific cross-examination of his own writings.

In this self-criticism there was not the slightest hint of excessive modesty. Barth was by no means only self-critical. He was also a polemicist whose criticism of others was exacting and sometimes outrageous. He hated false modesty and was not very fond of more than a little genuine modesty either. Only those are modest who have reason to be,* he would sometimes say with his Basel accent.

Barth's self-criticism was rather a reflection of his relationship to the subject matter of theology, and it consisted in always beginning anew with that subject matter. That is what made him great. Few theologians were so far from completing their work at the end than was Karl Barth.

---

*Literally, "Only rags are modest."—Trans.

For him, forging ahead in theology meant nothing other than starting again with the beginning. It is no accident that his *Church Dogmatics* is so large.

The subject which Barth contemplated for an entire lifetime is a simple one. His entire life revolved around a single word: the Yes that God says to himself—the Yes that (because he says it to himself) he says also to the human race. To this divine Yes, Barth replied with a thoughtful Yes. And, for the sake of this Yes, he said a No. Karl Barth brought the Word of God to light as the word Yes. That was his accomplishment.

His theological work began with the realization of the incomparability of the Yes of God. In order to be able to say an energetic Yes, he considered it necessary to say an even more energetic No. Barth's theological and political discernment were formed in his realization that the Yes of God heard in Jesus Christ, and only in him, could not be exchanged or supplemented. We are indebted to his realization of the unsurpassability of the divine Yes for what may be his most significant work: the doctrine of election. From his realization of the humanity of the God who says Yes came his masterwork, the Christology. And with the realization of how the divine Yes can be answered in a Christian life, his unfinished lifework came to its end.

Barth's lifework was a path of realization. On this path there are no finished results. The fundamental movement of his theological thought was always to return to the beginning. In his theology, to go forward always meant to begin once again with the beginning, which only as the beginning can also be the goal, only as the Alpha can also be the Omega. The essence of Barth's theological substance was his readiness for the beginning. That readiness kept him from becoming a Barthian, and led him from one realization to the next.

Was it this perpetual return to the beginning that made this scholar so uncommonly human and refreshing? Was it his temporal rejoicing over the eternal beginning that made a visitor sense in his presence something like, to use a pagan expression, a *daimonion?* Was that the source of his enigmatic, virile charm? Is that why he could only rarely laugh at himself? Was that the root of his determination to break with received wisdom, a determination which always produced outrage? Is that why he took criticism and opposition for granted and even relished them? And why he loved Mozart and always only Mozart?

In every case, the secret of Barth's theological substance is his well-practiced readiness to return to the beginning. "Theological work is distinguished from other kinds of work by the fact that anyone who desires to do it . . . [must] every day, in fact every hour, begin anew at the beginning."[5] Possessed by an irrepressible enthusiasm for the subject matter of theology, Barth diligently adhered to this insight. Diligence was the source of his genius. He was supremely a worker. He remained a man who was always beginning.

By this beginning, to which the theologian must always return, Barth meant a concrete, specific, understandable beginning. The general question of the beginning had little impact on him. *"Latet periculum in generalibus!"* "Danger lurks in generalities!" Barth's theology embodies a decisive turn in the direction of the particular, specific, and concrete, in order to make the universal into something concrete and specific as well. That, along with his rare gift of concentration and attentiveness, accounts for his historical inquisitiveness. In the beginning was the Word. Words must be audible. Barth took the beginning to be concrete, for the beginning has a name: Jesus Christ. Always to begin anew with Jesus Christ—that, for Barth, is certainly how one goes forward and, in going forward, can encounter the unexpected. To the end, without compromise, he held fast to this concrete beginning.

A proper theology makes no compromises. This distinguishes it from church governance, as well as from other things. Barth's theology is a theology without compromise. Was it to make room for the truth that he kept at such a great distance from the spirit of the times? The rich diversity of his linguistic expressions should warn us against thoughtlessly repeating accepted opinions, a practice which, paradoxically, is almost unique to theologians. It can be seen that this man looked into the world deeply. He demands to be read. And the refusal to compromise translates into concentration. When one concentrates on one thing, it does not follow that he or she is one-sided for long; it may be that he or she is a one-sided enemy of abstraction. Barth's refusal to compromise is directed against theological abstraction.

"Theology knows and practices only one truth."[6] Attacks on others and corrections of oneself serve this goal. The many twists and turns of Barth's theology; the thunderous attack against the so-called cultural Protestantism of both the Left and the Right; the retraction of the first *Dogmatics* volume; the break with his comrades-in-arms who had first gathered together "between the times"; the scornful "No!" directed against his friend Emil Brunner in Zurich; the vehement revulsion against the "Century of the Church" proclaimed by Otto Dibelius; and the decisive political struggle for the authority of freedom, not in any way a deterioration into something other, but rather with the utmost theological stringency, are all to be understood as the workings of an unfettered, concentrated mind. He concentrated on the gospel, from whence the law can be understood, and on the Yes of God, which says No only in the context of Yes.

Barth assailed the church and the world with the gospel. He pressed for enlightenment, not by the light of nature, but enlightenment by the light of the gospel. This assault distinguished him not only from liberal theology (as is well known), but also from every positivist orthodoxy (although this fact is blithely overlooked or obscured). When at the very last the man already acclaimed as a "church father of the twentieth century" directed his energetic attack against the doctrine and practice of Baptism, it was not only the Lutheran church leadership that held in him contempt. When a German professor of dogmatics, anxious for the cause of Christian unity, urged Barth not to publish his doctrine of Baptism, he reacted with scorn. "No dogma or article of the Creed can be simply taken over untested by theology from ecclesiastical antiquity. . . . There is no heresy worse than such orthodoxy!"[7]

The evangelical attack on the church and the world in the Theological Declaration of the Synod of Barmen was framed in a lapidary style. Every ecumenical appeal to Karl Barth will have to demonstrate its legitimacy by this touchstone: the uncompromising Yes to Jesus Christ.

Barth himself described the fundamental act of his theological existence with an Augustinian formulation: *Credo, ut intelligam,* "I believe in order to understand." He gave pointed expression to each part of that motto. *Credo*—that meant freedom from every dictation of an impertinent understanding; *ut intelligam*—that meant freedom for pertinent understanding. And Barth sought understanding. His faith sought knowledge. *Fides quaerens intellectum* [Faith seeking understanding] was the title he borrowed from Anselm of Canterbury for his favorite book. Barth's theology is intelligent. For him, the Holy Spirit was the dearest friend of a healthy human intelligence.[8] A profound impatience with human stupidity permeates many of Barth's writings. And the opinion that "we can't know anything" angered him just as much as the presumption that we can know everything. The renunciation of all understanding and the presumption of all understanding were, for him, simply two sides of the same foolishness. Barth's theology is intelligent precisely in that it understands its limits and, within those limits, takes great pleasure in knowledge. His theology won its freedom within these limits.

Barth's lifework is a free theology worthy of a free man. This is ultimately due to the fact that his work was nothing less than an essay in the theology of freedom, speaking of the sovereign freedom of a gracious God and of the justified freedom of the human being who receives that grace. Barth consciously responded with a Yes to both this freedom of God and this freedom of the human being. And it was on their behalf that he said No. He was an enemy of the enemies of freedom.

He was never shy about recruiting friends of freedom. Even in the last year of his life he sought and found the friendship of an author who had impressed him with his free candor. And the express purpose of his teaching was to cultivate students who would be friends of freedom.

The success of this undertaking is attested by the fact that Barth found friends of freedom, not only in Protestant Christianity, nor even simply in all Christian confessions, but even beyond the pale of the church. They by no means had to become Barthians.

The freedom of God: for Barth, that was God himself. The unmistakable greatness of his theology arises from his unwavering intention to think of God himself. The polemical aspect of his theology is directed against all surrogates. No idea, no ideology, no pious postulate, and especially no theological concept may take the place of God. God confides in no one. He speaks for himself. He reveals himself. Barth uncompromisingly demanded that we think of God himself!

It is only when our attention is directed to God himself that we can correspondingly think of the human being as a self. Here too, "the human being" is no general conception of humanity, no ideal humanity, no theoretical or practical substitute, no liturgical or sacramental surrogate, but the free person himself or herself, a living, irreplaceable, responding being.

Karl Barth lived a life of response. He was himself. His entire life and thought as a whole announced that "God" is a cheerful word.

With nothing more than this announcement, Karl Barth edified the community of Jesus Christ and helped to shape a century. At the very least, Barth's lifework was to provoke us—and not just us theologians—to continue to build in the same way.

One

Barth's Life and Work

Karl Barth is the most significant Protestant theologian since Schleiermacher, whom he sought to overcome and to whom he nevertheless remains indebted in many ways.[1] Barth's personal and literary influence profoundly changed the shape of Christian theology across confessional boundaries, significantly altered the direction of the Protestant church, and also left an unmistakable imprint on the political and cultural life of the twentieth century. Barth defied both the enduring and the passing currents of his time, even as he was conditioned by them. His unmistakable genius was a product of the times and their need for renewal, and at the same time it was a force behind the changes that occurred during this century. The developing controversy over whether his work marked the end of European and Eurocentric theological history (he himself willingly acknowledged that he was a child of the nineteenth century that he criticized so vehemently), or was rather a historical turning point, revolves around a false dichotomy. Barth's worldwide influence is not to be explained ultimately in terms of a contradiction between continuity and upheaval or between keeping tradition and breaking tradition. Both the radical title "spiritual revolutionary" as well as the patriarchal title "church father of the twentieth century" reflect the same misunderstanding. Barth's theological objectivity left that conflict behind. He understood himself as neither a revolutionary nor a church father, but rather as a witness to Jesus Christ after the manner of "theological existence," which he defined in 1933 as "our existence in the church, as we are called to be preachers and teachers in the church."[2]

During his lifetime, Barth's greatest influence came more from his actual pronouncements and his momentous impact on the theological "climate," both of which arose out of his theological existence, rather than from the *Church Dogmatics,* which was the most significant literary result of that existence. This is a factor which must not be neglected in research on Barth's influence on the immediate past. In addition, lighthearted and yet thoughtful recollections of Barth's life are to be found in his writings. The forewords and scattered autobiographical digressions in the *Church Dogmatics,* along with a number of essays, addresses, and letters, comprise a personal literary genre that forestalls any attempt to isolate Barth's writings and teachings from his person or historical situation. It is impossible to appreciate the cogency of Barth's truth-claims without understanding his theological biography, just as it is impossible to regard his writings as only the embodiment of his theological existence. This is attested by the fact that many of Barth's publications are clearly occasional writings and that every part of the *Church Dogmatics,* and several other books as well, were initially delivered as lectures.

His Life

Karl Barth was tied to the Basel theological milieu on both his father's side and his mother's side. When he was born in Basel on May 10, 1886, his father, Johann Friedrich Barth, had just taken a position on the faculty of a seminary which had been founded ten years earlier in express opposition to the liberal theology of the University. Barth's father had been one of the last students of J. T. Beck, and his grandfather had been one of the first; Beck's theology had a passing influence on Barth. Barth's mother was Anna Katharina née Sartorius. Her father was a pastor committed to Reformed orthodoxy. His father, who had a rationalist orientation, had left Germany to become a professor at the University, but he lost his position in 1832 because of a drinking problem. Barth, who was also related on his mother's side to Jacob Burckhardt, was a child of the urbane traditions of the Basel middle class, from which he later distanced himself.[3]

The spirit of Basel made its deepest impression on him in the simple form of the children's songs written in the local German dialect by Abel Burckhardt. Even in his later years, Barth gratefully recalled these songs, through which he received his "first theological instruction." In their "homely naturalness," they brought home the reality of the truth of faith and led him back "to the matter itself." It was for this reason that Barth later memorialized Burckhardt in the *Church Dogmatics.*[4]

The family moved to Bern in 1889, when Barth's father was called to succeed Adolf Schlatter. Here Barth spent his schooldays and began his advanced studies. The child was not reared without some "clashes," which originated primarily in his mother's maxim that one should practice love "while continuing to lay down the law."[5] This raised some questions for the boy, but they were always met—after the punishment —with a positive response: his mother's purpose was to raise a child "in a . . . good Christian spirit."[6] Recent depth-psychological interpretations have explained Barth's later theological departures and developments as arising from situations of conflict with his parents.[7] But such interpretations are plausible, if at all, only in reference to his mother and especially to his grandmother Sartorius.[8] The attempt to explain Barth's break with liberal theology as "deferred obedience" to his father has no more plausibility than the hypothesis that Barth, in his doctrine of the virgin birth in the *Church Dogmatics,* needed to work out dogmatically just what his father, despite his orthodoxy, refused to teach.[9]

Barth recalled his confirmation instruction under the Bern pastor Robert Aeschbacher as "a most extraordinary and enthralling, not to say thrilling, experience. It was then . . . that I learned that it could be good and pleasant, not only to learn and accept the great affirmations of the Christian faith, but also to understand them from the inside out."[10] It was there too that he came to understand the relevance of social issues. This instruction led him to the decision to become a theologian: "Not in the sense of preaching and pastoral care, but rather in the hope that in this way I might come to a clearer realization of what was then only a vague objective understanding of the affirmations of the Christian faith."[11] Studies in Bern gave him the opportunity "to comprehend the earlier 'historical-critical' school so thoroughly" that the later version of that school could "no longer get under my skin and certainly not into my heart, but, since I knew it only too well, could only get on my nerves."[12] On the other hand, Kant's *Critique of Practical Reason* (which he later reread many times) made a strong impression. His father successfully opposed a continuation of studies in liberal Marburg, so Barth went to Berlin, where he heard Kaftan, Gunkel, and, above all, Harnack, whose disciple Barth considered himself to be. "Alongside Kant, Schleiermacher took a clearer place in my thought than before,"[13] probably in connection with a reading of Wilhelm Herrmann's *Ethics.* It was with Herrmann that Barth concluded his studies in 1908, after he had studied once again in Bern and had attended Tübingen "with the pronounced obstinacy of a Schlatter."[14] Along with Herrmann, who became Barth's major professor, he was influenced by Heitmüller, Cohen, and Natorp, but also by Rade.

After a brief vicariate in the Jura Mountains near Bern and after his examinations, he returned to Marburg in 1908, where he served for one year as an editorial assistant for the journal *Die christliche Welt* [The Christian World]. He then went on to Geneva as a probationer and in 1911 became a pastor in Safenwil. It was there that Barth, confronted by the misery of the workers, was compelled both theoretically and practically to turn his attention to social issues. "It was the concrete class-conflict, taking place right before my eyes in my own congregation, which confronted me for the first time with the real problems of real life. As a result, my pursuit of theology . . . was for several years restricted to the most painstaking preparations for preaching and teaching."[15] In 1913 he married Nelly Hoffmann, who throughout his life was his faithful and loyal companion. During his years in Safenwil, Barth formed a close friendship with Eduard Thurneysen, who consistently participated in his theological development and even helped to stimulate it.

In 1915 Barth joined the Social Democratic Party, but at the same time, because of his twofold irritation over the pronouncements of his teachers and the posture of the European social democracies during World War I, he returned to intensive theological labors.[16] Then came not only the break with "liberal theology"[17] but also his rejection of the identification of the Kingdom of God with social action, which he had previously adopted from Kutter (and not from Ragaz). Meanwhile, the realistic hope in the Kingdom of God, as espoused by both Blumhardts, had become decisive for Barth, and it remained so. The "urgent need for preaching" both required and led to a new theological foundation,[18] so that Barth was able to call all of his subsequent theology "fundamentally a theology for pastors."[19]

The rediscovery of the Bible quickly bore literary fruit. In 1916 Barth began work on an exposition of the Epistle to the Romans, which, although dated 1919, was submitted to the publisher in December of 1918. Thus Barth could not possibly have known Lenin's *The State and Revolution* while he was writing the exposition of Romans 13, since the German translation of Lenin's piece had not yet been printed as of November 20, 1918.[20] This first edition of *The Epistle to the Romans* brought him an offer of a chair as associate professor of Reformed theology, with honors, at Göttingen, which he accepted in 1921. In 1922 the completely revised second edition of *The Epistle to the Romans* appeared, and it became the most influential text of the new theological movement. At Göttingen, he developed a critical but ardent relationship with Emanuel Hirsch.

In 1922, Barth, along with Friedrich Gogarten, Thurneysen, and Georg Merz, founded the journal *Zwischen den Zeiten* [Between the Times], which served as the leading forum for the "dialectical theology," and which also carried articles by Rudolf Bultmann. From 1925 to 1930, Barth was professor of dogmatics and New Testament exegesis at Münster, where he came into close and extended contact with the philosopher Heinrich Scholz. Here he produced the volume titled *Die christliche Dogmatik im Entwurf* [Christian Dogmatics in Outline].[21] Beginning in 1929, Barth found in Charlotte von Kirschbaum "a faithful colleague at my side, in every sense indispensable."[22]

In 1930 he accepted a call to the chair of systematic theology at Bonn. There he wrote the first volume of the *Church Dogmatics,* in which the disagreement with his erstwhile colleagues became unmistakable. *Zwischen den Zeiten* ceased publication in 1933, and Barth took a stand on the developing predicament in which theology and the church found themselves. His stand was expressed in his slogan "to the heart of the matter,"[23] which was contained in the pamphlet *Theologische Existenz heute!* [*Theological Existence Today!*]. More than 37,000 copies of this pamphlet were printed, including one sent to Hitler.

Hitler's seizure of power soon thereafter further sharpened the controversy between Barth (who in 1932 had been admitted to the Social Democratic Party) and Gogarten and several others. On May 5, 1934, the first synod of the "Confessing Church," held in Barmen, adopted a Theological Declaration which was largely drafted by Barth. Significant differences arose, however, between Barth and powerful forces in the Confessing Church. Theologically, these differences basically revolved around Barth's "No!" to Emil Brunner's postulate of a natural "point of contact" for the Christian proclamation.[24] Barth's refusal to take an unconditional oath of loyalty to the Führer resulted in disciplinary proceedings, which concluded with his dismissal in December of 1934. He successfully appealed; nevertheless, on June 21 of the next year he was pensioned off (not discharged) by the secretary of higher education for the Reich.[25] All publication of Barth's works in Germany was subsequently prohibited.

After his expulsion in June of 1935, Barth was called to Basel, where he remained until he attained the rank of professor emeritus. From Basel he encouraged the Christians of Europe, offering theological arguments for political resistance to National Socialism. His "Letter to Professor Hromádka of Prague," dated September 19, 1938, interpreted the thesis of his earlier essay "Church and State"[26] as signifying that every Czech soldier who fights now, fights "also for the church of Jesus Christ."[27] Barth demanded "evidence of political service to God."[28]

After the war, his opposition to both anticommunism and German rearmament aroused so much anger in Switzerland and West Germany that West German President Theodor Heuss successfully intervened and thwarted the planned presentation of the German Booksellers' Peace Prize. Barth's participation in the 1948 Assembly of the World Council of Churches intensified his interest in ecumenism. The volumes of the *Church Dogmatics,* which appeared at irregular intervals after first being delivered as lectures, were translated into many languages. Among the many honors Barth received, the British award "For Service in the Cause of Freedom" elicited a doctrinal response.[29]

His official teaching career came to a close with the lectures *Evangelical Theology: An Introduction,* delivered in the winter semester of 1961–62. Nevertheless, after a visit to the United States, he continued to offer a series of seminars, as his health would permit, until the last year of his life. One of these seminars dealt with the Second Vatican Council, on which Barth spoke in Rome at the invitation of the Vatican in 1966. His "irenic and critical observations"[30] were later published in a small volume, under the not merely ironic title *Ad Limina Apostolorum* [At the Threshold of the Apostles], in which he proclaimed that "The Pope is not the Antichrist!"[31] His last efforts as a teacher were devoted once again to a consideration of Schleiermacher,[32] as was his last publication.[33] Karl Barth died on December 10, 1968, in Basel. In an interview shortly before his death—in which he combined the organizing principle of his life and thought, always to begin anew with the beginning, with listening to his beloved Mozart[34]—he recapitulated the substance of his theology: "God for the world, God for humanity, heaven for the earth."[35]

His Theology

Barth's theology was, from the beginning, an avowed enemy of systems. It remained so even in the very systematically written *Church Dogmatics.*[36] What is systematic about this theology is that it resolves to make progress precisely by constantly correcting, or else completely changing, its direction. Barth's enormous theological productivity and the massive dimensions of his work are ultimately to be understood as the result of his categorical demand always "to begin anew at the beginning." "In theological study, continuation always means 'beginning once again at the beginning.' "[37] This precept explains the important shifts in Barth's theological development. It led to his break with the then dominant liberal theology and with the so-called positive theology. It was later expressed in more radical self-corrections—once again partly in connection with his rejection of other theological movements—and was finally represented by the mostly tacit changes of direction within the apparently seamless fabric of the *Church Dogmatics.*

The changes in direction which Barth did acknowledge allow us to identify the following phases in his theological development: (1) Beginnings, to the first edition of the commentary on Romans, 1919; (2) Dialectical theology, to *Die christliche Dogmatik im Entwurf,* 1927; (3) Dogmatic theology, the *Church Dogmatics* and an abundance of shorter writings, some of which were occasional and some of which were significant texts in which the key questions of the *Dogmatics* took shape. But during each of these periods Barth's theology was always being reshaped, so that these divisions cannot be applied with precision. It is one of the tasks of future research to determine the extent to which Barth's contemporary experiences ("praxis") helped to shape his knowledge. A reciprocal relationship between knowledge and praxis can be clearly seen in the striking reversals which punctuated his theological development. Here too, Barth's own testimony—whether offered at the time or in his later years—may be read, with the necessary critical reserve, as an authentic commentary.

Theological Beginnings

The theological beginnings which led to Barth's own particular theological disposition and to his consequent rejection of the then dominant theology extend back into different phases of his life. Even in his later years, Barth was aware of the fundamental role played by the children's songs of Abel Burckhardt and by the confirmation class taught by Robert Aeschbacher. An unmistakable tension with his father's theological views developed during Barth's studies. It became manifest in a dispute over where he was to pursue his education. His father only reluctantly agreed to enrollment at Marburg, where Barth studied with Wilhelm Herrmann and carefully read Kant and Schleiermacher. Herrmann made a lasting impression on the young Barth. And even after his break with liberal theology, Barth retained one thing he had learned from Herrmann: the (at least relative) independence of theology as a discipline, the "conviction of Christian truth as based on itself,"[38] needing no apologetic, that is, "the christocentric impulse."[39]

In 1909, when Barth was promoted from the study of "modern theology" to full participation in the "task of building the Kingdom of God,"[40] he was a "wholehearted Marburger."[41] He was therefore fully immunized against Seeberg's school of "mediating theology," only slightly influenced by Troeltsch,[42] and quite unaffected by Ritschl and his students.[43] When, in that year, he gave an account of what he had learned in school, he simply repeated and endorsed the chief characteristics of the theology he had been taught: "religious individualism" and "historical relativism." The legitimate plurality of theological formulations corresponded to their verifiability through a present, "personally experienced reality."[44] He refuted in advance the expected objection that such a theology is unsuitable for praxis,[45] arguing that such a criticism was intended to make us forget that "scholarship . . . is method, not matter."[46] In his first sermon in Geneva, the new vicar commended himself to the congregation as a guide "to the sphere of the inner life . . . ; we can do no more."[47] While Barth was in Geneva, his study of Calvin's *Institutes,* accompanied by another reading of Schleiermacher, issued in the 1910 lecture "Der christliche Glaube und die Geschichte" [The Christian Faith and History], in which he claimed to formulate the "general problem of Christian theology."[48] In this essay, Barth called for further development of the Marburg theology.

This essay is distinguished primarily by its radical style of expression, a style that was to reappear with Rudolf Bultmann. It is taken for granted that "the method of faith" obviously must determine "the method of theology"* in any treatment of the subject.[49] In his exposition, Barth distances himself from Troeltsch, who is able to "make only the vaguest generalizations about the matter."[50] At the same time he dryly concludes that the history of religions school, which stemmed from Ritschl, sought "to cultivate history only as history" and thus "lost sight of the revelation." "God is not found in history"[51]—all that scholarly study can show is that "God, revelation, and miracle . . . are scientific non-concepts."[52] Adolf von Harnack later used the same argument against Barth: "The concept of revelation is not a scientific concept."[53] Barth knew that only too well. He had learned it from Harnack and especially from Herrmann: "Faith and revelation are possible only with the presupposition of an absolute relation to an absolute history."[54] But by now faith had come to be explained as a "social fact,"[55] held to be Christian only insofar "as the personality of Jesus" has a historically mediated "presence within human society."[56] Here Barth is already saying that faith cannot be "something *presupposed* in the essence of humanity,"[57] for "the Christ intended by faith is a Christ who is utterly beyond us." Just as there is no faith which is proper to our nature, so too there can be "no 'Christ in us' which is proper to our nature."[58] Christ is rather to be understood, with reference to Melanchthon and Calvin, as "the effective-affective Christ," and thus the "source and substance of the Christian faith,"[59] mediated through the perception of the inner life of Jesus. It is only in this sense that "the Christ outside us is the Christ in us."[60]

It may seem that Barth is speaking of a christological self-mediation of the Word, but he expressly describes faith itself as the real mediation and rejects the "opposition" of faith and history in favor of their "coincidence."[61] And all this takes place with reference to the doctrine of the inward witness of the Holy Spirit, which even in this early essay is described as a "patron saint of dynamite" that "will necessarily" blow "the entire orthodox edifice into the air."[62] Faith cannot be traced to a historical foundation. It is more like a closed circuit, scorning "any diversion, that is, any necessity other than its own internal necessity."[63] Alongside the Bible there stands "a complete line of mediating individuals" who are "sources of revelation." Their individual characteristics are muted in interest of the universality of faith: "The activity of the Spirit of Christ has, thank God, still other channels: . . . Francis of Assisi and Bodelschwingh . . . in their deeds, as well . . . as Paul and Luther in their thoughts. But also the works of a Michelangelo, of a J. S. Bach, a Mozart, and a Beethoven . . . , Schiller as a preacher of the cross of Christ.

---

*Literally: "the method of *Glauben*" obviously must determine "the method of Glaubens*lehre.*" —TRANS.

. . . And, even in the mightily impressive works of Goethe, is it not something of . . . Christ's self-denying obedience in love that impresses us? . . ."[64] One should remember that Barth later concluded that this essay "would have been better left unpublished."[65] But there are enduring insights here as well, inextricably interwoven with expressions which he would later find intolerable. Particularly significant are the coincidence of faith and history, the analysis of the truth of faith in terms of its own inner necessity,[66] and the movement from Christ outside us to Christ within us. But Barth's interest in the universal Christ, the Christ who is effective outside the church, would also keep returning, albeit in greatly altered forms.

For a young Swiss pastor with a Marburg education, a close connection with the Swiss religious socialist movement, as represented by Hermann Kutter and Leonhard Ragaz, was almost to be taken for granted.[67] Barth learned, especially from Kutter's language about the living God, "to say again that great word 'God,' earnestly, responsibly, and momentously."[68] Kutter took the familiar antiecclesiastical resentment of liberal theology and put it to a positive use: "The realm of God's power is greater than the realm of the church"; God may well confront Christendom "right in the midst of the persons and events of the profane world process."[69] Kutter had a strong and lasting influence on Barth, but Ragaz's "theory that the church must take a position toward socialism as a preliminary manifestation of the Kingdom of God"[70] also briefly claimed Barth's allegiance. Barth's encounter with class conflict in his Safenwil congregation of peasants and workers led him to write a series of essays on social problems. One of these essays, published under the title "Jesus Christus und die soziale Bewegung" [Jesus Christ and the Social Movement] in *Der Freie Aargauer* ["The Free Aargauer," the official voice of the Workers' Party of Aargau Canton], endorsed Kutter's trenchant thesis:[71] "Jesus *is* the social movement, and the social movement *is* Jesus in the present."

Barth expounds both aspects of Kutter's thesis in terms of "a movement from the bottom up." A polemic against Idealism dominates: in the eyes of God, spirit is a social force which "transforms matter" on behalf of loving-kindness (F. C. Oetinger). Jesus shatters the proprietary tautology "What is mine, is mine" even for familiar relationships, proving himself to be "more socialist than the socialists." The divine power of the gospel is to be found in the organizational genius of social democracy. It follows from the "Our Father" of the Lord's Prayer that "for Jesus, there is no God except a God of social solidarity, and no religion except a religion of social solidarity." Thus, "one must become a comrade if one is to be human at all."[72]

Disillusioned with both liberal theology and socialism, Barth sought a new theological foundation. He also broke with Kutter and Ragaz, who wanted "to have nothing to do with theology at all,"[73] but at the same time he joined the Social Democratic Party of Switzerland. Indeed, he wanted to be neither a "religious" nor a "political" pastor. Barth explained why in a lecture he gave on the assigned topic of "Religion and Socialism."[74] Basic motifs of his later theology can be seen in this lecture. It is here that we first encounter his theological criticism of religion, insofar as the "great, fundamental, and living reality" of the Kingdom of God is opposed to the one-sidedly anthropological concept of religion. However, the Kingdom is said to have its human "reflection" in socialism.

In this lecture, Barth announces new ideas in the old forms he had learned from Kutter and his teachers at Marburg. "Revelation" is still used in the broadest possible sense, and socialism is understood as "God's revelation," but the "Kingdom of God" is interpreted emphatically as the living majesty of God, not to be identified with religion. Reflections, symptoms, and signs of the Kingdom of God are distinguished from the Kingdom itself and refer back to it. God himself is at work in such a way that his work corresponds to a world-transforming praxis—the praxis which socialism so vigorously postulates. Nevertheless: "The world is the world. But God is God."[75] Barth now begins to work with fundamental differentiations and relations which will later appear in a new form. At first they return simply as contrasts; later they are fully elaborated in the doctrine of analogy set forth in the *Church Dogmatics.* In a 1916 sermon on Genesis 15:6, Barth's persistent determination to "begin joyfully with the beginning" and to "recognize that God is God"[76] appears for the first time.

Barth's first attempts to find a new theological foundation were stimulated by his study of Johann Christoph Blumhardt and his son Christoph Blumhardt (prompted in part by Thurneysen and Kutter[77]). Barth praised the younger Blumhardt's *Haus-Andachten* [Household Devotions] in a 1916 review, calling it "the most immediate and compelling word of God that has yet come to light in this time of war."[78]

Barth finds it noteworthy that Blumhardt believes he can "love the world and still be completely true to God."[79] "He starts with God"[80] and can therefore respond to God with a "revolutionary"[81] expectancy. Writing on the occasion of the deaths of Friedrich Naumann and Christoph Blumhardt, Barth rejoices that "the unhappy word 'religion' . . . was no longer heard in Möttlingen and Boll."[82] Christoph Blumhardt taught Barth that the Kingdom of God is antagonistic to religion: "Nothing is more inimical to the progress of the Kingdom of God than a religion."[83]

Instead of religion, Barth discovered a hope "for humanity" and "for the physical side of life"[84] in Blumhardt. Barth later specifically identified the eschatological orientation of both Blumhardts as the real turning point in his development.[85] The certainty of Easter that "Jesus is Victor" (even if it was scarcely more than an abstract philosophical axiom) became the material starting point of the first commentary on Romans: "You have Easter behind you."[86] But even the doctrine of reconciliation in the *Church Dogmatics* was expounded under the elder Blumhardt's watchword "Jesus is Victor."[87]

Nevertheless, it was the Bible that provided the decisive impetus for a properly theological beginning, in the sense of the "concrete biblical exegesis" which arose from the influence of Christoph Blumhardt.[88] Barth's inability to discover an "organic connection" between "the daily newspaper and the New Testament" was rooted in deficient biblical knowledge: "If only we had returned to the Bible sooner!"[89] The view that Barth's socialism constituted the theoretical framework of his theology is untenable. It is rather the case that socialism and liberal theology found themselves together in a crisis and yet emerged from it separately. What was constitutive for the development of a proper theology was a new style of biblical exegesis, from which the socialist option was by no means excluded. Barth and Thurneysen joined in an "attempt to begin to learn our theological ABC's anew . . . with the reading and exposition of the scriptures of the Old and New Testaments." This attempt bore fruit in Barth's study of the Epistle to the Romans: "I began to read it as if I had never read it before."[90] Barth's commentary grew out of that reading. The first edition of that commentary was written "under the strong influence of Bengel, Oetinger, and Beck (and Schelling, by way of Kutter); but their ideas later proved to be incapable of conveying what had to be said."[91]

Barth's commentary begins with an already familiar opposition: "Tidings from God . . . , not any human religious teaching";[92] "not *a* truth, but *the* truth." This truth sees to its own victory: it is "the heart of the matter itself," "our knowledge of God, realized in Christ, whereby God is not represented to us, but is creatively and immediately present to us."[93] Thus it is that "God can be known and found by those who seek him."[94] "The concept of God is given to us as immediately as our own being."[95] Barth expounds the gospel dialectically in terms of the category of origin. On the one hand it is "nothing new, but the oldest; not particular, but the most universal; not historical, but the presupposition of all history," while on the other hand it is "not an old acquaintance, but a new one; not universal, but the most particular; not a mere presupposition, but history itself."[96]

The initial, starkly paradoxical assertion of the unity of these opposites yields to the task of showing how "the most particular" is, or can be, also "the most universal," a task that Barth would henceforth repeatedly reformulate and reconstruct. Here Barth constructs an eschatological argument, using the metaphor of the revolution of God: a "cosmic intrusion into the cosmic order,"[97] the "elimination of all dependency" in favor of a "republic" of "freedom in God"—a "realm of no one but kings."[98] The "revolutionary" can therefore be a sign of the divine,[99] showing that the "return of all things to their source"[100] is the work of the dissolver of all bonds who intrudes into the dying world, and not a chance at "reform"[101] for the dying world.

The revolution of God is a concrete event which does not proceed from this world but breaks into this world from the beyond. This event transforms the entire human race, not just particular individuals. It is a "divine worldwide revolution!"[102] And, correspondingly, the "living spirit" of this world "in the present time" can be "nothing other than revolution, including the revolution of what today is called revolution."[103] Barth asserts an eschatological immediacy: neither "trust in God," nor "solving the riddle of life," nor "certainty of salvation" can be divorced from eschatology.[104]

This leads up to a trenchant, effective treatment of justification which eliminates the possibility of an ethic. "From the viewpoint of the last things, which is the viewpoint we must take in Christ, there is no ethic. There is only the activity of God."[105] But this is itself the best "foundation for an ethic,"[106] for it signifies that God "himself is not finished," that God is love and goodness, that God acts with "the greatest freedom and vitality. He wishes to involve us in this activity."[107] In the meanwhile, however, Barth's criticism of the old order soon proved to be too radical for him, while the criticism of the "old school" was not radical enough. "What was needed was a crisis . . . that would bring the criticism to an end."[108]

Dialectical Theology

The term "dialectical theology" was simply "tacked on"[109] to the movement represented by Barth, Brunner, Bultmann, Gogarten, et al., but their language was genuinely dialectical. Barth's lecture on "The Christian's Place in Society," delivered in Tambach after the appearance of his first commentary on Romans, belabors harsh antitheses and emphasizes the "totally other" which comes "down . . . out of heaven" (Zündel).[110] Barth's reputation was quickly established in Germany by this lecture. "The Christian is that within us which is not ourselves but Christ in us."[111]

"The greatest insight into things" comes "from the greatest distance."[112] For that reason, Barth rejects all combinations ("social-Christian," "social-evangelical," "social-religious") and describes the "divine" as "complete in itself . . . with no ties to our common social life." He condemns any attempt "to secularize Christ for the umpteenth time"[113] or to erect "a new church with democratic manners and socialist motives."[114] There is no such thing as religious experience. "The Immediate, the Original, is never experienced as such."[115] The "breakthrough of the divine into the human"[116] is "a movement, so to speak, from above" whose "power and import are revealed in the resurrection of Jesus Christ."[117] "Interest in the personal life of the so-called historical Jesus" is not even permitted.[118] Barth describes this christological-eschatological movement as the "miracle of the revelation of God,"[119] the key concept of Barth's theology in all its phases. "And that is why the synoptic accounts of Jesus can be properly understood only with Bengel's insight: 'They breathe the resurrection.' "[120] Barth's theological negation of the values of society—authority, family, art, work, and religion, each for its own sake—is really an affirmation: "The negation which issues from God, and means God, is positive, and all positives which are not built upon God are negative."[121] It is precisely the person who "stands over against life in an absolutely critical role" that can then "recognize in the worldly the analogy of the heavenly and take pleasure in it."[122] This is the person who is free for a "view of life" oriented to "the parables of the synoptic Gospels,"[123] even though "there is no continuity leading from analogy over into divine reality."[124] "It is only in God that the synthesis can be found."[125]

Barth's meetings in Tambach—with Gogarten, among others—intensified "the question of the biblical sense of the 'Kingdom of God.' " Under the influence of Overbeck, Kant, Plato, Kierkegaard, and Dostoevsky, Barth came to a further, fully completed "turn," now in "open opposition to Schleiermacher." This "turn" was first documented in the lecture "Biblical Questions, Insights, and Vistas," given at the conference in Aargau.[126]

His previous movement toward a biblical understanding now becomes an explicit working hypothesis: "What does the Bible have to offer? It has already offered. . . . We are not outside, as it were, but inside,"[127] so that "our question . . . contains its own answer . . . and is taken captive by a presupposed and original Yes."[128] The priority of the answer over the question[129] becomes the indispensable hermeneutic of Barth's subsequent theological work. Henceforth, questions of method coincide with questions of content. The Word which permeates Barth's theology is really a Yes, even if "the reality of the Yes," because it "causes us such unrest," is first manifested in a theological No.[130] Barth increasingly emphasized the Bible as the competent material witness in his theology of "the permanent crisis of the relation between time and eternity."[131] As a result, the critical response to his theology developed primarily into a dispute over hermeneutics, as can be seen in the forewords to the second and third editions of *Romans*.

In the second edition of the commentary on Romans, written under the influence of yet another meeting with Gogarten,[132] Barth's tautology "God is God" now becomes an expression for the " 'infinite qualitative difference' between time and eternity."[133] This latter phrase is yet another expression for the difference between the Here [*Diesseits*] and the Beyond [*Jenseits*]: God is not "tied to the contradiction between 'here' and 'there,' but is the pure negation—and therefore the Beyond—of both the 'Here' and the 'Beyond,' the negation of negation. He signifies the Here of the Beyond and the Beyond of the Here, the death of our death, and the nonbeing of our nonbeing."[134] Hans Urs von Balthasar therefore claims that a presupposition of the "original identity" of creator and creature stands behind "the Reformed pathos of the absolute distance between creator and creature."[135] On the contrary (and despite Przywara[136]): "Within a historical perspective," God can be known only as a No, only in the "bomb-craters and voids"[137] he has produced, in a faith defined by "the impossibility of God." This faith is impossible and unhistorical; it "can be represented in history only as crisis and in the forms of myth and mysticism."[138]

Faith participates in the character of Jesus Christ, who can "be understood within history" only as "Paradox," "Victor," "primal history, only as a problem, only as a myth." We know him only as "an unknown plane . . . that intersects perpendicularly from above."[139] The concept of "primal history," which Barth appropriated from Overbeck but used in a way Overbeck had never intended, signifies an "impossible possibility," a " 'Moment' which has no before or after,"[140] reminiscent of Plato's *exaiphnēs* (that which is between motion and rest and thus not in the time sequence).[141] This "primal history" constitutes the proper context of theology. Barth ties protology [first things] so closely to eschatology [last things] that he, once again in reliance on Overbeck, was able to write the following sentence, which he later retracted[142] as mistaken: "Any Christianity which is not utterly and absolutely eschatological has utterly and absolutely nothing to do with Christ."[143]

Barth insisted on raising the question of the "inner dialectic of the subject matter" in Paul's Epistle to the Romans,[144] using his own thorough, sharply dialectical approach. He demanded more criticism from critical exegesis: "The historical-critical school must be more critical in order to suit me!"[145] He insists that the interpreter "enter as freely and eagerly as possible into the . . . concepts presented by the text," so that "the connection of the words to the Word in the words can be exposed."[146]

In the foreword to the first edition, Barth had already expressed a preference for the "doctrine of inspiration" over against historical-critical exegesis, because the former is more closely tied to the "task of understanding itself."[147] In the second edition, the doctrine of inspiration is paradoxically construed as a universal hermeneutic. The imperative "Consider well!" taken together with the presupposition that the book in question is a "good book," whose ideas should be taken "at least as seriously" as one's own, constitutes a hermeneutic which can be applied to any worthwhile text, including the Bible.[148] The interpreter's "relationship of faithfulness" to the author[149] signifies that, in the Bible, "everything is *litera* [2 Cor. 3:6]." But the Bible must be read in terms of the question "whether and how far everything can be understood also in the context of the 'subject matter' as the voice of the *spiritus* (of Christ)."[150] "What is there" in the epistle must "be rethought,"[151] because it "awaits working out" itself.[152] Barth thought that this determination to understand the text was even more radical than the radical criticism of the subject matter which Bultmann demanded of him.[153]

Barth's approach to hermeneutics unquestionably constituted a breakthrough to a new relationship between theology and its subject matter. It can be traced back "to his unyielding posture in the discussion," a discussion which was "itself part of the heritage" of "liberal theology."[154] (A certain kinship to phenomenology and to Heidegger has now been established.[155]) But this new hermeneutic also involved the danger that one's attention could be so exclusively concentrated on the more important task—the subject matter—that the less significant but still important task of formulating the questions could be dismissed.

Barth's move to an academic position in 1921 resulted in changes in his theological style. In particular, it led him to a greater awareness of the distinctive characteristics of Reformed theology.[156] His historical and exegetical lectures issued in the dogmatic judgment—understood simply as a mere corrective—that the situation of "the man in the pulpit" is not a standpoint, but a mathematical point between the Bible and the hearer.[157] For Barth, this was the fundamental significance of exegesis for all theology. Both the "way of dogmatism," with its objective representations, and the "way of criticism," with its self-negation, are transformed into the "way of the dialectic," which is the way of Paul and the Reformers.[158] It is intrinsically the best way because it "looks from one side to the other, both from positive to negative and from negative to positive."[159] Thus the true task of theology may be formulated: "As theologians we ought to speak of God. We are human, however, and so cannot speak of God. We ought therefore to recognize both our obligation and our inability and by that very recognition give God the glory."[160] This formula expressed the theological intention shared by the founders of *Zwischen den Zeiten* when they established the journal in 1922–23. They thought of themselves as "theologians of controversy"[161] in two senses: (1) polemically, as opponents of the prevailing theology in all its tendencies; and (2) dialectically, as theologians of the Word of God, the Word which identifies all human beings as sinners. Despite all their protestations to the contrary,[162] they grew into the most influential theological "school" since Schleiermacher, first united, and later divided, by the ever more vexatious question of the relationship between revelation and history.

Gogarten[163] had already proclaimed his solidarity with Barth in a rejoinder to Jülicher's critical review of the first commentary on Romans; [164] meanwhile, Brunner[165] gave his approval to the first edition, Bultmann[166] expressed his appreciation for the second edition, and Tillich announced his "spiritual companionship"[167] with Barth and Gogarten. Bultmann[168] particularly identified with Barth's "Fifteen Answers"[169] to Adolf von Harnack's "Fifteen Questions to Those Among the Theologians Who Are Contemptuous of the Scientific Theology."[170] Bultmann especially appreciated Barth's response to Harnack's claim that "a reliable and common knowledge" of Jesus Christ cannot be achieved except through "critical historical study."[171] Barth replied: "The reliability and common nature of the knowledge of the person of Jesus Christ as the midpoint of the gospel can be no other than that of a faith awakened by God,"[172] which is why "the task of theology is the same as that of preaching," to awaken faith.[173]

This school was unified by its rejection of any attempt to objectify the unobjectifiable God, and by its concomitant rejection of the liberal synthesis of revelation and history. It denied any attempt to isolate a special history of God in a salvation history distilled from universal history,[174] but it was also held together by its rejection of any attempt to identify revelation with the church and thereby to avoid the question of truth.[175] Nevertheless, despite the unity within the school, the problem of history divided it. The question of the theological meaning of the specifically modern experience of history (Gogarten), and the corresponding philosophical question of the consciousness of truth (Tillich), proved to be the most troublesome point of contention; and the longer the dispute went on, the worse it became. The discussion finally issued in the hermeneutical controversy over the place and function of anthropology in theology —that is, the question of preunderstanding (Bultmann)—and in the dogmatic quarrel over the relationship of nature and grace (Brunner).

Barth described the modern history of theology as a progressive deterioration that reached its logical conclusion in Ludwig Feuerbach's thesis: "Theology is anthropology—that is to say, in the object of religion, in what we call . . . 'God,' nothing is specified except the essence of man."[176] Feuerbach only drew out the logical consequence of the shift in theology's "attention from what God is in himself to what God is for men."[177] Luther's "talk of faith as almost a divine hypostasis which moved and worked independently"; the doctrine of the Real Presence in the Lutheran teaching of the Lord's Supper; and the orthodox Lutheran doctrine of the *communicatio idiomatum* [the interchange of attributes in the divine-human Christ], which took no notice of the Reformed reservation *Finitum non capax infiniti* [The finite cannot contain the infinite]— all these signified, Barth held, "the possibility of a reversal . . . of God and man."[178] Barth believed that this possibility had become a reality in the modern era and was completely accomplished in Feuerbach.[179]

Barth's new orientation to the Reformation thus became eminently critical and objective, in express opposition to Karl Holl's and Reinhold Seeberg's interpretation of Luther. As a rule, Holl and Seeberg took Luther and Calvin (but not Zwingli) together, and then opposed them to Catholicism and Neo-Protestantism. Barth charged both scholars with disregarding the presupposition, maintained only by H. F. Kohlbrügge, "that there is no being a Christian except by being a lost sinner," that the grace which makes a Christian is "free grace and always remains free grace."[180] Barth thus elicited the genuinely Catholic objection—although not just a Catholic objection—that he thereby made the "concepts of nature and sin coincide."[181] For Barth, the "modern Protestantism of both the Left and the Right" represented "a Catholicism tempered by negligible heresies,"[182] sharing a common "Semi-Pelagianism which entered . . . in the eighteenth century by the two open doors of Rationalism and Pietism."[183] Barth found Catholic opposition all the more interesting because of its principled argumentation: "In its presuppositions," Catholicism "is closer to the Reformation" than modern Protestantism.[184] Barth's theology was increasingly characterized by an intense interest in Catholic theology and thereby took on major significance for ecumenism.

Barth prepared his lectures on dogmatics with reference to the old Protestant dogmatics, but also with constructive attention to Orthodox and scholastic theology.[185] He engaged, too, in an increasingly energetic dialogue with the church fathers, and came to be impressed by the truth of the supposedly passé propositions of the old dogmatics. In this way he came to see, for example, that the doctrine of the Trinity should be formulated in terms of "the problem of the inalienable subjectivity of God in his revelation."[186] His understanding of theology as an ecclesiastical science grew correspondingly. In this connection, a telling influence may have been exerted by Erik Peterson, among others. In opposition to the dialectical method, Peterson insisted on the necessity of a "real even though analogous knowledge of God" and called for a "theology which presupposes that dogma," taking seriously "God's undialectical presence."[187] Barth pondered this objection and the similar criticisms of, among others, Erich Przywara, just as seriously as he had earlier sought to appropriate Overbeck's *aperçu* that "theology can no longer be established through anything but audacity."[188]

Barth opposed any attempt to find a nontheological basis for speech about God—something that the dialectical theologians were also beginning to attempt. Barth affirmed ever more strongly that the Word of God is dependent on no preconditions, and that the same is true of any valid scientific theory about it. He now began a sustained exposition of this unconditioned Word, "neither entitled nor obligated . . . to remain with the gestures of the prophet or the deportment of an outburst."[189] Thus was born *Die christliche Dogmatik im Entwurf* [Christian Dogmatics in Outline], of which only the Prolegomena appeared. But this Prolegomena, in opposition to the established understanding of the genre, set forth a dogmatics in brief compass— including a doctrine of the Trinity! It was a Prolegomena which was "illustrative of the whole, a part of the dogmatic Legomena itself."[190] In 1922, Barth had wondered whether theology could or should ever get beyond the Prolegomena to the Christology, and he conjectured that perhaps "everything is said in the Prolegomena."[191] Now he defined the Prolegomena as the theological genre in which everything must be said in anticipation, so that it can thereafter be said adequately and methodically. This definition of the Prolegomena as "the dogmatic Legomena itself" is meant to demonstrate that dogmatics is possible only on a dogmatic basis, that theology is possible only on a theological basis. A "natural theology," no matter how extensive or limited, is the essence of a misbegotten theology—as he learned from Wilhelm Herrmann. As Werner Elert ironically observed, Barth's refusal to locate revelation in either the "book of nature" or the "book of history" earned them both a place on "Karl Barth's Index of Forbidden Books."[192] Theological theory participates in the irreducibility of its object, the revelation. And Barth describes that revelation as an "unhistorical event"[193] in which "our 'I' is addressed by God in the form of a human 'You.' "[194] The category of "primal history" [*Urgeschichte*] establishes that "history . . . is a predicate of revelation, while revelation . . . is not a predicate of history."[195] Revelation is a unique category, as "attested by the unity of happening, speaking, and hearing in the Bible."[196] This category too is drawn from the dialectic: "Revelation both establishes and proceeds from the upper limit of the dialectic of our existence."[197] This upper limit, by itself, victoriously penetrates the "sinfulness" of the fallen world, so that "our entire existence . . . must . . . be understood as a single *vestigium trinitatis* [trace of the Trinity]."[198] But the history which participates in, and attests to, that primal history attains the rank of a "qualified history of the second degree," constituting a "history of God on earth as the church—already begun in the Old Testament, grounded once for all in Jesus Christ. It encompasses the rest of history even as it is in history itself."[199] Dogmatics is carried on in the sphere of the church, in the service of preaching from "a biblical posture." It is fully aware of the inevitability of philosophical, psychological, and sociological implications, etc., but it "presupposes unproblematically that God has spoken," and that one "must learn dogmatics in the same way as anything else, through practice."[200]

Barth delivered a series of lectures on ethics in 1928–29 and again in 1930–31, but he never published them because of their reliance on the doctrine of the orders of Creation, which he was soon to reject. Ethics

is an "auxiliary dogmatic science"—also based on the Word of God—
in which an answer "to the question of the goodness of human conduct"
is sought.[201] But "good" here means "sanctified through God's Word,"[202]
so that the theme of ethics is not the saintly person, but rather the
sanctifying demand made on the human person (as a creature of God,
as a redeemed sinner, and as an inheritor of the riches of God) by the
proclaimed command of God. Theology, as ethics, must repeat what it
has already said as dogmatics. This constitutes "a practical confession
of humility on the part of theology,"[203] recognizing that it is very different
from the actual event of the Word of God itself. The concept of God's
legitimate claim on humanity raises the possibility of a positive critical
assessment of human nature, culture, and philosophy, as attested in the
two lectures "Church and Culture"[204] and "Schicksal und Idee in der
Theologie" [Fate and Idea in Theology].[205] "The relationship between
theology and philosophy (when it remains philosophy in the strict sense)
can and will be not merely that of a benevolent neutrality . . . but rather
one of . . . most instructive partnership,"[206] as long as philosophy does
not become theosophy and theology does not abandon its "theological
axiom," the First Commandment.[207]

Barth suspected that Brunner, Bultmann, and Gogarten had all abandoned this very axiom.[208] Correspondingly, they objected that Barth had
neglected "the necessary business of attending to the presuppositions" of
theological statements.[209] And so the dialectical theology came to an end.
Although the fronts of the beginning battle for the church were drawn
along somewhat different lines (Bultmann), Barth's suspicion spelled the
end for *Zwischen den Zeiten.* The "last piece of advice" that Barth left
his students in Bonn distinctively expressed his positive critical concern:
"Exegesis, exegesis, and again, exegesis!"[210] Barth could identify this last
piece of advice as the criterion which separated him from Brunner and
Gogarten. His dogmatics had no other aim than to be consistent exegesis.
But this parting advice, "Exegesis, exegesis, and again, exegesis!" was
followed by the remark: "Then, certainly, take care for systematics and
dogmatics."[211] That is why Barth declined to identify his Reformed
affiliation, his Swiss nationality, or his political preference for social
democracy as a presupposition of his theological arguments. "I warn
you. Of course I have my own ideas about such things. But if that is how
I am to be interpreted, I could upset the German religious socialists just
as well. . . . And then my theological and ecclesiastical affinity with
Marxism, liberalism, etc., even during the notorious fourteen years,
would have to become visible in some way. And then now—in this year
1933—my politically overwhelming opponents would also have to listen
to me with this evil causal nexus of my theology in mind, and act
accordingly. They may demonstrate this nexus on the basis of my books,
essays, and sermons, or, if they are so inclined, they may inquire in

Göttingen, Münster, and Bonn about everything I did and did not do during all those years— but they should attend first to what I say, not to my political backgrounds. Until that is done, I shall view this activity as conduct unworthy of gentlemen."[212] Today, renewed attempts to repeat the same mistake will have to pass off these sentences as "self-misunderstandings."[213] Furthermore, they will find it necessary to distort Barth's remark that "theological existence today" will be politically effective[214] precisely because it decides "to practice theology and only theology . . . now as in the past, as though nothing has changed."[215] They will claim that this marks a concession by Barth that his earlier "extraordinarily incisive, entirely political manifesto" is being displaced by the "politically accommodating" *Theological Existence Today!*[216] This is a historically untenable interpretation.[217] Politics was a predicate—the "political side"—of his theology,[218] but his theology was never a predicate of politics.[219]

Barth's life and thought now became "much more churchly" and therefore also "much more worldly."[220] This process is documented in the *Church Dogmatics,* which replaced *Die christliche Dogmatik im Entwurf,* now retracted by Barth as a "false start."[221]

Dogmatic Theology

Barth's formal preparation for the task of dogmatic theology was his teaching assignment, but his material preparation dated back to the hermeneutical dispute provoked by his exegesis of Paul. He demanded that both thought and speech, with "their own responsibility in the present,"[222] be judged by the text of the Bible. His dogmatic turn was expressed by another change in style, from dialectic to assertion. His dialectical style had been assertive, and his new assertive style was by no means undialectical—but it did undialectically affirm the Word of God.[223] Barth's new style combined material relevance with contemporary relevance. He combined an ability to make fine intellectual distinctions with an ability to make courageous and unambiguous declarations of position. His scholarly rejection of any attempt to discredit precise thought as " 'intellectualistic' "[224] matched his polemic declaration: "Now I must make myself clear."[225]

As soon as he had finished his first attempt at a dogmatic style, Barth quickly decided that a revision was necessary—a revision that would eliminate every vestige of appearing "to give theology a basis, support, or even a mere justification by means of existential philosophy."[226] But he could not reach that goal by simply eliminating the objectionable material. A complete reorientation of the previous "direction" of his thought was necessary. He found this reorientation in his study of Anselm of Canterbury, whose influence was already apparent in *Die christ-*

liche Dogmatik im Entwurf. Barth's study of Anselm resulted in a book[227] whose historical accuracy was questioned, but which Barth regarded "with the greatest satisfaction."[228] Barth himself described this book as "the key to an understanding of that whole process of thought that has impressed me more and more in my *Church Dogmatics* as the only one proper to theology."[229]

Barth's thinking now follows the direction of faith, which wishes to understand its own truth on its own premises. "*Intelligere* comes about by reflection on the *credo* that has already been spoken and affirmed." The "theologian asks, 'To what extent is reality as the Christian believes it to be?' "[230] Hence the theologian needs to "consider the factuality of Christian truth alongside the demonstration of its inner necessity. This factuality is derived from no external necessity, and must be understood as the impetus of its inner necessity."[231] In express opposition to the modern philosophical and theological turn to the subject and to consciousness, Barth presupposes an ontic necessity and rationality which is ontologically prior to the corresponding noetic necessity and rationality. Furthermore, he firmly anchors this ontological priority in a truth which is identical with God. "It is in the truth and by the truth . . . that the basis is a basis and that rationality possesses rationality."[232] That is how the truth "by analogy can be made manifest" in the world. "With its knowledge of God the church realizes a possibility open to humankind," a truth which "cannot be put into practice because of the Fall—and yet, for that very reason, . . . it is a possibility whose truth must be insisted upon."[233] Barth thus expresses a "confidence based on faith,"[234] proceeding "by the roundabout way of an argument for the rationality and necessity of the object, moving from noetic necessity to noetic rationality."[235] The Bible is the criterion of the theological propositions which are developed in this way. But the Bible is not to be grasped merely as a fact (in the manner of positivism). It is to be approached as the truth, in the context of its well-grounded meaning. "Not only the objective truth as such, but also its inner meaning, its basis and its context, as we discern them, ought to bear witness that what Scripture declares is in fact so."[236]

Therefore, even as Barth abandoned the circular style of the dialectic, his theology increasingly came to exhibit a hermeneutical circle. This circle established the increasingly confessional and narrative character of his dogmatic argumentation. A confessional theology explains the reality of the articles of faith on the basis of the ground of reality itself. Argumentative, conceptual, and kerygmatic language are now woven together in a most individual, inimitable style. More and more,[237] analogy now becomes the formal foundation and structure of Barth's dogmatic assertions: the analogy (a) between the triune God who even in all his differentiation and separation (for example, between commanding and obeying!) remains self-consistent, and his relationship to his creation (definitively realized in the person of the God-man Jesus Christ and ontologically true for all human beings in him); (b) between the revelation of God and the biblical language of faith which interprets it; and (c) between the expressive power of the revelation and that of the dogmatic assertions. Analogy brings the formal activity of theological thought in line with the material activity of the theological object, God. That is why Barth waged an extended war against the *analogia entis* [analogy between human and divine being], which presumes to usurp the activity of God himself, calling it "the invention of Antichrist."[238] He opposed the *analogia entis* by stressing the authentic analogy, which he construed ontologically as the analogy of relationship and theologically as the analogy of faith—without, however, a sufficient concern for clarity.[239]

The formal-material structure of the analogy made it possible for Barth to overcome his earlier dialectical fear of any "objectification" of revelation. He now understood the inviolable objectivity of God as an .event (history), as a revelation in which God himself is present in the three corresponding "modes of being," the Father, the Son, and the Spirit.[240] He could also "unabashedly" employ the concept of Being once he reconceived it in terms of God's activity, self-relatedness, and primal history.[241] The tautology "God is God," once thoroughly obscure,[242] now, without losing its original truth, opens up: God is God, in that he corresponds to himself and makes human beings correspond to him. Barth expressed this dogmatically in a "christological concentration" which dominated both the form and the content of his theology. It led him "to a critical (in a better sense of the word) discussion of church tradition, and as well of the Reformers, and especially of Calvin."[243] The most important ecclesiastical expression of Barth's christological concentration came during the battle for the church in the Theological Declaration of Barmen, which can truly be read as the basic text of Barth's theology.

The direction now taken by Barth's thought is manifested in the structure of the monumental *Church Dogmatics.* The revelation has a "most specific" christological identity. But this "most specific" revelation is now traced back to a corresponding[244] reality, a reality which possesses a given, "most universal" validity. The possibility of this reality rests on no basis other than itself.[245] Indeed, the possibility is itself the most original reality. Barth's exposition of the reality of the Word of God in its three forms—as the revealed, written, and proclaimed Word—constitutes the content of the Prolegomena. In the doctrines of the Trinity, the Incarnation, and the outpouring of the Holy Spirit, the Prolegomena communicates the specific character of the revelation. This, in turn, is followed by the doctrines of the Holy Scriptures and the proclamation of the church.[246] Barth describes the relationship of the Old and New Testaments christologically: both Testaments represent the "time of the revelation." The Old Testament is the "time of anticipation," in which Christ was revealed in anticipation, and the New Testament is the "time of remembrance," in which the same Christ is the subject of the narrative. From this perspective, the distinction between law and gospel recedes into the background and cannot serve in any way as a criterion for differentiating the two Testaments. The resurrection of Jesus Christ is the quintessence of the time of the revelation and, as such, is a mystery; and the sign of this mystery is the miracle of the birth of Christ from the Virgin Mary. The reality of God, christologically identified as the one who loves in freedom, constitutes the subject of the doctrine of God[247] in the narrower sense.[248] This doctrine includes the doctrine of election,[249] which is the sum of the gospel. But the doctrine of God also serves as the basis for an ethic of the command of God,[250] that is, the law. And this law is nothing other than "the gospel itself . . . insofar as it has the form of a claim addressed to us."[251]

The basic thrust of the Christology—expounded briefly in CD I/2, §15 —is fully developed in the doctrine of election,[252] which completely reconstructs the traditional doctrine of predestination. Here Barth describes Jesus Christ as both the God who elects and the human being who is elected, already having his "place-holder"[253] in the eternal "Logos" of John 1:1–18. His history—carrying out God's primal decision "within our universe and time"[254]—signifies that God on the one hand ordained the death of the sinner in Christ himself, but on the other hand also ordained the life and salvation of humankind,[255] a humankind dialectically represented by Israel and the church. Barth's emphasis now shifts from Christology to the "full reciprocity"[256] of God's essence with his triune existence, freedom, and love, and to the correlation of the inner divine mystery and the revelation. The "aseity of God"[257] in his Trinity is manifested by this revelation "as ours in advance, so to speak."[258]

Barth therefore vigorously rejects both the Calvinistic abstraction of a double predestination in the absolute decree of God[259] and the ostensibly Lutheran problematic of a "primal decision of divine grace" or a "self-determination"[260] of God. He was consequently also bound to reject the abstract distinction between God revealed and hidden: "There is no greater depth in God's being and work than that [which is] revealed."[261] On the contrary, the presence of the eternal God in the world corresponds to an eternity that is conceived in terms of an interpenetration of the three modes of time,[262] in a manner analogous to that of the intra-Trinitarian *perichoresis* [coinherence].[263] Barth's universalist formulation of the doctrine of predestination implies the primacy of the election of the community over that of the individual. Barth thought that it was safer to risk the danger of implicitly teaching the *apokatastasis panton* [Acts 3:21] ("I do not teach it, but I also do not not teach it," as he once said)[264]—than to risk the greater peril of restricting the power of the gospel and the sovereign will for salvation. He also expressed this fundamentally christological orientation in the ethics of the doctrine of God, where Jesus Christ is described as both the sanctifying God and the sanctified human being—parallel to the dialectic of the electing God and the elected human being.[265]

Barth also bases the doctrine of creation, analogically and christologically, on the *concretissimum universale* [absolutely concrete universal] of God's will for salvation. He describes "The Covenant as the Internal Basis of Creation" and expounds creation as "The External Basis of the Covenant"[266] which is fulfilled in Jesus Christ. The world is therefore described as the stage of revelation. In his exposition of nature and its forms of time and space and its material history, Barth holds that both time and space entail the possibility, on the basis of grace, of a history of the love of God for the human race. This perspective also determines the anthropology[267] and the doctrines of providence, nothingness, and angels.[268] In addition, it forms the basis of Barth's now more concrete ethics, which takes the form of the doctrine of the freedom of the creature: freedom before God, in community, for life, and in limitation.[269]

The history of the covenant of grace "follows creation, but does not derive from it," because creation itself follows from "the history of the covenant of grace" as the covenant's express presupposition.[270] Hence Barth can hold that the creation as such is a "sign and witness of the event which will follow";[271] indeed, it is "a true sacrament."[272] The relationships within creation, e.g., between heaven and earth and between man and woman, correspond to the original relationship of God to himself and to the creation.[273] The analogy between God's being and human being "is simply the existence of the I and the Thou in confrontation. . . . To remove it is tantamount to removing the divine from God as well as the human from man."[274] Barth's anthropology consistently develops this ontological relationship, which, even though it is "distorted by sin, is not structurally altered by sin."[275] The ontological and epistemological basis for this relationship is the true and complete human being Jesus, who exists enhypostatically in the ontological mode of the Word of God which becomes flesh. Jesus is the man for God and for his fellow human beings, and is therefore the likeness *(imago)* of the God who, in his three-in-oneness, is for himself and for his creation. Hence Jesus is the original image of the human person, whose being *with* (not *for*) fulfills the ontological, basic form of his or her humanity. And *"si quis dixerit hominem esse solitarium, anathema sit"* [if anyone says that man is a solitary being, let him be accursed].[276] The human being is the one who is addressed by God and thus has spirit,[277] the "soul of his body."[278] He or she is therefore a whole person, with the capacity to "rule one's self" (soul) and to "serve one's self" (body)—"an authentic, free subject,"[279]—finite and mortal in the time given to him or her, and over whom Jesus rules. "Man as such, therefore, has no beyond. Nor does he need one, for God is his beyond."[280] Human nature is therefore no "point of contact"[281] for grace. Human beings are not created *as* covenant-partners, but *"to be* God's covenant-partners."[282]

Barth's doctrine of nothingness and sin illustrates the overall pattern of his dogmatics. Here too, he begins with the specific reality of the Yes which God says to being, and which is victorious in Jesus. Thence he proceeds to evil as that which is denied by the No that is implied in the Yes. This denial becomes definitive and final in Jesus Christ. Hence evil is determined as nothingness: an "impossible possibility."[283] This victory over nothingness justifies the "fatherly lordship" of God, by which he "preserves, accompanies, and rules" his creation.[284]

Finally, with the doctrine of reconcilation the *Church Dogmatics* arrived at the "center of all Christian knowledge."[285] This doctrine was both a massive recapitulation and a thorough revision of Barth's entire dogmatics, broken off in the midst of the section on the ethics of the Christian life.[286] Barth undertook this exposition of the doctrine of reconciliation as part of "broad and intensive . . . debate with Rudolf Bultmann"[287] and as "an attempted Evangelical answer to the Marian dogma of Romanism."[288] The nucleus of Barth's Christology had been set forth in *Church Dogmatics* I/2. Now, critically referring back to the orthodox dogma and especially to the propositions of the old Protestant orthodoxy, Barth broadly deploys his Christology as the basis of his treatment of sin, justification, sanctification, and vocation. Christology also forms the basis of the doctrine of the work of the Holy Spirit as he gathers, edifies, and sends forth the community even as he ordains the individual Christian to faith, love, and hope.

Barth intensifies his antimetaphysical, trinitarian formulation of the concept of God by identifying Christ's humiliation and obedience unto death as a movement in God's own being.[289] At the same time, his language about God now extends to include the elevation of the human Jesus to the right hand of the Father. Jesus' exaltation ontologically benefits human being as such; Barth now affirms a "theanthropology"[290] in opposition to any "abstract theomonism."[291] In both respects, Barth was issuing a retraction of his one-sided proclamation, made forty years earlier, of the "deity of God"; he now acknowledges the element of truth in the liberal theology that he had once so bitterly opposed: "God's deity, . . . rightly understood, includes his humanity."[292] "Nietzsche's statement that man is something that must be overcome is an impudent lie."[293] Now, with reference to the language of the New Testament—but also in connection with a methodical study of the hymnbook, and in a certain measure of agreement with Hegel—Barth discusses the christological mediation of Lordship and servanthood. He describes the event in which

God became a human being under the heading of "Jesus Christ, the Lord as Servant,"[294] while he expresses the exaltation (*not* divinization) of humanity under the heading of "Jesus Christ, the Servant as Lord."[295] This event is also christologically attested by "Jesus Christ, the True Witness,"[296] who first discloses the event to the world. Correspondingly, the Christian community is described as "The Community for the World."[297]

Only two sections of the ethics of the doctrine of reconciliation were completed: the doctrine of Baptism[298] as the foundation of the Christian life, and the posthumously published groundwork for the ethics of reconcilation, accompanied by an exposition of the Lord's Prayer, which describes the Christian life as consummated in prayer.[299] The ecclesiology and the doctrine of Baptism developed in CD IV/4 resulted in an unacknowledged revision of Barth's earlier position (formulated in the Prolegomena) concerning the threefold form of the Word of God and the relationship of Word and Sacrament. This, in turn, led him to revise the stand he had taken in *The Teaching of the Church Regarding Baptism.* [300] Barth now reserves the concept of a sacrament for Christ and therefore construes Baptism as a human act. As a result, he rejects infant Baptism.

The architecture (see diagram) of this genuine masterpiece demonstrates that Barth knew how to put what Anselm called the beauty of theology into practice. The old Protestant doctrines of the person, office, and states of Jesus Christ are rearranged and reformulated, with the result that the being of the unity of the person in the two natures is narrated as history.[301] Barth can then describe this being in terms of historical activity, using the categories of the threefold work or office of Christ. The point of this Christology is that Jesus Christ manifests his divinity in his humiliation, his humanity in his exaltation, and the unity of the God-man in his self-manifestation as the mediator. Barth construes this not only noetically but also—supremely—ontically. This threefold division simultaneously structures the doctrine of sin, the soteriology, and the ecclesiology: (a) the humiliation of the divine contradicts the sin of human pride, and yet corresponds to justification by faith alone and to the gathering of the community; (b) the exaltation of the human contradicts the sin of human sloth, and yet corresponds to sanctification in love and to the upbuilding of the community; and (c) the manifestation of this being and work *extra nos* [outside us] by the true witness unites (a) and (b), contradicts the sin of human falsehood, and yet corresponds to the human vocation of hope and to the sending of the community into the world. The ethics of CD IV, based on the divinely mandated appeal to God (Ps. 50:15), was to have expounded: (a) Baptism, culminating in prayer for the Holy Spirit, as the foundation of the Christian life; (b) the life of prayer, guided by the Lord's Prayer, as the fulfillment of the Christian life; and (c) the Lord's Supper, celebrated in

CHURCH DOGMATICS IV

DOGMATICS	CD IV/1	CD IV/2	CD IV/3
Christology:			
Person	The Lord as Servant: *vere deus* (true God)	The Servant as Lord: *vere homo* (true man)	The true Witness
Office	The Judge judged in our place: The obedience of the Son of God=*munus sacerdotale* (priestly office)	The Royal Man: The exaltation of the Son of Man=*munus regale* (royal office)	Jesus is Victor: The glory of the Mediator=*munus propheticum* (prophetic office)
State/Way	The way of the Son of God into the far country=*status exinanitionis* (state of self-emptying)	The homecoming of the Son of Man=*status exaltationis* (state of exaltation)	The Light of life=the unity of both states
Doctrine of Sin:			
Sin as	Pride and Fall	Sloth and misery	Falsehood and condemnation
Soteriology:	The judgment of God as the justification of humanity	The direction of God as the sanctification of humanity	The promise of God as the vocation of humanity

Pneumatology:

The work of the Holy Spirit

in the community

in the individual

	Gathering the community	Upbuilding the community	Sending the community
	Faith	Love	Hope

ETHICS CD IV/4

The Christian life as an appeal to God

Baptism—with water—as the foundation of the Christian life in prayer for the Holy Spirit ↓	The Lord's Prayer—Our Father —as (instruction in) the fulfillment of the Christian life ↑	(The Lord's Supper—Eucharist —as the renewal of the Christian life in thanksgiving) ↓ ↑

thanksgiving (Eucharist), as the renewal of the Christian life. Thus the
appeal to God is interpreted on the basis of the imperative which it
implies. Characteristically, Barth increasingly understands this appeal as
a human action which is intersected "directly from below" by the ambiguity of *simul justus et peccator* [being righteous and sinful at the same
time].[302]

Barth postpones his exposition of sin until after the Christology. This
is the result of his programmatic reversal of the customary Lutheran
sequence of "law and gospel," a reversal already accomplished in 1935
and reiterated in 1952 by the programmatic essay *Christ and Adam*. In
that essay, Barth argues—"to the left of every collectivism and to the
right of every individualism"—that humanity, as represented by Adam
and present in every human being, is "to be understood in Christ."[303] In
much the same way, "the law can be known only from the gospel, and
not vice versa."[304] Therefore, sin is known to be sin only when it is also
known to be vanquished. Barth thought it wise to "abandon" the concept
of hereditary sin, which he viewed as a contradiction in terms, and to
replace it with the concept of "primal sin" [*Ursünde*] *(peccatum origi-
nale)*. [305]

The transitional concepts (judgment of the Father, direction of the
Son, and the promise of the Holy Spirit) are determinative for the Christology and also open the way to the soteriology. These concepts ordain
an "ontological connection between the man Jesus on the one side and
all other men on the other," so that his work, accomplished *extra nos*
and *pro nobis,* makes all human beings into "virtual" (and not anony-
mous) Christians.[306] Jesus Christ *in nobis* is "the principle . . . of spontaneous being" in human persons.[307] This resulted in sweeping changes
for Barth's critique of religion and natural theology, which had played
such a momentous role in his previous theology.[308] Previously, particularly in the early stages of his dogmatic theology, Barth had been concerned to emphasize the element of truth in that which he nevertheless
sharply criticized: for example, religion, which he described as unbelief,
was held to be justified in Christ, so that Christianity could be identified
as the true religion.[309] But now[310] Barth speaks of "true words . . . *extra
muros ecclesiae* [outside the walls of the church]"[311] and even of lights
in the world which, because they reflect the one light of life, illuminate
the creaturely world in *esse* and *nosse* [being and nonbeing].[312] These
lights, like the Christian witnesses—although they are strictly to be
distinguished—are "given to be parables of the kingdom of heaven."[313]
The fact that Barth says this under the heading of the first thesis of the
Theological Declaration of Barmen[314] demonstrates that his new teaching is a positive extension of his old critique of religion and not a
retraction of it.[315]

Moreover, the christological premises of the doctrine of justification now led Barth to conclude that justification is both the pronouncement of righteousness and the making of righteousness,[316] so that even from a Catholic perspective there is "no genuine argument for schism."[317] Similarly, Barth's doctrine of Baptism with water as a "saving" human action[318] (by no means to be understood as a sacrament[319]) can be "fully and entirely" affirmed, with respect to its intention, from a Catholic standpoint.[320] It can also be a stimulus to Catholic theologians to develop their thought along ecumenical lines.[321] Barth's description of the church as "the earthly-historical form of [the] existence of Jesus Christ"[322] provides additional opportunities for ecumenical discussion. He goes so far as to call the church a "provisional representation,"[323] consummated in the world by the power of the Holy Spirit, of the "sanctification of all humanity and human life as it has already taken place *de jure* in Jesus Christ,"[324] and, as such, "necessary for salvation."[325]

On the basis of this understanding of the church—which follows from the relationship of Christ and Adam—Barth raises the issue of a necessary, inner relationship between the justification of sinners and human justice,[326] between "the Christian community and the civil community."[327] "An interest in this question begins where the interest of the Reformation confessional writings and Reformation theology as a whole ceases, or rather wanes."[328] Barth answers this question along the "line" of the analogy. There is certainly no comparison, but rather a fundamental difference between the state and the church; hence the church "will beware of playing off one political concept—even the 'democratic' concept—as the Christian concept."[329] But, nevertheless, there is "an analogous capacity and an analogous need in the essence of politics" which does permit "the rightful existence of the State" to be viewed "as . . . an analogue to the Kingdom of God . . . in which the church believes."[330] This allows the political activity of the Christian to be understood as a confession of faith.[331]

Underlying all these formulations is the lapidary affirmation—which, like many of Barth's ideas, recalls Schleiermacher even as it repudiates him—that there is "indeed a godlessness in humanity, . . . but according to the Word of reconciliation there is no absence of humanity in God."[332]

His Impact

The impact made by Barth's theology is inseparable from both the understanding and the misunderstanding that it encountered. Its primary impact on Protestant theology came first through the "dialectical theology" and then through the Theological Declaration of Barmen. The Barmen declaration became the theological basis of the Confessing Church in the battle for the church during the Third Reich, and after 1945 it served the same function for the territorial churches, despite the assaults made on it. As such, it has attained the rank of a major event in church history. Beyond that, however, Barth's dogmatic theology has received remarkably little consideration in Protestant theology and remains largely unknown, despite the constructive criticism of H. J. Iwand, H. Vogel, G. C. Berkouwer, G. Gloege, et al., and despite the critical mediation of H. Gollwitzer, E. Wolf, O. Weber, and W. Kreck. Meanwhile, it has met with increasing interest in Catholic and ecumenical circles.[333] If the early, often sterile Protestant reception of Barth (which neglected the material issues in favor of the hermeneutical rebuttal begun by F. Gogarten and later vigorously pursued by R. Bultmann and E. Fuchs) was a hindrance to any fruitful discussion, then the Catholic discussion (to which G. Söhngen, H. U. von Balthasar, H. Bouillard,[334] and H. Küng have made particular contributions[335]) and the now growing Protestant contributions to the discussion signify an important new development.

Investigation of the specific problems of Barth's theology—Gloege has compiled a list of the basic problems[336]—will lead back to its unmistakable christological concentration and the universal expansion implied thereby: "Jesus is Victor!"[337] It should also call attention to the freedom of God as well as the freedom of humankind that Barth's theology describes. The attempts made shortly after Barth's death to interpret his theology as "socialistically" conditioned, or as a faulty theory of modern autonomous subjectivity which lapsed into a "positionality," do show that neglected issues have won a place in the discussion. But this should be possible without the violence which distorts the intention of his work. Despite the monumental dimensions of Barth's literary output (which has also restricted its impact), we will also have to reckon with the unfinished character of the *Church Dogmatics.* However, there are several possible starting points for the missing eschatology, and they call into question the sometimes proffered interpretation that his theology makes any doctrine of *eschatos/eschaton* impossible. Equally important for an adequate understanding of Barth's theology are the historical studies contained in his digressions in the *Church Dogmatics* and in his history of Protestant theology in the nineteenth century.[338] The same holds true for his theological existence, which made him "the pastoral counselor of oppressed peoples and the conscience of Christendom,"[339] but which also provoked vehement hostility.

It is indisputable that his literary work effected a fundamental change in theology, but it also ranks as one of the most significant literary achievements in the cultural history of the twentieth century. Yet Barth could still make the point of his theology in two words: "Ah, yes!" "Everything depends on, and everything must return to, this small sigh, in which we say to God, 'Ah, yes!' "[340]

Two

Barth's
Theological Beginnings

Anyone at all familiar with the scholarly debate over the *initia Lutheri* [Luther's beginnings] might well be horrified at the suggestion of a study of Karl Barth's theological beginnings. But the debate over the beginnings of Barth's ideas should not obscure the fact that it is only his later, developed theology which makes these beginnings, however they are interpreted, interesting in the first place. At any rate, Barth's beginnings have already become the object of theological study, and hence also an object of controversy, in which I too may be permitted to join. I do so with peaceful intent. At the same time, as a kind of admonition, I recall the slightly ironic tone of voice with which the older Karl Barth himself occasionally referred to his own *initia*—and to others' interest in them.

I do not claim that these observations about Barth's theological beginnings can explain his later work wholly in terms of the beginnings. I will simply highlight a few matters which might prevent a misinterpretation of Barth's theology. Thus the first stage in Barth's development will assume particular importance for a systematic perspective. I will focus on three convictions that emerged by the end of this first stage: first, the recognition that theology, in that historical situation (but only in that historical situation?) is actually conceivable only as an "impossible possibility"; second, the understanding of theology as a kind of hermeneutical metacriticism; and, finally, the insight that theology is a "theory of praxis"—an insight that is subject to all kinds of misunderstandings, but which can be clarified by an examination of Barth's discourse about the "revolution of God."

Beginnings are points of departure and must be left behind if we wish to move on. Barth research will have to adopt this view if it wishes to avoid drawing false conclusions from the beginnings. It should be remembered, however, that Barth's beginnings are not irrelevant to his historical development. Like "every word," so too every curriculum vitae "is still conditioned by its origin." And much of what is left behind at the point of departure continues to be influential, returning again and again in ever-changing forms. Therefore it is crucial, for a full understanding of Barth's theology, to take account of both the beginnings and the later developments, and to do so, we might say, dialectically. Otherwise, Barth research would probably subject him to the same gruesome fate that was supposedly prepared for a Turkish enemy of the Holy Roman Emperor Barbarossa: "to the right and to the left, half of a Turk is seen falling to the ground." Heaven forbid!

Theology as an "Impossible Possibility": Between Overbeck and the Two Blumhardts

"Theology can no longer be established through anything but audacity." This sentence signaled the end of Karl Barth's theological beginnings. He was formulating a new theological approach which intentionally departed from the then established theology. Assuming full responsibility for his actions, he began to search for ways in which theology might be reestablished. The fact that as a theologian one must reason "for oneself" is taken for granted; even the follower of a school is not released from this personal responsibility. Thinking always involves personal responsibility, whether it takes place in a school of one or of many. "I think that I have learned a few things from Schleiermacher and Biedermann, from Buber and Ragaz, but I personally am incapable of any responsible thinking on the basis of their common presupposition,"[1] wrote Barth in 1960. He was at the time attempting to fulfill "one of the most peculiar" commissions he had ever received: to "comment on the tendencies of liberal theology" which he, its notorious antagonist and exterminator, would consider viable today.[2] Barth, who incidentally considered the case "difficult but not hopeless,"[3] was unable to go along with the basis of liberal theology, given what should be self-evident to every theologian, namely, the need to think responsibly for oneself. It was when he was seeking a completely new foundation for theology that Barth apparently realized how audacious such an undertaking must not only appear, but indeed really be. Reflecting on "The Possibilities of Liberal Theology for Today" in 1960, he told its advocates, "It was over forty years ago that I read this remark by Franz Overbeck, 'Theology can no longer be established through anything but audacity.' I paid attention to it. The liberal theologians will have to pay attention to it as well."[4]

Barth's understanding of this remark of Franz Overbeck (1837–1905), however, missed Overbeck's point. In fact, it was rather a grotesque misunderstanding. Overbeck, in one of his numerous sketches, as malicious as they were apt (a few of which, poorly edited, were posthumously published by Carl Albrecht Bernoulli under the title *Christentum und Kultur*[5] [Christianity and Culture]), had sneered at an announcement by his Berlin colleague G. Runze, who was publicizing his upcoming lectures on no less a topic than "The Best That There Is to Know in the History of Religions." Overbeck, having soberly observed that the discipline of the history of religions is "at this point still in its cradle," went on to remark derisively: "The simple knowledge that these lectures are to be delivered is like a breath of fresh air, even before they begin. It may be true that a theology can no longer be reestablished except with audacity. But what help is that to a person who has already lost faith in theology as a result of studying early church history!"[6] By no means, then, did Overbeck ever think that theology could—even with audacity —be "reestablished." The bitter irony of his remark makes it an argument *ad absurdum.* Either Barth did not notice this irony or he consciously ignored it. As early as 1920, in his essay "Unsettled Questions for Theology Today," Barth cited Overbeck's comment about audacity, describing it as one of those remarks "which escaped the author almost against his will and which deal with at least the possibility of a more clear-headed and open-eyed theology."[7] This was certainly not what Overbeck had in mind. But someone who was searching for a theology more clear-headed and open-eyed than the reigning "liberal theology" could well find in Overbeck's ironic comment an unintentional suggestion concerning how theology might be established after all. In any case, Barth appropriated the remark as a most earnest assessment and earnestly applied it in his own way: "Theology can no longer be reestablished except with[8] audacity."

This remark, as Barth used it, clearly marked the end of his previous theological pilgrimage. Methodologically, we read it as the turning point in Barth's theological development: He had moved beyond his previous theological thinking, but had not yet discovered a new foundation for theology. When it became clear to him that this would be impossible except with, or through, audacity, his early theological work had irretrievably come to an end. Our method, then, will be to trace Barth's theological beginnings as they lead up to this end.

There are two different ways in which this might be done. We could attempt to portray the beginnings from their own beginning—*ab ovo,* so to speak. This would chart Barth's development over time and attempt to relate how he came to his theological positions, and how and why he moved from one position to another. In this process the storyteller already knows the outcome and runs the risk of steering each of the preceding events toward just this outcome, all the while pretending not to know how the story ends and remaining open for all possible endings —or if not for all, at least for some different endings. It therefore makes sense to take a different approach, to begin the study with the admission that one already knows its outcome and wishes to explain it in terms of the events which lead up to it. But that means that the end, the *telos* of the story, must come first, before the history which leads up to it.

Although the former approach obviously has its advantages and attractions, I consider this latter procedure systematically more appropriate and historically more hygienic. It is better protected against the danger of suggesting more than it really accomplishes. We are, so to speak, playing with our cards on the table.

We will therefore proceed directly to an examination of Barth's theological reversal, which drew attention to him as a noteworthy theologian in his own right, and which is perhaps most significantly expressed in his idiosyncratic appropriation of Overbeck's inane remark that theology cannot be reestablished except with audacity.

The end of Barth's theological beginnings, and the dawn of the new era of the so-called dialectical theology, can be seen most clearly in Barth's lecture "Unsettled Questions for Theology Today," which took the form of a review of Overbeck's aphorisms in *Christentum und Kultur.*

Overbeck has such great significance for Barth's theology because he made the aporia of the theology of his day exceptionally clear. In Overbeck, Barth found that which he himself had at first only sensed and then had tried to articulate ever more clearly: the profound impotence of "modern theology," hidden only too well behind the fig leaf of culture-Protestantism. Overbeck bluntly denied that the theology of his day was Christian. He called attention to that which his theological contemporaries and colleagues did not wish to admit, that which they wished to prevent and instead were largely promoting: the end of Christianity. Overbeck was a diagnostician of the end of Christianity, not a proclaimer like his friend Nietzsche, but something more like a learned historian and analyst. It was this diagnosis of the end of Christianity that aroused Barth's enthusiasm. This is highly significant for any understanding of Barth's theological development, regardless of whether or not Barth understood Overbeck correctly.[9] And so we ask, What did Franz Overbeck want? What was it about him that led Barth to claim that he was so important?

Barth's first reference to Overbeck, in those texts available to me at any rate, appears after the posthumous publication in 1919 of some of Overbeck's "thoughts and remarks on modern theology" under the title *Christentum und Kultur.* In a letter to Eduard Thurneysen on January 5, 1920, Barth writes, "Our Melchizedek is probably—Overbeck. I may write something about him."[10] Barth did in fact write something about Overbeck that same year, the essay "Unsettled Questions for Theology Today." Overbeck's "thoughts and remarks" must have had considerable impact on Barth, apparently helping him to understand himself better. Barth probably first became acquainted with Overbeck's work by reading *Christentum und Kultur,* and had probably not read the controversial essay of 1873 (which appeared in an expanded second edition in

1903), *Über die Christlichkeit unserer heutigen Theologie* [How Christian Is Our Theology Today?].[11] In this article, Overbeck had already argued that modern theology, instead of distinguishing between faith and knowledge as strictly as possible, had hopelessly mixed the two and thereby done serious damage to both religion and science. I shall illustrate Overbeck's thesis with several of his remarks. Although these remarks (like the papers selected from his estate for the publication of *Christentum und Kultur*) were not published during his lifetime,[12] they say nothing fundamentally different from what was known, or could have been known, about the antitheological professor of theology at Basel.

As a historian, Overbeck had an especially sharp eye for the peculiar character of religion and for the loss of this character through historical development. "As long as a religion is alive among us, everything connected with it is taken for granted, and it is not defended, because it needs no defense. As soon as it moves out into our culture, however, it dies as a religion and must draw its life from the vitality of the culture."[13] But theology belongs to culture, insofar as it wishes to be scholarly. "Therefore every theology, insofar as it relates faith to knowledge, is itself irreligious."[14] This is completely true of the Christian faith, inasmuch as Christianity's original expectations were neither for a theology nor for the continuation of earthly history, since it "came into the world proclaiming the world's impending destruction."[15] Nearly two decades before Johannes Weiss, Overbeck outlined the eschatological basis of Christianity and, unlike Weiss, stood firmly by it. An eschatological faith cannot tolerate any theology; on the other hand, "theology, insofar as it is a scholarly discipline, does not itself possess any proper principles of knowledge." And since theology can no longer dictate to other disciplines as it did in the Middle Ages, it must derive from them, so that "even the delusion that [theology] is Christian is no longer possible."[16] "Theology can demonstrate that it is an academic discipline only by selling out completely."[17] "Christianity has fundamentally always been an academic problem for theology; today, however, it is clear that this means nothing less than questioning the very existence of Christianity as a religion."[18] If an apologetic theology "were to justify Christianity in scholarly terms," Christianity would cease to exist as a religion.[19]

Overbeck turns this argument primarily against the liberal theologians of his day and their historical apologetic. Nothing shows theology's estrangement from religion, its distance from Christianity, "more clearly than today's exaggerated overestimation of the value of history for the [supposedly] positive aims of theology."[20] While the early church was still free of the "superstition . . . that a holy record attains its religious status through the application of historical interpretation" and therefore made constant use of allegory, modern theology "pays homage to the nearly inconceivable delusion that it can become sure of Christianity again by historical means; however, should it succeed, it would at best result in a religion for scholars, that is, nothing that could seriously be compared with true religion."[21]

Therefore, "the worst thing that can happen to a text is to suffer this type of interpretation. The more zealously this method [historical theological interpretation] is applied, the worse it is for the text. . . . A text which has been confined behind a wall of commentary might be regarded as something by the world, but it has in fact been strangled, and even though it might seem alive it is merely a corpse. This alone warrants a judgment against theology as an academic discipline. Theology (Protestant theology, at any rate) lives largely on exegesis, that is, by the death of a book. Almost all its activity is devoted to spreading thick clouds over this truth and to piling up mountains of commentaries; that is its basic wisdom and art. It pretends to preserve the life of the holy texts from which it draws its life, and by so doing only throws sand into the eyes of the world. But this is precisely what true scholarship would never pretend to do, since it cannot ever create life[22] and therefore can never give life to a text through exegesis." "With exegesis, if one is honest about it, one can only free oneself from the text, not do justice to it."[23]

But modern theology does not see through its self-deception. It does not recognize its own "unhappy, hybrid, internally fragmented nature" and "does not comprehend the confusion in which it is entangled."[24] According to Overbeck, this is its essential characteristic. He knows how distant he is from it, because he has seen through it and recognized its essential inability to be a Christian theology. His claim to be the only one who has realized this makes his remarks sound rather pointed and bold. As result, his honorable scholarly erudition approached precisely that audacity which Barth (wrongly) read as an indirect invitation to reestablish theology. Anyone who observes things carefully—meaning, of course, more carefully than usual—will in fact see and depict them in a way that will seem audacious to the less precise observer. How could the Christian world *not* be astounded when, in the book *Christentum und Kultur,* among the thoughts and remarks, it was forced to see the greatest of all great modern theologians, Adolf von Harnack, described in a "Lexicon" with entries for every letter of the alphabet (except D, Q, X, and Y), with every entry resembling a public execution? Harnack under A for "Protestant Abbé," in whom the elegance of Catholicism is replaced by coarseness! Harnack as the "perfect salon professor"![25] Harnack under A for "Arbeit" [work], as the "apostle of work," who could not comprehend that it was not the work itself that counted, but its quality![26] Harnack under B for "Biedermann" [middle-class], as the "popularizer" whose "light, even when it only flickered, appeared to flash like lightning"![27] And so on. No question about it—Overbeck stood out from the crowd. And so he interested Barth.

His precise observations and his thorough iconoclasm made this prosecutor of an irrelevant theology into an advocate, in Barth's eyes, for the cause of theology. "The cause was too great and the situation too complicated for him to be able to do more than cast his net widely. The net will someday be drawn in, who knows when? and by whom? Overbeck simply cast it out. In this fruitful epoch, which strongly reflects the sense of the Hellenistic or pre-Reformation ages,[28] we need to take careful note of him." What was posthumously published under the title "Christianity and Culture" could just as well have been called "An Introduction to Theology,"[29] according to Barth. Even if it could scarcely have been Overbeck's intention, this book is de facto—for Barth at any rate—"an extremely impressive restatement of the commandment 'Thou shalt not take the name of the Lord thy God in vain.' If it is read and understood, the normal effect would be that ninety-nine percent of us . . . will discover that it is impossible for anyone really to be such a thing as a theologian."[30] Indeed, this was already evident in the polemical essay that Overbeck did publish during his lifetime. And Barth was also amazed "that the theology that is dominant today could . . . remain so indifferent to and untroubled by the questions he [Overbeck] put" to it.[31]

In the same year that he wrote this, Barth once again encountered this "theology that is today dominant" in the person of his teacher, Harnack. At the Aarau Students' Conference of April 1920, he and Harnack, among others, lectured on "The Meaning of World History." Barth gave a lecture entitled "Biblical Questions, Insights, and Vistas." In it he vigorously distanced himself from the usual method of religious studies, which approaches the substance of religion from the outside. "We are inside and not outside, . . . inside the knowledge of God, inside the knowledge of the last things,"[32] and that is what makes us bold and allows us to become inquiring and critical. Because we presuppose a Yes, we are restless.[33]

This sort of critical approach comes closer to its object than do critical religious studies, which approach it from the outside. That is to say, Barth's approach, which begins with a Yes, sees that the biblical history of religion is "neither religion nor history in its deepest essence: not religion, but reality; not history, but truth. . . . Religion forgets that it has a right to exist only when it constantly does away with itself."[34] Religion attains truth only through self-dissolution [*Selbstaufhebung*]. Barth sees this self-dissolution of religion in the Bible. Barth reads the Bible as, so to speak, a self-demythologizing book. "The biblical piety is not really pious; one must rather characterize it as a well-considered, qualified worldliness."[35] This explains why Barth and Gogarten saw each other as kindred spirits.

Harnack may well have shaken his head at such utterances. But there was more: "Jesus simply has nothing to do with religion. The meaning of his life is the actuality of that which is not actually present in any religion—the actuality of the unapproachable, the unreachable, the incomprehensible, the realization of the possibility, which is not a matter of speculation: 'Behold, I make all things new!' "[36] When Harnack heard that, the conflict came to a head. Barth later described Harnack's response in a letter to Harnack's daughter, Agnes von Zahn, written after his death: "I can remember very clearly the horror which he expressed in the discussion after my lecture: The state of affairs was now worse than it had ever been since Kierkegaard (I can still hear the Baltic sound of the name on his lips)."[37] The next day Harnack (together with Eberhard Vischer) told his former student that he would do better to keep his "concept of God ('a new creation')" to himself and "not make it an 'export article.'" He finally dismissed Barth with the prophecy that "according to all the experience of church history [Barth] would found a sect and claim inspiration."[38] Barth, on the other hand, could see that Harnack was just as undismayed and unaffected as all others who thought they could evade Overbeck. Yet it was just this kind of reaction which Barth hoped he could confound with the help of Overbeck's unsettled questions. He believed the time had come: "It is clear that the idol totters."[39]

The idol totters—this was how Karl Barth, inspired by the impetus received from Overbeck, dared to refer to the liberal theology of his time. It was an eye for the essence of Christianity that had led Overbeck to become a sharp critic of liberal theology. He accused it, on the one hand, of falsifying the essence of Christianity—and doing so precisely when it attempted to determine this essence, as in Harnack's famous lectures at the turn of the century on "The Essence of Christianity,"[40] later translated into several languages. On the other hand, he also accused it of failing to recognize the contemporary situation of Christianity, insofar as the liberal theologians "delude themselves about what is happening to Christianity." They treat it like a living religion instead of letting "Christianity die in dignity." Indeed, it is already de facto about to give up the ghost. The two accusations belong together, insofar as there is now "so little room anymore for the very concept of the return of Christ" that no one can "even conceive of it historically as a part of early Christianity, or at least treat it as a negligible quantity."[41] But without this concept, Christianity becomes nonessential, loses its driving force, and dies. Liberal theology, which thinks it can portray the essence of Christianity and prove it contemporary without "the entire concept of the return of Christ," is, according to Overbeck, consequently "living . . . with a corpse."[42]

Barth was evidently quite convinced by Overbeck's argument. In particular, he believed that Overbeck had repudiated liberal theology's synthesis of Christianity and world, of faith and world history. Overbeck had written: "The contradiction between the original Christian eschatology and the contemporary hope for the future is fundamental."[43] And Barth commented: "The challenge of Matthew 18:3 ['Unless you turn and become like children, you will not enter the kingdom of heaven'] by itself either eliminates Christianity or unhinges the church."[44] As Overbeck had said: "Christians *must* be children, but they *cannot*. That is the way it should be, for the challenge is meant for a different world from the one in which the contemporary church and Christianity exist."[45]

Barth was in substantial agreement with Overbeck that an authentic Christianity must be eschatologically oriented. "Any Christianity which is not utterly and absolutely eschatological has utterly and absolutely nothing to do with Christ,"[46] he later wrote in his exposition of Romans 8:24 in the second edition of his commentary on Romans. A statement as radical as this is in the spirit of Overbeck. It corresponds to the formal structure of Barth's theology in its "dialectical" phase, prefigured in Overbeck's figure of speech, "Christians *must* be children, but they *cannot*."

The contradiction between a real necessity and a factual impossibility became a motif of Barth's style of argument and dominated his thinking for some time: "As theologians we ought to speak of God. We are human, however, and so cannot speak about God."[47] In this style of argumentation, Barth juxtaposes two antithetical statements and, at the same time, formulates a most dialectical concept. He speaks of an "impossible possibility." The concept of an "impossible possibility" in theology is known today primarily from the *Church Dogmatics,* where Barth uses it to characterize sin and nothingness. According to Barth these phenomena, which are defined in themselves through negativity, have their empty existence merely insofar as they are "only on the left hand of God, under his No," only as "the object of his . . . wrath and judgment," and that means "only as inherent contradiction, as impossible possibility."[48] This usage in the "late" Barth has been much criticized for minimizing the reality of sin and evil by characterizing them as an impossible possibility, or—as Barth can also say—as an ontological impossibility. We can leave this accusation (an erroneous one) aside, since we are now concerned with Barth's earlier use of the expression under the influence of his study of Overbeck. "It is most interesting, and seldom noted, that this central concept of Barth's doctrine of sin still retains its function of describing the human condition under the Word of God."[49] This phrase, which in the *Church Dogmatics* appears simply as a fitting characterization of the ontological peculiarity of negative phenomena, is in Barth's earlier writings an indispensable expression for the essence of Christianity. In the second edition of *The Epistle to the Romans,* the justification of the practice of religion by faith is described as "the

impossible possibility"[50]—and, at that, in a context which expressly recalls the antireligious Overbeck. He wrote that the word "God" can,
correspondingly, be considered the "last word, . . . if we mean the
impossible possibility of the faithfulness of God."[51] In fact, with reference
to the oracles of God which were entrusted to the Jews according to
Romans 3:2, Barth says that God surely "stands within the realm of
possibility, not as one possibility among others, but . . . as the impossible
possibility."[52]

Barth follows Overbeck in both form and content. With Overbeck, he
denies that the Christian faith can be mediated through the world or
world history in the manner of liberal theology. And so also for Barth
there can be no synthesis of God and man. Absolutely not: "In this world
no human union with God is possible."[53] Yet Barth did not appropriate
Overbeck's critique of liberal theology simply in order to destroy liberal
theology the way Overbeck had done,[54] although he did consider that
necessary. Barth knew that he differed from Overbeck precisely in that
he took the latter's ironic remark seriously, that theology cannot be
established again except with audacity. We should probably put this
more tentatively: he *considered* taking it seriously. For Barth knew well
that a theology "which would dare to become eschatology . . . would be
not only a new theology but also a new Christianity, it would be a new
being, itself already a piece of the 'last things,' towering above the Reformation and all 'religious' movements."[55] That is probably why Barth did
not wish to make "positive proposals" but preferred to content himself
with the realization "that only the impossible can save us from the
impossible."[56] Barth concurred with Overbeck's diagnosis of "liberal
theology" and "modern Christianity": the idol totters.

In Barth's judgment, however, the idol was tottering because it was
time to think about the divine God. Barth studied Overbeck as an
example of someone who feels "forced under the pressure of present
events to make decisions and breakthroughs."[57] Overbeck's unsettled
questions for theology—and above all the "question of the practical
significance of the 'last things' "[58]—made Barth feel that it was his task
to reflect anew on the presuppositions of Christian theology, to begin
anew with the beginning. While Overbeck would have thought that the
insight "that only the impossible can save us from the impossible"
pointed to the absolute impossibility of Christian existence, Barth took
it to be an expression of hope. In fact, he thought of it as a paraphrase
of theological existence: a "wandering in the desert"[59]—a wandering,
however, which held out the hope of the promised land. Barth was not
unaware that "the matters dealt with in this audacious undertaking" are
massive, indeed "too massive for the theologian to be able to pass
through the narrow door of Overbeck's negation."[60] But he looked the
audacity of this undertaking straight in the eye. What he saw in the

"impossible possibility" was the inner disposition and structure of a hope which, with Paul (Rom. 4:18), may be somewhat aptly described as a faith in hope against all hope. We will need to clarify this further meaning of the concept "impossible possibility." What gives it support? What is its basis?

The reason for Barth's not merely negative attitude toward the task of theology—that is, toward the task of freshly establishing theology in the face of the undeniable failure of liberal theology—is surely to be sought in Barth's fundamental preoccupation with the Bible. But this objective basis was, however, at the same time theologically and historically mediated. By the time Barth began to stray from his teachers' theology, he had read not only Overbeck, but also the two Blumhardts and Friedrich Zündel. And Barth remained theologically close to the two Blumhardts for the rest of his life. He knew that he was in their debt. In fact, in his last lectures on the *Church Dogmatics,* which expounded his ethics of the doctrine of reconciliation (later published as a fragment from his literary remains), Barth offered a thankful testimony to how much his own theology was influenced by "the two Württembergers, Johann Christoph Blumhardt (1805–1880) and his son Christoph Blumhardt (1842–1919), who preached in Möttlingen and later in Bad Boll, and stood out in contrast to all the academic theology of their day. They did not so much teach as testify, in sermons, meditations, and other 'edifying' utterances—but still with the highest theological relevance—to the reality contained in the word and concept of the 'Kingdom of God.' "[61] Barth took this opportunity to summarize once again what the two Blumhardts and their proclamation of the Kingdom of God meant to him. "They clearly distinguished themselves from that tradition which goes back to the second century [the at least indirect identification of the Kingdom of God with the church or some other aspect of this life] and, as a result, they were unalterably opposed to identification of the Kingdom of God with the life and ministry of the church or with any of the other Christian communities within or outside the church [the *ecclesiolae in ecclesia*]. This still gives offense even today to their fellow Christians, whether scholastic or pietistic. When they spoke of the Kingdom of God, they saw far beyond even the best that has taken place or may yet take place within any church or chapel walls. They were, nevertheless, still close enough to that tradition that they thought they could still recognize a dawning of the Kingdom in certain historical changes and occurrences, in part already begun and in part still awaited. In this way the elder Blumhardt, until the end of his life, looked back again and again on the most extraordinary events he had witnessed in Möttlingen and later in Boll as well [the healing of Gottliebin Dittus—'Jesus is Victor!'—and the movement of repentance it triggered, along with further healings of the sick and 'possessed']. . . . He also looked forward in hope to a general outpouring of the Holy Spirit that would awaken the graveyard of his day's Christendom to a new life. . . . And so too, the younger Blumhardt in his middle years thought that he had discovered a more than natural light in the developments of . . . modern natural science, in social democracy, . . . indeed . . . briefly even in the Eastern religions. At that time, he had an unmistakable tendency to attribute to the world precisely that which he more and more denied to Christianity. He lacked, on the whole, the always rather corrosive scorn of Kierkegaard, but he was in fact no less decisive. One must, however, immediately offer the caution that in his last days he became quite selective about these matters and similar discoveries. . . . Both Blumhardts lacked nothing in vitality, in energy, or in a healthy self-consciousness." Yet a "peculiar, increasing restlessness about all the realizations [of the Kingdom of God on earth] which they themselves had known and experienced is unmistakable in the old age of both Blumhardts, father and son."[62] What really mattered to them both was "an Other which not only defines the boundaries of the world and illuminates it from beginning to end in all its dimensions, but which also breaks into the world and shakes it with superior strength and goodness. . . . The Other to which they looked . . . existed in its *coming* . . . . But what is this 'Other'? When the two Blumhardts spoke, with the greatest seriousness, of the Kingdom of God, they pronounced— startlingly, simply and directly—the name Jesus. This name illuminated and yet infinitely outshone all of the miracles of Möttlingen and the experiences of Boll, the long-awaited fresh outpouring of the Spirit, and, later, all auspicious scientific, or even religious . . . and political possibilities. It was neither the God-man of orthodox Christology, nor the . . . so-called 'historical' Jesus, that they had in mind. They meant very naively, but for that reason very surely, the reality of the resurrected, the living Jesus; the Jesus himself who today as yesterday acts, creates, and speaks as a real, quite specific, agent."[63] Christoph Blumhardt states clearly in his household devotions that the certainty of the resurrection must accompany all talk about Jesus: "As whenever Jesus is mentioned, it must mean that he is truly risen and bestows power through his words and his deeds."[64] In this sense "the entire story of the Blumhardts stood under this sign: 'Jesus is Victor!' The father told of having heard this sign with several other witnesses in a forest on a December day in 1843, only to hear it again, to his surprise, immediately afterwards, from the mouth of Gottliebin Dittus' sister, herself similarly possessed.* This time it resounded . . . like an agonized confession by a capitulating demon. No doctrine, then, no definition, but rather the unmistakable call from the

---

*Gottliebin Dittus was the name of a girl in Johann Christoph Blumhardt's congregation in Möttlingen who was healed of an apparent demonic possession.—TRANS.

heights and from the depths: 'Jesus—is—Victor!' . . . This is—if you have ears to hear, then hear! . . .—the characteristic thrust of the Blumhardts' thinking, their 'theology,' their message of the Kingdom of God, a message with such gravity that none who have heard it, even from afar, will be able to extricate themselves, despite their personal and historical limitations."[65]

Barth certainly had ears to hear the two Blumhardts. He published a review[66] of the Blumhardts' household devotions under the title "Auf das Reich Gottes warten" [Waiting for the Kingdom of God]. [67] And so by the time that he was confronted with Overbeck's insistence on the eschatological character of Christianity and his conclusion that modern Christianity was beginning to decay because it had betrayed this basic eschatological character, Barth already knew of a living Christianity whose "theology" was a proclamation of the Kingdom of God which hinged on the resurrection of Jesus. And now Barth apparently found in Overbeck the scholar who made it possible for him to radicalize what he had learned from the theology of the two Blumhardts. On the other hand, he had already found in the Blumhardts those Christians and nonscholarly theologians who made it possible for him to stand up to "the Overbeckian negation" and even to recommend it as "an introduction to theology." The contradiction between Overbeck and his contemporary, the younger Blumhardt, can, to be sure, scarcely be overestimated. What one declared to be (or to have become) historically impossible, the other fulfilled with complete naiveté. "Both lived in very different worlds; they scarcely knew each other, and had they known each other, each would surely have been a source of the greatest amazement for the other." Yet Barth still thought that "that which drove 'scientific' theology one way at the end of the nineteenth century must be taken together with that which the two Blumhardts . . . very unscientifically, but therefore quite positively, represented."[68] And so, when he discovered Overbeck, he had also immediately seen him as a counterpoint to the Blumhardts. "They stood next to each other . . . , back to back, if you like, differing greatly in habit, vocabulary, in their conceptual worlds, in experience, but together in substance—Blumhardt as the forward-looking, hopeful Overbeck, Overbeck as the backward-looking, critical Blumhardt, each as a witness for the other's mission."[69] Barth knew that he was called "to the matter" through both of them, precisely because they were a stumbling block, a *skandalon,* to the theology of that day.[70]

It cannot be overlooked that Barth's study of Overbeck enabled him to radicalize what he had learned from the two Blumhardts. The previously quoted comment on Romans 8:24 from the second edition of his commentary on Romans (that any Christianity which is not utterly and absolutely eschatological has utterly and absolutely nothing to do with

Christ) does not, significantly, appear in the first edition. But Barth had already expressed Christianity's eschatological basis in a somewhat less radical fashion in the first edition with his comment on Romans 8:17f.: "Trust in God cannot be separated from eschatology."[71] Again, commenting on Romans 8:19–22, he continued: "*Solving the riddle* of the world cannot be separated from eschatology."[72] And on Romans 8:23–25 comes the declaration "that *certainty of salvation* and *eschatology* are inseparably united."[73] "For the sake of our connection with the coming world, God takes us and uses us as we are."[74] The radicalization that Barth's thought underwent as a result of his study of Overbeck (along with his reading of Kierkegaard and Dostoevsky, among others) is most forcefully expressed in the distance between God and humanity, between the coming Kingdom and present world reality. Overbeck taught him to keep "the negative significance" of "what Kierkegaard called the 'infinite qualitative distinction' between time and eternity in view as persistently as possible."[75] Overbeck sharpened Barth's eye for the impossible.

Yet Barth wanted to keep "what Kierkegaard called the 'infinite qualitative distinction' between time and eternity in view as persistently as possible" not only for its "negative" but also for its "positive" significance.[76] And he could do that because he dared to read Overbeck as a "backward-looking, critical Blumhardt" and Blumhardt as a "forward-looking, hopeful Overbeck." The two Blumhardts opened his eyes to see that the impossible becomes possible. And so the possibility of "righteousness before God, righteousness which comes from him,"[77] is interpreted in the second edition of *The Epistle to the Romans* as the "inconceivable breaking-in of God as God, of the unknown God, into our known context of reality, the impossible possibility of the new world! Humanly impossible, but possible with God."[78] This possibility, described with the most paradoxical expression "impossible possibility," is conceived as something foreign to the reality of the world, an alien power whose potency can in no way derive from the energy (as the Greeks called reality) of the world; it is indeed impossible within the context of the world. Within the reality of the world, this possibility *must* appear as a paradox. For this reason "the impossible possibility of the faithfulness of God" reveals itself for Barth "in the paradox of faith." Yet "the faithfulness of God in the paradox of faith" is sufficient. "It suffices for us because with it we stand on sure ground and walk a sure path."[79] Paradoxically, this ground and this path are safe because they are not founded or constructed on this world. In a certain proximity to Plato's understanding of the moment which ever and anon instantly occurs, Barth affirms that "the possibility of clothing the divine in a human garment, the eternal in a temporal parable, can be permitted only when the possibility is recognized as an *impossible* possibility, a moment with no before and no after. We must not conclude from this that we have achieved a secure place to stand. That is a decision which can only be made by God as God, in God alone. We cannot claim that we have attained this possibility. We can only, in fear and trembling, determine that it can occur."[80]

This peculiar category of "impossible possibility," with which Barth seeks to describe the formal essence of Christianity, initially had a polemic function: to declare impossible (at least humanly impossible) what liberal theology had taken to be all too possible, indeed self-evident. And if, according to Barth, it should nevertheless be possible, it is only as a possibility for God which does not proceed from the context of earthly reality, and which is indeed impossible within that context. The characterization of the impossible possibility as a moment "with no before and no after,"[81] however, transcends any polemic intent, and is in fact best understood in terms of Barth's study of Plato (influenced by his brother Heinrich Barth). Indeed, Barth referred explicitly to Plato—as well as to Overbeck and others—in the foreword to the second edition of *The Epistle to the Romans.*[82] Kierkegaard plays a role as well, with his emphasis on the "moment" as crucial to any understanding of Christianity, and so also does Schleiermacher's famous declaration (well known to Barth) at the conclusion of his second speech on religion: "To be eternal in a moment, that is the immortality of religion."[83] But both of these formulations are also indebted to the Platonic model. And so it will be helpful to clarify Barth's description of the impossible possibility of God as a moment with no before and no after in terms of Plato's *exaiphnēs.*

Plato speaks of the *exaiphnēs* in the *Parmenides,* where he raises the question of how, in the context of our reality, something at rest can change to something in motion, and conversely, how something in motion can come to be at rest. The question is of primary importance for any understanding of reality, for the real confronts us either in a state of rest or in motion. We are not, however, confronted by the transition from the one to the other. But it is precisely this transition which is decisive for the context of our reality, which depends on constant transition from rest to movement and from movement to rest. How is this possible, how can it become possible? Rest does not wish to be disturbed. And it certainly cannot set itself in motion alone. The transition to movement is, then, not explicable on the basis of rest. Motion, similarly, does not wish to come to rest. And above all, it cannot cease to move by itself and cannot come to rest. Rest and motion are by definition so completely opposed to each other that each excludes the other. Rest permits no motion, and motion no rest. But the reality of the world consists not least in this, that rest is set in motion and motion is brought to rest. The reality of the world is constituted by the transition from the one to the other. And so the question becomes all the more pressing: from whence does this transition, and with it the context which is constitutive of the reality of the world, draw its being at all? Plato answers: The moment which ever and anon instantly occurs makes that transition. But this concept can be only negatively illustrated: "this thing with no place, the moment,"[84] this sudden essence which is in no place, or, as Schleiermacher translated it, "this incomprehensible essence, the moment." And this queer moment is an intermediate which lies between rest and motion and does not itself belong to any time: "situated between the motion and the rest, it occupies no time at all."[85] Therefore, "with no place" and "occupying no time at all," the transition from rest to motion and from motion to rest takes place without spatial or temporal identity. With neither a location in space nor a place in time, that sudden, instantaneous moment which is constitutive of the context of space and time occurs as the transition between rest and motion. This moment is not constituted by a possibility proceeding from this reality, but is rather a potency which confronts it, ever and anon suddenly occurring. That which cannot be identified spatially or temporally in this world is that which holds the world together at its core.

This is something like the way Karl Barth, tutored by his philosophical brother Heinrich, might have received Plato. Karl Barth's concern, however, was not to grasp what ultimately holds the world together, but to understand how God can confront the context of world reality. He used the Platonic framework to insist polemically that the temporal (finite) cannot by itself conceive of the eternal (infinite): *Finitum non capax infiniti.* At the same time, that Platonic framework enabled him to express the worldly impossibility as a divine possibility: the moment with no before and no after. Drawing on Plato's moment, Barth can make sense out of what was simply an absurdity for Overbeck. That which is necessary is that which is impossible: "Christians must be children, but they cannot." For Barth, Overbeck's statement now gains a more than paradoxical meaning, because now, with help from Plato, it becomes formally conceivable. He now traces this apparent absurdity —that that which must be, cannot be—back to Jesus' assertion: "humanly impossible, but possible for God" (paraphrase of Mark 10:27); and he can elevate this saying, usually taken to be merely edifying, to the rank of a category, indeed to the rank of a theological axiom of ontological relevance.

"Impossible possibility" now becomes something more than self-contradiction. This peculiar combination of words hints at a way of thinking which God requires of the world—indeed, not only requires but also permits. The assertion that such thoughts are impossible is posted like a guard at the shrine. The category of "impossible possibility" in this phase of Barth's thought does not mean to stifle theological thinking, or even thinking itself. Rather, the process of thought should be set right:

the divine possibility in question can only be conceived (and therefore should be so conceived) through the needle's eye of recognizing its human and earthly impossibility. Barth does not simply stop with the antithesis of worldly impossibility and divine possibility. He was not interested in this sort of abstract dialectic. It did take some time before he found the conceptual and theological framework (and the corresponding positions) which would lead out of the exciting, but also rather too excited and gruff dialectic, with its precipitous contrasts and its rather too formal *sic et non* [yes and no]. It is clear that Barth was not interested in the antithesis for its own sake; he was not trying to demonstrate the impossibility of theology, but its possibility. This was already evident by the time that the beginnings of his theological development came to an end. He did not remain satisfied with the bald contradiction that Overbeck had intended as an argument *ad absurdum:* Christians must—but they cannot. Barth's thinking certainly did not run in the direction of a synthesis, let alone a compromise. He did not say "either-or" in order to add "both-and" right away, and then to connect both phrases with a third, most dearly beloved by theologians of compromise, "not only–but also." If there is any continuity in Barth's thought, then it lies in his lifelong suspicion of "not only either-or but also both-and." Barth was never inclined to compromise. He certainly did not want Overbeck's antithesis to perish in a compromise. But he likewise refused to accept Overbeck's blunt antithesis of necessity and impossibility as final.

We have already seen one of Barth's own antitheses. In the lecture "The Word of God and the Task of the Ministry" (1922), Barth said: "As theologians we ought to speak of God. We are human, however, and so cannot speak of God." But Barth was just as little satisfied with this blunt opposition as he would have been with a "higher" synthesis or compromise. He continued: "We ought to recognize both our obligation and our inability, and by that very recognition give God the glory."[86] It is this recognition that separated Barth from the theology he had been taught. This recognition is a matter of aporia [perplexity or doubt]. The theology he had learned recognized no systematic theological aporia; it only knew how to escape before getting trapped in a situation from which there was no escape. Barth thought these means of escape were too commonplace, an all too smoothly paved boulevard which he was not prepared to travel. He sought paths that stood up to aporia. For this reason his thought, his knowledge, became above all aporetic. And with this aporetic knowledge, his theological beginnings came to an end.

Meanwhile, he wanted this recognition to give God the glory, and here is the beginning point of a theology which would go beyond an aporetic basis. For to "give God the glory" is not some kind of a pious vault over aporia, and is certainly not an edifying phrase designed to silence it. Instead, to give God the glory by recognizing our obligation and inability

—that is Barth's outrageous demand on our thought and knowledge. And now it most certainly demands the exertion of thought. As we have said, it took some time before Barth's efforts led, in his own judgment, to a somewhat serviceable theological groundwork. He was now unceasingly moving toward that end, searching and testing, erring and discarding, immersed in criticism and self-criticism.

Theology as Metacriticism:
Toward a Hermeneutic of Theological Exegesis

"The historical-critical school must become more critical in order to suit me!"[87] This was Barth's response to a critic of the first edition of his commentary on Romans who charged him with being a "declared enemy of historical criticism."[88] The accusation gave Barth an opportunity, in the foreword to the second edition, to expound his own understanding of "criticism" more precisely. He did so by meeting the historical-critical theology of that day with theological criticism. This occasion marked a new beginning for theology with the recognition that liberal theology had reached a state of aporia, even though liberal theology would not admit it. This merits closer analysis, for it brings the end of Barth's theological beginnings into exceptionally sharp focus.

The Epistle to the Romans had provoked the liberal theologians (insofar as they took notice of it at all) to accuse Barth of eliminating history from his interpretation of Paul. Since the theology Barth advocated was in fact antihistorical, they charged, his exegesis was necessarily antihistorical as well. Biblicism and pneumatic exegesis had replaced historical-critical exegesis. I shall amplify this accusation with reference to Adolf Jülicher's brilliant review of the first edition of the commentary on Romans. The review appeared under the title "A Modern Interpreter of Paul."[89]

Jülicher's review is especially impressive because it is involuntarily dialectical. It is essentially a sharp rejoinder to Barth's book. But it is also a recommendation. The scholar, the critical historian, the learned theologian Adolf Jülicher raises protest; but Adolf Jülicher the Christian, as I see it, is edified. At any rate, Jülicher wishes Barth's book many readers, even if they for the time being will skip his "presumptuous" foreword.[90] Barth had concluded that foreword with the assurance that if his interpretation elicited no immediate response, it had "time to wait; the Epistle to the Romans waits also."[91] Jülicher, at the close of his review, grants him as much: "The Epistle to the Romans does not need to wait." And although Jülicher the historian must criticize Barth as an advocate "of a period in the history of culture that is not attuned to history," he also observes that Barth's book illustrates how "Christianity the religion will not perish, . . . and the letters of Paul will not die."[92] Nevertheless, Barth's foreword makes the entire work suspect.

In the terse foreword to the first edition, Barth emphasizes that Paul "addressed his contemporaries as a child of his age." But it is "far more important that he speaks as a prophet and apostle of the Kingdom of God to people of every age."[93] It is noteworthy that Barth calls Paul (contrary to Paul's own self-understanding) not only an apostle but also a prophet, and not an apostle of Jesus Christ (as Paul calls himself) but an apostle of the Kingdom of God. This would have been completely unthinkable to Paul (the expression "Kingdom of God" plays almost no part in his letters). It is noteworthy, moreover, that Barth considers it "far more important" that Paul speaks, than that he once spoke. Of course "the difference between then and now" must be noted, but "the purpose of such investigation can only be to demonstrate that these differences make no difference. The historical-critical method of biblical investigation has its rightful place. It is concerned with the preparation of the intelligence, and this can never be superfluous. But, were I driven to choose between it and the venerable doctrine of inspiration, I should without hesitation adopt the latter, which has a broader, deeper, more important justification, for it is concerned with the task of understanding as such. . . . Fortunately, I am not compelled to choose between the two. Nevertheless, my energy has been entirely directed toward the task of seeing through the historical to the spirit of the Bible, which is the eternal spirit. What was once of great importance is still so today. What is today of great importance, and is not just accidental and faddish, stands in a direct relation to that which was once of such importance. Our questions, if we ourselves understand them aright, are Paul's questions; and Paul's answers, if we let them cast their light upon us, must be our answers."[94] In this sense, this book is "written with a joyful sense of discovery," and, correspondingly, "in objective partnership beside Paul, not set apart from him as a serene spectator."[95]

That is a hermeneutical declaration of principle. One could call it the declaration of a hermeneutic of simultaneity. But the liberal theologians had to understand it as a declaration of war, and Jülicher retaliated quickly and decisively. Anyone who claims that he does not have to choose between the historical-critical method of biblical study and the old doctrine of inspiration has already, as far as that day's historical-critical method is concerned, decided against the former and must therefore be a biblicist or a pneumatic. Whoever dares to see *"through* the historical" and claims "to stand in objective partnership beside Paul" must be suspected of ignoring history. As early as 1916, Barth wrote that he had become "frightfully indifferent" to historical questions. "Of course that is nothing new for me. Already under the influence of Herrmann, I always thought of historical criticism as merely a means of attaining freedom over against tradition, not, however, as a constitutive factor in a new liberal tradition."[96] Jülicher also concludes that one could learn "scarcely anything new" from Barth's book "for the understanding of the 'historical' Paul." And, not unlike Harnack's judgment that Barth would be a better object than a subject of scientific theology,[97] Jülicher also concludes that one may learn "much, perhaps even very much" from this book "for the understanding of our time."[98] This time, an era which is "not attuned to history," is moving toward a denial of history. "In Barth there is no room for the impulse of even a limited respect for what the gospel has accomplished in the 1900 years before the Letter to the Romans was rediscovered"[99]—rediscovered by Barth, that is! The hermeneutic of simultaneity, while it does not fully embrace the old doctrine of inspiration, nevertheless attests that that doctrine "is concerned with the task of understanding,"[100] rather than merely preparing for understanding; and to Jülicher that seemed to be a denial of history.[101] He described Barth and Friedrich Gogarten as theologians for whom "there is nothing more sure than that there is no more progress in history, that development is forever at an end, and that no optimism in the interest of culture moves us anymore."[102] And because they do not look for any progress in the future, they see the past as something to be left behind. Gogarten even " 'rejoices at the downfall [of history], for no one likes to live among corpses.' "[103]

What outraged Jülicher was the separation of Christianity from history which lay behind such pronouncements. For Jülicher, Christianity was finally identical with its historical impact. But Gogarten rejected that: "We," he wrote, "do not equate Christianity with its historical expression,"[104] outlining a position which, in Jülicher's eyes, was utterly incapable of providing a scientifically adequate account of the origins of Christianity, and such an account was, in turn, essential to any account of the essence of Christianity. The immediacy claimed by Gogarten and Barth for their relationship to Paul was fundamentally nothing more than "holy egoism." For Jülicher, this fundamentally unhistorical claim —to share in Paul's problems and thereby to understand his answers in partnership with him—threatens to make any real understanding of Paul impossible. Whoever expects to learn nothing from the subsequent history can also gain nothing from the original history. "Anyone who in holy egoism thinks only of his own questions and chides the dead, who can no longer answer back, can surely not demand that a product of the past—as the Letter to the Romans most surely still is—should become alive for him. . . . My own questions I answer as well as I can in the privacy of my own room. I do not pretend that, as a historical researcher, I can give an answer to anyone else's questions."[105]

The fact that Barth and Gogarten believed that they could give this answer betrayed, as Jülicher saw it, their radical nonhistoricity. They already claimed to stand beyond this world. "That is actual denial of history. . . . And this lack of reverence for the past's greatness . . . makes it impossible for even the most ardent admirer of Paul in the no longer Christian Christendom to explain Paul impartially and correctly."[106] For Jülicher, this is a decidedly Gnostic position. And so Jülicher the historian offered a historical diagnosis of the disease of the deniers of history: they were neo-Gnostics. He saw Gogarten as a "Basilides wandering between the aeons,[107] or a new Valentinus," and in Barth he recognized "the half-Gnostic Marcion with his radical dualism of all or nothing and his wrath on those who go only halfway."[108]

If Jülicher wished Barth's *Romans* many readers anyway, it was because the book was still important "as a stimulus for the direction that thought must take if it is to keep Paul alive [!] and arouse the spirits of present-day readers."[109] Barth stands "with passionate commitment in the midst of the struggle with the problem" and commands "superb gifts" for reproducing "the basic thought of that letter in the language of our time."[110] That is precisely why Jülicher categorizes the book as practical, not scientific theology. "Barth forced me point-blank to make a decision about the question of the significance of practical exegesis of scripture compared to strictly scientific exegesis. His *Epistle to the Romans* is well suited to showing its necessity."[111]

Barth, to be sure, was not exactly enthusiastic about this. He was sharply critical of Jülicher's eagerness "to turn me out into the quiet pastures of practical theology"[112]—an eagerness that was just as suspicious as it was significant—and took that opportunity to reopen the question of understanding. It is still surprising that neither Jülicher nor Barth seems to have wondered whether theology is not, in its inmost essence, "practical," as the old Lutheran theology had taught. If the true purpose of theology is practical,[113] then Jülicher's eagerness to banish Barth into the supposedly quiet pastures of practical theology would have been an involuntary but first-class testimony to the scientific relevance of Barth's effort to understand Paul's letter to the Romans.

"I am no 'pneumatic.' . . . I am no 'declared enemy of historical criticism.' "[114] Barth had no intention of letting the theologians of the historical-critical school pressure him into rejecting historical criticism. On the contrary, he understood himself as a critical theologian throughout his life; in the year before his death, he amiably but firmly rejected Rudolf Smend's call for a "postcritical interpretation of scripture." He demurred, without having properly understood the proposal, because of the term "postcritical." Similarly, when he took his leave of liberal theology, he did not wish to leave historical criticism behind. Instead, he wanted to press on to the real hermeneutical task, "the task of understanding." This is why he summons up the old doctrine of verbal inspiration, for it had always pointed to the necessity of this task. This is why he demands that the historical critics be more critical. At any rate, some kind of a criticism of historical criticism itself is necessary, a hermeneutical metacriticism that can direct historical criticism to its proper task. In his dispute with the historical critics of that day, Barth's theology proves to be very much a metacritical theology. This can be seen in his reaction to the charge that he was a "declared enemy of historical criticism."

The most important thing about Barth's hermeneutic is its universality. Significantly, he does not plead for the special theological method or hermeneutic that his opponents probably expected from him. His "biblicist" method is by his own admission not restricted to the Bible. He would apply it to Lao-Tzu or Goethe if it were his "job to explain Lao-Tzu or Goethe."[115] At the same time, he confesses that it would be difficult to apply this method "to some other books of the Bible."[116] One may surmise that this is because not all the biblical writers seemed to recognize the questions of the present as their own, so that their answers would ultimately not be our answers. Barth recognizes, then, something like a relevance criticism *[Sachkritik]* of both nonbiblical and biblical writings. His purported "biblicism" consists in his openly admitted "prejudice that the Bible is a good book, and that it is worthwhile to take its thoughts at least as seriously as our own."[117] But that is true of any good book. There can be no question, therefore, of a special, let alone even pneumatic, method of exegesis. Barth condenses his hermeneutical method to the short imperative: "Consider well!"[118] What does that mean? What must we consider in order to understand what someone else has written?

Surely one must consider oneself! "If we rightly understand ourselves, our questions [should be] Paul's questions," as Barth says in the foreword to the first edition.[119] He thus assumes that there are such things as basic human questions which endure throughout all historical vicissitudes. He shares this premise with liberal theologians. The problem is that he cannot agree with them on just what these basic questions are. He knows of other questions more urgent than theirs. Now a shrewd thinker might reason: If even contemporaries cannot agree on these basic human questions, their identity throughout all historical vicissitudes must be rather tentative. But Barth does not think that these questions are, so to speak, just sitting around, waiting to be asked. Indeed, he added the clear reservation "if we rightly understand ourselves." Yet we do not always rightly understand ourselves. Hence the hermeneutical imperative: Consider well! Consider yourself!

For Barth, the dispute over the correct method of biblical exegesis was —then, at least—identical to the dispute over what constitutes a proper self-understanding. That was why he could not accept Adolf Jülicher's description of his work as "practical biblical exegesis." Behind this he saw an inadequate theory of historical understanding, which limits self-understanding to the realm of practical theology. Self-understanding can then occur only in the immediate present, while historical understanding is kept free from any attempt at self-understanding. Barth denies that this will lead to better historical understanding. "It is consistent with my principle of exposition that I cannot see how the contemporary parallels, which in other commentaries are just about all there is, should be more instructive . . . than the events of which we ourselves are witnesses" for the purpose of "understanding and explaining the Letter to the Romans."[120] His principle of exegesis forbade him to carry "respect for history" so far that history itself can no longer be understood. Barth charged that those who tried to teach him "respect for history" had themselves abandoned the task of "earnest, respectful understanding and explanation."[121] His charge can also be understood as a rejection of the false dichotomy between the historical explanation of historically transmitted texts, on the one hand, and the practical clarification of one's own relationship to the subject matter of those texts, on the other. This dichotomy makes real understanding impossible. What Jülicher assigns to practical theology is, for Barth, constitutive of the historical process of understanding. In an allusion to Lietzmann's *Handbuch zum Neuen Testament* [Handbook of the New Testament], in which some space had been given to the work of a practical theologian, Barth sarcastically asks: "Do the historians really suppose that they have fulfilled their duty to human society in that as a nice gesture, they permit Niebergall to speak —in the fifth volume?"[122] And using one of his critic's favorite words, Barth insists that "there are texts—for example, those of the New Testament—the hearing of which, no matter what the cost, can be termed an ultimate and profound concern of (to say the word for once) culture."[123]

The point, therefore, about which the controversy swirled was that both sides, although they based their arguments on diametrically opposite premises, accused each other of the same thing: making historical understanding impossible. Barth's understanding, according to his critics, was not historical understanding, while he maintained that the "historical-critical" exegetes never arrived at any understanding truly worthy of the name. Jülicher and others maintained that Barth wished to allow the texts to speak "no matter what the cost," and yet only really succeeded in allowing himself to speak. Barth maintained that they, in explaining the texts historically, did not even try to let them speak. For if a text is to speak, it must have hearers who are willing to be confronted by what the text has to say. But for that to occur there must be some kind of material relationship between the listener and the message of the text. This relationship, for Barth, is part of the task of historical understanding. "As one who would understand, I must press forward to the point where insofar as possible I confront the riddle of the *subject matter* and no longer merely the riddle of the *document* as such, where I can almost forget that I am not the author, where I have almost understood him so well that I let him speak in my name, and can myself speak in his name. . . . Or are these historians, whom I truly respect as scholars, quite unaware that there is content, a cardinal question, a Word in the words?"[124]

Now these scholars certainly thought that they recognized a content, a Word in the words. Their difference from Barth was only that they must have thought this matter was largely foreign to history, something that it was their duty as scholars to separate from history. For this reason they insisted on critical distance in method, so that the interpreter could never forget that he was not the author of the text to be interpreted. For them, historical criticism meant maintaining the historical distance between the interpreter and the text and its content. In light of this understanding of historical criticism, Barth thought it necessary to elevate criticism to metacriticism. He sought a closer relationship between the text and its interpreter, despite their undeniable historical distance. For him, real understanding begins where the explanations of "the historical critics" end, in a second stage, different in principle: "practical application."

The difference can be seen in Barth's metacriticism of Paul Wernle's criticism of his exegesis. Barth begins by reciting the litany of Wernle's objections: " 'There is absolutely no point in the thought of Paul that he [Barth] finds disagreeable . . . ; no remnant conditioned by the history of the times, however modest, is left out,' Wernle writes with a certain bitterness, and then he lists what should have been 'left out' as 'disagreeable points' and 'remnants conditioned by the history of the times,' namely: the Pauline 'belittling' of the earthly lifework of Jesus, Christ as the Son of God, reconciliation through the blood of Christ, Christ and Adam, Pauline scriptural proofs, the so-called 'baptism sacramentalism,' double predestination, and Paul's relation to the magistrate."[125] Barth lists these Pauline concepts—which he had indecently failed to relegate to the inscrutable past—in order to register a point, not without rancor, but pertinent nevertheless: "Let us imagine a commentary on Romans in which these eight little points remain unexplained, that is, are declared to be 'disagreeable points' which are 'left out' under a scrollwork of contemporary parallels! How could that be called a 'commentary'? In contrast to this agreeable ignoring of disagreeable points," Barth emphasizes that he senses "more or less clearly in the background a 'remnant' that is not understood and not explained and which awaits working out. But it awaits working out—not being left out."[126]

It is this intractable, penetrating desire to understand Paul directly that makes Barth's exegesis a theological interpretation, "a part of the conversation of a theologian with theologians."[127] This desire to understand all biblical contexts and matters theologically distinguishes him just as much from the liberal theologians as from the so-called positive [orthodox] theologians. The latter are, to be sure, "better off" in Barth's judgment "than their 'liberal' colleagues, in that the more or less powerful orthodoxy or other historical form of Christianity to which they customarily withdraw is always a somewhat more stately haven of refuge than cultural Protestantism's religion of conscience. Strictly speaking," however, "this means only that they have been more successful in concealing their lack of will to understand and explain."[128] For his part, though, Barth would never give up that will. He was later compared to Hegel for his intellectualism and indulgence in speculation. But no one could accuse him of being an advocate for a cause which he had not himself thoughtfully considered and theologically pondered. If the Bible is to have meaning, then what is there must be "not only . . . repeated" but "rethought."[129]

There is a further dimension to this kind of rethinking. We would completely misunderstand Barth's lapidary formulation of his method, "Consider well!" if we stopped with our previous answer to the question, "What must we consider?" We have already answered: "Consider yourself!" And that is correct. But we cannot really deny that both the liberal and the positive theologians were willing to do that. It was precisely because they did know themselves well that a Wernle, for example, was sensitive to Paul's "disagreeable points." The problem here was that the requisite self-knowledge was entirely removed from the task of exegesis and understanding.

And that was exactly what Barth called into question. For him, "Consider well!" meant: Consider yourself well by considering someone else and opening yourself to the cause he advocates. Barth's principle of interpretation is a hermeneutical circle between that which is understood and that which is to be understood. In Paul's letter to the Romans, what is to be understood is, as Barth saw it then, the "permanent crisis of time and eternity."[130] This is because he presupposes that Paul "spoke of Jesus Christ and not of anything else." For that reason, he is worth taking seriously. "Paul knows something about God which we as a rule do not know, but which we certainly could know."[131]

With this statement, Barth's general hermeneutic now becomes particular, a specifically theological hermeneutic. But this is not a reversal of his general hermeneutical principles; it is their consequence. The general hermeneutical rule instructs the interpreter to be open to the particular and peculiar subject of the text. With all texts, not just "religious" ones, the essential question must be whether the subject that they express in their own language is to be taken seriously; and if it is, then the general method of understanding must be subordinated to this particular subject. In this sense, Barth takes it as a serious matter that Paul knows something about God. "That I know Paul knew this is my 'system,' my 'dogmatic presupposition.' . . . I have found that, even considered from the point of view of historical criticism, this is relatively more effective."[132]

But how does Barth know that Paul knows something about God? That Paul claims to speak of God is clear. But is this claim justified? How does Barth know that Paul's language about God truly speaks of God? How is speech about God to be verified? Barth does not, on principle, answer such questions—at any rate not with a proposition. At that time, he responded to it with another question, but this counterquestion does conceal an axiom within it. It extends far beyond the issue of Paul's letter to the Romans and touches it at the same time. The counterquestion asks "whether an earnest person can approach a text [note: not only this text] which is not patently frivolous with any other assumption than this— that God is God."[133]

God is God—that is Barth's axiom. At that time, when his theological beginnings came to an end, this axiom was still a general presupposition, presupposed largely in the sense of natural theology. For if one should be able to approach any text worth taking seriously with the assumption that God is God, then this assumption is to be taken as a given. Thurneysen put it much the same way in a sermon which appeared in an anthology of sermons which he and Barth had written: "I cannot conceive of anyone in whom this questioning and searching and calling for God was not in some way present."[134] Later, Barth would vehemently dispute the possibility of a general knowledge of God apart from the revelation of God in Jesus Christ. But for the time being he still worked with the premises of natural theology—with a characteristic difference. Whereas the so-called natural theology of Reformed dogmatics concerned itself only with the question of the existence of God and with the knowledge of some of the divine attributes, Barth was scarcely interested in those matters. He simply took the statement that God is God as a universal presupposition. This tautology highlights more the essence of God than the existence of God, and only in a rather negative form. Its function is not to establish some kind of divine existence or essence, but rather to underscore the absolute otherness of the divine essence, the deity of God, in opposition to all that is not God. According to Barth, one must read every text worth taking seriously on the premise that God is not world, not finite, not human, but simply God—every text, not just biblical or religious writings!

We must describe, if only briefly, what this presupposition implies. If one can, may, and indeed must approach all objects of human understanding and explanation with the assumption that God is God, then all of these objects would necessarily have to respond, to resonate to this assumption. They would have to begin to speak of God themselves, or at least be capable of doing so. Taken seriously, this would mean that there is no real need for the specific science of theology; indeed, all sciences would be concerned with the business of theology as they sought understanding and clarification. Barth later realized this conclusion himself, if only in the form of a hypothesis, in the first few paragraphs of the *Church Dogmatics,* asserting that the "independence of theology over against the other sciences is at least not to be proved as a matter of necessary principle. As for treating the question of the truth of language about God as a special question belonging to a particular faculty," he continues, "that is a difficulty which we should desire to make the best of by acknowledging seriously its true inevitability, but not to justify on final grounds. Only theological arrogance would dream of arguing here otherwise than practically. It could be that philosophy, or historical science or sociology or psychology or pedagogics, or all of them working toether, working in the sphere of the church, would undertake the task . . . and thus render a special theology superfluous. Theology does not really find itself in possession of special keys for special doors! . . . Philosophy and 'secular' scholarship in general really need not be 'secular,' need not be heathen; they could be Christian philosophy."[135] This later explication indicates how seriously Barth intended the earlier counterquestion: "whether an earnest person can approach a text which is not patently frivolous with any other assumption than this—that God is God."[136]

Turning back to the Barth of the foreword to the second edition, we see that he construes the axiom that God is God as a prejudgment that anyone can arrive at. (This is something he will later dispute, asserting that this "axiom" corresponds to the First Commandment and is therefore a concrete promise—not something that can be conceived a priori!) His specifically theological hermeneutic is also a consequence of his general concept of understanding. Indeed, he returns to it in the end. If all understanding takes place in the context of this prejudgment, then the problem of historical understanding becomes something very different from what it was for the liberal theologians. They approached biblical texts just as they approached all secular texts, that is, with the presupposition of the three essential elements of the historical method enumerated by Troeltsch:[137] (1) the basic principle of criticism, that all judgments are only probable; (2) the analogy between historical events and our own experience, as well as the analogy between historical events themselves; and (3) the principle of correlation, according to which all phenomena are interconnected and every event in history has its antecedents and consequences. Barth, on the other hand, insists that all secular texts be explained in the same way as biblical texts—under the presupposition that God is God. That changes the problem of historical understanding in principle. The task of understanding Paul becomes the task of understanding God, since Paul—and not only Paul!—can only be correctly understood on the premise that God is God.

The subject of Paul's letter coincides with the hermeneutical presupposition that God is God, and that is what makes it so theologically instructive. A critical interpretation of Paul must lie within this hermeneutical circle, moving from this presupposition to his subject. The interpreter personally considers Paul's subject and also considers himself. But that means that the problem of historical understanding now becomes the problem of faith and knowledge. This makes the question all the more pointed; it is more critical for Barth than the criticism of the historical-critical school. Not that he thought the problem was solved. "I know that the problem is not simple."[138] But he would not accept a simpler formulation of the problem. Only when the other side would acknowledge this problem would Barth consider it possible to agree on "the difficulties and dangers, not unknown to me, of what I call critical theology."[139]

It is one of the missed opportunities of twentieth-century theology that Barth could at that time find no one to debate this with him; and when just such a competent critic and opponent later appeared in Rudolf Bultmann, he was no longer prepared to engage Bultmann's different approach to the hermeneutical problem, despite the fact that he had applauded Bultmann's review of the second edition of *Romans* because it corresponded to his own formulation of the problem.[140]

Barth's exchange with Bultmann was critical, but it also embraced a far-reaching consensus. The debate with Bultmann shows how radical Barth's consciousness of the problem had become at that revolutionary time, more so even than his dispute with Jülicher and Wernle indicates. For that reason it too merits our attention.

In his "for the most part friendly" review of the second edition of *Romans,* Bultmann had objected that Barth, despite his radical efforts to understand the subject of the letter, was not radical enough[141] because he did not criticize Paul, who, according to Barth's hermeneutic, was supposed to have retreated completely behind the subject matter. Bultmann maintains that even Paul does not always speak to the subject: "In him there are other spirits speaking besides the Spirit of Christ."[142]

Barth responded by suggesting that those other spirits speak in all of Paul's utterances. "Or, at what place could one point his finger with the observation that *there* assuredly the Spirit of Christ speaks? Or to turn the matter around, is the Spirit of Christ perhaps a spirit which can be presented as competing *along with* other spirits?"[143] Barth therefore wants to follow an even more radical procedure than Bultmann's, refusing to identify the spirit of Christ with any specific biblical texts. The human words of Paul all express other spirits, as can be discerned by the history of culture and the history of religions. Paul speaks throughout as a child of his time. But it is in just this way that he puts the subject matter into words as best he can. As a result, spot criticism of the subject matter here and there makes no sense. The spirit of Christ is rather "the crisis in which the whole finds itself. Everything is *litera*" [2 Cor. 3:6]. Therefore everything must be read with the premise and with the question, whether it might not "be understood . . . as the voice of the *spiritus* (of Christ)."[144]

In this way Barth demands, once again as a general hermeneutical rule, that the exegete "enter into a relationship of faithfulness to the author," intending to "read him with the hypothesis that the author also knew with more or less clarity down to the last word . . . what it was all about. . . . The exegete spares no pains to show the degree to which what is scattered is still paradoxically part of the context of the one subject matter, and how all the 'other' spirits really are somehow subject to the Spirit of Christ."[145] Bultmann also had attributed a "modern dogma of inspiration"[146] to Barth because of this basic hermeneutical position; this was, of course, close to how Barth saw it himself. But the exchange with Bultmann clarifies how Barth understood his hermeneutical procedure as a certain analogy to "the old teaching of verbal inspiration."[147] It was not his intention (as tended to be the case with this doctrine) to distinguish the biblical texts from others, but rather to establish the hypothesis, appropriate for every author, that the author spoke of his subject matter throughout, and that his language is thoroughly relevant. "I hold that it is impossible for anyone to do justice to any writer, to be able really to bring any writer to speak again, without daring to assume that hypothesis, without entering into that relationship of faithfulness to the writer."[148] The spirit of the subject matter inspires —that is how Barth's unique version of the dogma of inspiration can be formulated. But it must be applied to all serious texts. And because the spirit of the subject matter inspires the writer, Barth cannot apply a spot criticism, but simply always an alert, implicit, continuous criticism (an interpretation *with* Paul, if "not without sighs and shaking of the head"[149]). That is why he cannot understand how Bultmann can invite him to think for the time being "*with* Paul . . . *in* the entirely foreign language of his Jewish-popular-Christian-Hellenistic thought world, and then suddenly, when this may get to be too much for me—as if something struck me especially strange where everything is strange!—to speak 'critically' *about* and *against* Paul."[150]

This style of argumentation is characteristic of Barth. He would later argue in much the same way about very different issues (for example, the challenge of Ludwig Feuerbach), radicalizing the particular objections in order to force a new and direct approach to the subject at stake. An unfriendly observer might call this procedure self-defense through radicalization. And, in fact, we cannot simply dismiss the danger that Barth's radicalization often leads to a "peaceful haven"[151] where the torrents that all too often buffet other scholars are never felt. On the other hand, one should not underestimate the value of this procedure. The radicalization of the oblique intention exposes a new direct intention: a second or, better, a new naiveté (here Barth is comparable to Heidegger) emerges from the energetic response; a childlike, immediate anticipation of the story that is being told results from the "more critical" style he demanded of the historical-critical school. And that could well be the real point of his exclamation: "The historical critics must be more critical to suit me!"—i.e., that grown-up scholars whose reflective exegetical labors have made them rigid must become as children, who see and hear more because they know less.

Theology as the "Theory of Praxis"—Political Theology?

"If only we had been converted to the Bible earlier so that we would now have solid ground under our feet: One broods alternately over the newspaper and the New Testament and actually sees fearfully little of the organic connection between the two worlds concerning which one should now be able to give a clear and powerful witness. Or is it different for you?"[152]

Barth directed these remarks to Eduard Thurneysen in a letter written from Safenwil on November 11, 1918. We will understand them better if we first consider the situation in which Barth wrote and its historical antecedents. We will then understand that they allude to the fact that the New Testament and the newspaper represent two worlds which cannot be understood apart from one another. This is because any theory about the subject matter of the New Testament is a theory of praxis, a praxis objectified for the present in, for example, a newspaper. In the second edition of *Romans,* Barth comments on Romans 12:1 (the beginning of Paul's parenesis: "I appeal to you, therefore, brethren"): "Paul is not recommending some 'praxis' in addition to theory, but rather establishes that precisely the 'theory' which precedes this passage [chapters 1–11] is a theory of praxis."[153] To be able to describe adequately this understanding of theology as a "theory of praxis," we must look first at the praxis which occupied Barth in Safenwil.[154]

"One broods alternately over the newspaper and the New Testament" —that remark is to be understood first in terms of the situation in which it was uttered. In November of 1918, revolution broke out in Germany and a general strike was announced in Switzerland. Newspapers have special value in such times. Barth complained in the same letter that

"The post arrives—again without a newspaper."[155] At the same time, he was reading the proofs of the first edition of his commentary on Romans. Yet Barth feels that he has "come too late," both to the New Testament and to current events. He knows that he is in this respect no different from the capitalist manufacturers of Safenwil, who funded an "emergency commission" (partly to combat the results of the flu raging in Europe at that time): "All at once at the eleventh hour mammon begins to totter on its throne and it is a life-or-death matter for soup to be prepared in the schoolhouse for everyone who wants it. Other helpful projects are to follow with clothing, etc. The question is, can such measures prevent the Bolshevist infiltration of Safenwil?"[156] Barth's question is sarcastic. He had already had a series of disputes with these manufacturers because, as pastor of his congregation in Safenwil, he had become an advocate for their employees. A letter dated September 9, 1917, describes one example: "In the Letter to the Romans I have come to the magnificent passage, 5:12–21. . . . Decisive events here have broken right into the middle of it: fifty-five women employees in the knitting mill organized themselves last Monday. And now the factory owner [F. Hochuli] threatens to fire all of them! In regard to this I visited him this afternoon in his villa, like Moses with Pharaoh, asking him to let the people go out into the wilderness. Polite men's talk in deep easy chairs which unfortunately ended with a flat rejection and declaration of war, during which I had to hear that I am the 'worst enemy' he has had in his whole life. Now we shall have to see how the fifty-five and the town that stands behind them will behave. Naturally I am more than ready for a collapse, but beforehand I will certainly do what I can. The manufacturer took his stand on the well-known 'a man's home is his castle,' and declared that he would rather close the factory or sell it to a racketeer (!) than to give a single inch."[157] The owner's declaration of war to the pastor made sense, considering that Barth believed himself compelled "by the situation in the congregation" to concern himself both theoretically and practically "with socialism, and especially with the labor movement."[158] This commitment can be best explained by comparing it with the other activities in Safenwil to which Barth also felt compelled "by the situation in the congregation." For similar reasons he not only vigorously supported the *Blaukreuz* [Blue Cross] temperance organization but also, like half of all pastors at that time, became a practicing member and was even a temporary president of the Safenwil branch. Later on, to be sure, he had to endure the Blue Crossers identifying him, like all backsliders, as a "continuing drunk." Barth's commitment to socialism and the labor movement was no less than his commitment to the Blue Cross. He himself drew the parallel between the two in 1915, declaring that he had to side with the socialists for the same reason that he had sided with the abstainers, primarily from the sense of duty that he belonged there if he was serious about God. This comparison clearly shows the practical basis of his commitment. The pastor who had firmly refused to be the kind of pastor "who complies with people's wishes"[159] was also the pastor who wondered what caused his people's suffering. And that also determined his own behavior in theory and in praxis. It was the suffering of the people in his "congregation of farmers and workers" that, along with "the influence of Kutter and Ragaz, whose proclamations were at their peak," made him realize "the burning importance of the social question and movement. . . . In the class conflict that I saw concretely in my congregation, I was touched for the first time by the real problems of real life. This led me . . . to devote my studies to industrial codes, insurance, union news, etc., and to get involved in the fierce battles which raged through both town and canton when I took my stand on the side of the workers."[160] From the beginning of his pastorate in 1911, Barth spoke before the Safenwil *Arbeiterverein* [Workers' Union] on, for example, "Human Rights and Civil Duties," "Earn, Work, Live," but also on "Religion and Scholarship." His lecture on "Jesus Christ and the Social Movement"[161] was published during that time. We shall analyze it briefly.

Barth began his lecture with an explanation of his topic. He was delighted to be able to speak to the workers about Jesus Christ. "The best and the greatest that I as a pastor can bring you will always be Jesus Christ." But the second half of the topic—the social movement—also touched his heart, and was, in fact, "just as important." Indeed, Barth agreed with Leonhard Ragaz[162] and, above all, with Hermann Kutter,[163] that one cannot separate Jesus Christ and the social movement, that to distinguish between them would limit them to a merely superficial relationship. Even more: "Jesus Christ *is* the social movement, and the social movement *is* Jesus in the present." Barth, to be sure, wishes to interpret this thesis in his own way,[164] but he proceeds on the supposition that the "real substance of the person of Jesus . . . can be summed up in the two words 'social movement,' " and conversely, "the social movement of the nineteenth and twentieth centuries is not only the most important and urgent word of God for the present day, but is actually the direct result of the continuing . . . spiritual power which Jesus brought into life and history."[165]

Barth proceeds to dismiss two objections. Opposition to the identification of Jesus Christ with the social movement comes, on the one hand, from "the narrowly so-called 'Christian' circles to which, in this situation, the majority of middle-class churchgoers belong."[166] Opposition comes from the other side as well, from the "comrades." The "Christian"-bourgeois objection holds that Jesus does not belong to the Social Democratic Party because he belongs to no party. "He is nonpartisan, indeed a different entity, aloof from all social battles."[167] To identify Jesus with a political movement is "to profane the eternal." It is not unusual for these critics to recite a litany of the activities and failings of the Left and to ask what that can possibly have to do with Jesus Christ. Barth counters these all too comfortable arguments by demanding that one must first of all take the goals of the social movement seriously, instead of merely being concerned and agitated about what its advocates do, just as we Christians also want Christianity to be judged by "what we want, not by what we do."[168] To ask what the Social Democrats want is to ask about the "eternal, lasting, universal aspects of modern social democracy," not about its "temporal and accidental" aspects. In that respect one can "demonstrate an inner connection" between "modern social democracy and the eternal Word of God, which became flesh in Jesus."[169] Barth does not seem to find it logically scandalous that this implies that Jesus stands in the same temporal and accidental relationship to the eternal Word of God.

Opposition also comes from the labor movement itself, fearing "a conservative maneuver in [this] combination of Christianity and socialism" which is intended to make the workers " 'pious lambs' again."[170] Barth admits that "much of the 'Christian' response to socialism" does look like such a " 'maneuver,' designed to 'turn the people around' "[171] and bring them back to the church. But he desired nothing of the sort, for "the church is not Jesus, and Jesus is not the church."[172] One is not even converted to a "Christian worldview" nor obligated by any duty to believe when one accepts Jesus Christ: "If you see the connection between your socialist convictions and the person of Jesus, and if you wish to arrange your life correspondingly, that surely does not mean that you must accept this or that 'belief.' What Jesus brings us is not ideas, but a way of life. You can have Christian ideas about God and the world and humanity and salvation and still be a perfect heathen. And you can be a true follower and disciple of Jesus as an atheist and materialist and Darwinist. Jesus is not the Christian worldview, and the Christian worldview is not Jesus."[173] Barth rigorously applies the Protestant distinction (which he learned from Wilhelm Herrmann) between the person of Jesus Christ on the one side, and dogma and dogmatics (i.e., the Christian world view) on the other; everything that dogmatics teaches must be subordinated to the confrontation with the person of Jesus Christ and the praxis which results.

After carefully picking apart the current objections, Barth turns to the explication of the matter at hand. He compares socialism and Jesus Christ. Both are described as "a movement from below to above": socialism, "the movement of the proletariat," is a movement from below to above insofar as it seeks "independence for the dependent" along with "all the consequences for external, moral, and spiritual life which must accompany it."[174] Jesus Christ, at least as "seen from the human side,"

as Barth carefully qualifies, is also "thoroughly a movement from
below."[175] Jesus himself came from a lower social class and turned to
those who were miserable and dependent, preaching and living in their
midst. "There was no one too low and too mean for him."[176] And he had
not brought these miserable and dependent people a "comfortable pity
from above." It is the rich who need pity, not the poor; the pious, not
the godless. Jesus' movement was from below to above, "a volcanic
eruption from below."[177]

It is not only in its essential movement that the history of Jesus Christ
coincides with the socialist movement. Jesus' judgments "on the relationship between spirit and matter, between inner and outer, between heaven
and earth"[178] also do not contradict socialist intention. Barth sharply
distinguishes Jesus' own point of view from the ordinary Christian understanding of these relationships, which is its direct opposite. The
church believes the Kingdom of God to be otherworldly, to be spiritual
and internal, and assigns politics to this world; the church proclaims
conversion where social democracy preaches revolution; but for Jesus
there is only one reality. "He knows nothing of these two worlds, but
only the one reality of the Kingdom of God."[179] Significantly, for Jesus,
this one and only reality, the Kingdom of God, finds opposition "not in
the world, not in matter, not in the external, but rather in evil, . . . in
the devil that lives within."[180] He is not interested in being freed from
matter in order to rise to heaven, but in the opposite movement: "The
Kingdom of God comes to us in matter and on the earth. The Word
became flesh (John 1:14) and not the other way around!"[181] Barth illustrates this thesis with the parable of the Kingdom of God as a table
fellowship (Luke 13:29) and with the texts that describe discipleship as
social aid (e.g., Matt. 25:32–46). "The spirit that stands before God is
the social spirit."[182] It is a spirit "that transforms matter."[183] Barth
praises social democracy (despite the fact that it still has much to learn
from Jesus in this respect) because it has assumed his attitude "toward
material needs more energetically than anything seen since Jesus himself."[184] "It tells us that we really should believe what we constantly pray:
Thy Kingdom come! It preaches to us with its 'materialism,' a word that
does not come from Jesus yet fully accords with his spirit," that "the end
of God's ways is corporeality"[185] (F. C. Oetinger).

Barth then turns his attention to capitalism. Socialism demands the
abolition of private ownership of the means of production. But Jesus
demands the abolition of all private ownership. The socialist argues: "As
work is collective, a common endeavor, so also profit must be a common
possession. But for that to happen, unchecked competition between individual producers must come to an end, and the state, the collective itself,
must become the producer and therefore the owner of the means of
production."[186] This argument does not call private property itself into

question. But Jesus is, even considering all historical differences, "more socialist than the socialists."[187] He even rejected the basis of all property: whatever is mine, is mine. Indeed, he even stripped away private family ties, actually implying a "stripping away of everything that is private." Jesus "tells us: You must become free of everything that begins with 'I' and 'my,' absolutely free, in order to be free for social aid."[188]

W. Hüssy, an Aargau manufacturer, attacked this position, as indeed he had to. In an open letter[189] he took the "still very young" pastor to task for his speech, contrasted his utopian theory with the reality of economic life, and insisted that this difference "cannot be solved by even the oldest and therefore most outdated Bible verses."[190] The manufacturer, at any rate, understood neither the New Testament nor socialism, as Barth sharply observed in his reply.[191]

But let us continue with our analysis of the lecture. Barth further sharpens his thesis by arguing that the socialist *means* of attaining the end of capitalist productive relationships, organization, is justified by Jesus. With reference to the closing exhortation of the Communist Manifesto of 1848 ("Workers of the world, unite!"), he identifies solidarity as "the law and gospel of socialism,"[192] concluding that the *"Our Father"* means that "for Jesus there existed only a social God of solidarity and therefore only a social religion of solidarity."[193] Here too, the church, with its individualism and its limitation of religion to the relationship of God and the soul, has corrupted the gospel of Jesus. According to Barth, German Lutheranism is especially blameworthy in this regard, while the Swiss reformers Zwingli and Calvin are somewhat less at fault in that they believed religion was "from the start something cooperative, something social."[194] They better preserved what was obvious for Jesus, that "the rule of cooperative action" flows all by itself from "the consciousness of a collective, cooperative, social God of solidarity."[195] Barth finally makes the matter most acute by formulating it in the light of the cross: "We approach here the Holy of Holies of our faith."[196] The death of Jesus Christ on the cross is, as the risk of one's own life for others, the highest value that one can conceive in life. And Barth sees the ultimate expression of the "consciousness of solidarity" in this risk. "Let whoever can, understand this: that one must lose one's life to find it, that one must stop being for oneself; one must become a member of the human community, a comrade, if one is to be human at all."[197]

Those are serious words, and they were meant seriously. Barth thought he saw the divine power of the gospel reflected in the organizational concepts of socialism. "I see it in other places as well, but here more clearly and purely, and I see it here in the way that it must work in our time."[198] He said this on December 17, 1911.

It took, however, all of three years and two months before Barth himself chose to become human as well, before he decided to become a comrade. He reported his decision rather undramatically in a letter from Safenwil to Eduard Thurneysen, dated February 5, 1915: "I have now become a member of the Social Democratic Party. Just because I set such emphasis Sunday by Sunday upon the last things, it was no longer possible for me personally to remain suspended in the clouds above the present evil world. Rather it had to be demonstrated here and now that faith in the Greatest does not exclude, but includes work and suffering in the realm of the imperfect." He continues: "The socialists in my congregation will now, I hope, have a right understanding of my public criticisms of the party. And I myself hope now to avoid becoming unfaithful to our 'essential' orientation, as might very well have happened had I taken this step two years ago. I have for now refused all partisan political activity; my involvement consists of paying dues and giving lectures."[199]

To understand correctly Barth's decision to join the Social Democratic Party, one must note that it took place at a time when, in his judgment, socialism—judged now by its actions as well as its intentions—had become just as "hopelessly compromised" as liberal theology, even though he "had innocently enough . . . expected more from socialism than from the Christian church: that it would shun that ideology [i.e., war]." And now he saw socialism, to his "outrage, doing just the opposite in every country."[200] A few months after he joined the party, Barth began a sketch on "The Intrinsic Future of Social Democracy," dated August 12, 1915, with the lapidary observation that the failure of social democracy was more intrinsic than extrinsic.*

In light of this judgment, Barth's membership in the Social Democratic Party is doubly significant. He proceeded directly from criticism of the party he had just joined to observations on its own intrinsic future: reflections on the failure of social democracy form the basis for anticipations of its future. Barth charges the Social Democratic Party with abandoning its revolutionary goals at the very moment when the old social structure was yielding its most horrible harvest. It had now become just another nationalist-bourgeois party.[201] What Barth was talking about can be seen clearly in Friedrich Naumann's declaration of 1914: "The Social Democratic Party stands with both feet firmly planted on the ground of facts and has become a patriotic workers' movement. It approves the war expenditures and joins in our common task without any difference. We had always expected that from the party, but we were called dreamers for it. Now, in the storm of the European war, it fulfills

---

*That is, more from its own shortcomings than from the assaults of its enemies.—TRANS.

the national aspirations of German idealists."[202] The fulfillment of Naumann's aspirations was the mockery of Barth's hopes.[203] Nevertheless, Barth immediately directed his attention toward social democracy's intrinsic future, toward the socialist spirit that must develop if it is ever to be any different; but he did not do so without first raising the question, which he answered with a yes, whether socialism, i.e., materialism in Marx's sense, even permits the category of spirit.

According to Barth, if social democracy is to have a future, it must develop a new social disposition. And to do that, it must accept these three basic principles of the content, means, and goal of socialism. (1) The *essence* or the content of socialism must be identified as justice for humanity, and not merely as improvement of the lot of the working class. Barth characteristically cites Romans 3:28, "by faith alone" [Luther's translation], against the perversions of "egotistical socialism." The innermost essence of socialism should surely be a passion for justice for each and every person, in opposition to the concessions on the level of "works," which was just where the party was compromising itself. (2) The *means* of socialism must reflect a trust in the power of its truth for victory. For that reason, socialism must not draw its strength from the struggle for political and economic power, but from an entirely different source. If the movement does not draw its strength from this other source, which is unfortunately not further described, it will be merely one "bickering, foul-smelling, compromising party among others." (3) The *aim* of socialism must be the free, pure personality, and the future state can only be a means to the attainment of that end. The free, pure personality is to be freed, indeed "redeemed" from bourgeois egoism, with its false idealism and half-serious Christianity, and it is to be grasped by the power of socialist truth, which Barth explicitly calls transcendent. These three principles for a new socialist disposition will not, according to Barth, lead to some kind of sectarian division with the political party—that would lead to "the error of anarchy." Barth's approach would lead to a party firmly grounded in its true content. In 1934 Barth would argue in a similar vein about the church.

The sketch on "The Intrinsic Future of Social Democracy" has a theological counterpart in the lecture on "Religion and Socialism," also given in the same year that Barth joined the party. We must also consider this lecture in order to clarify why Barth became a socialist despite his bitter disappointment with the socialist parties. Only then will it also become clear why he later departed from this course.

The lecture opens with a startling assertion: "I am glad to be a pastor." Barth immediately interprets this assertion with reference to the tension between his joy and his burden, a burden which consists in the magnitude of his task. Yet it is just that burden, which sometimes almost frightens him about his calling, that makes him glad to be a pastor.[204] Barth's avowal of joy over his calling has more than a private confessional function. It expresses the integral connection between "Religion and Socialism." For, Barth continues, he became a socialist and a Social Democrat precisely because he is glad to be a pastor, not because he is more or less bored with his calling. The "great cause" for which he lives, and for which he works as a pastor, is also that which allowed him to become a socialist. The path which leads into the Social Democratic Party does not lead away from that cause, which "is and remains the main thing" for him.

I think that Barth's self-assessment is decisive for a proper understanding of his "theology-politics connection,"[205] not only during his beginnings but through all his later development. It plays a key role. It makes it clear that Barth's political activity springs from his "theological existence" and that his political choices must be judged on the basis of his theological attitude. Therefore, all attempts to explain his theology on the basis of his early socialism fly in the face of his own professed self-understanding. His joy over the "great cause" of his theological calling allowed him to become a socialist because, as he continues, socialism had become for him one of the most important reflections of the Kingdom of God, the Kingdom which is the great fact and basis of life. Barth affirmed socialism then as such a reflection, but only after he had first become aware of the challenge and opportunity it posed as a result of the crisis faced by the workers in his congregation. He understands it as one "reflection," one "symptom" of the Kingdom of God, but not as the only one. Barth lists an entire series of such reflections and symptoms—both in nature, i.e., the starry heavens above, and in history, i.e., the state, science, the Enlightenment's fanatical devotion to truth, the Reformation, the Renaissance, and the French Revolution. It is somewhat startling that he includes religion. Religion must therefore not be "the great cause" itself, but its symptom. For that reason he also criticized the assigned topic for the lecture, "Religion and Socialism." It connects two phenomena that, from a theological perspective, are on the same level. For Barth understands religion in much the same way as Schleiermacher, as a pious feeling within the solitary person, along with the particular morality and worship that proceed from this feeling. Barth does not deny that each of us achieves a certain purity and sublimity every now and then. But that same feeling also illustrates the weaknesses and delusions and plain aberrations of the religious person. It is this one-sidedly anthropological, and therefore always ambiguous, religion which Barth includes in his list of the reflections and symptoms of the Kingdom of God. But the Kingdom has the dignity of fact, indeed the basic fact of life, over against mere feeling. The pastoral calling is concerned with this fact, with working for the Kingdom of God and speaking of God himself, but not with religion. Barth explicitly questions whether it can be the task of a pastor to cultivate religion. But to speak of God—that is what the task is.

These are the earliest comments I can find in which Barth practices theological criticism of religion. Barth considers religion not something essential but rather merely a human response to the "basic fact of life" of the Kingdom of God.[206] And so one might think that he would welcome the topic "Religion and Socialism" all the more, since it concerns two comparable phenomena that are related in principle. But Barth does not want to compare two ways of life; he wants to explicate the foundational relationship between theology and socialism. For that reason he corrects the assigned topic and lectures on "the Kingdom of God and Socialism," two very different orders of magnitude, one of which (the Kingdom of God) is the basis for the other (socialism), while the latter can only be a reflection of the former.

That is the first trace of Barth's new theological starting point. It appears where he was still in the process of separating himself from his teachers and their theology, a theology which still determines to too large a degree the rest of his lecture. For example, he identifies conscience and Jesus Christ as sources for human knowledge of the Kingdom of God. And the Kingdom of God is described as, among other things, that "holy, radiant, majestic essence above us, which greets us from afar, now as truth, now as beauty, now as love." Observe that love greets us from afar! But new strains can be heard among the old. We do not only hear that the Kingdom of God is to be "simply the restoration of the original, direct life that we . . . have lost," but also that this Kingdom of God derives from the concept of God as an expression of the divine life itself, which is in turn understood as the sovereignty of the living God. The Lordship of God is, following Kutter, an expression of the fact that God lives. Therefore it can be said: The Kingdom of God is coming. And therefore it can be declared, in unmistakable proximity to Paul's joining of indicative and imperative: God is alive and at work. Rejoice and join in!

The joy with which Barth begins his lecture is thus the joy that God lives and works. One should not misunderstand this joy. Barth rejects the misunderstanding (to which he had himself briefly succumbed) that he wished to confuse theology with politics. He does not wish to be a "political pastor."

What then? A pastor who is a socialist, but not a "political pastor"? The logic seems strange, but it is worth following the argument carefully. Barth asserts that he became a socialist not for the sake of religion, but because of the Kingdom of God. The difference between the Kingdom of God and religion should be the basis for the socialist option. For all of socialism's mistakes, Barth sees a revelation of God, as he somewhat carelessly formulates it, in socialism's "essential struggles." I say "carelessly" because he uses the word "revelation" in the widest possible sense, indeed in precisely the same sense as his prior use of the term "reflections." For Barth no longer presumes to identify them the way he did as recently as 1911 with the thesis "Jesus *is* the social movement."[207] For him, the Kingdom of God stands head and shoulders above all its signs, and therefore above socialism as well. And he would not think of equating socialism with the Kingdom of God and preaching it instead of the gospel. And that is why he considers the "political pastor" in any form, even the socialist, to be in error. Henceforth he is a socialist, not as a pastor, but as a human being and a citizen.

Barth is beginning to work with fundamental differences here. Yet he does not seek to set up some sort of irrelevance. It is theologically far more relevant that socialism is a "reflection," "symptom," or "signpost" of the Kingdom of God, so much so that Barth can be thoroughly glad of it. Socialism is for him one of the happiest signs that the Kingdom of God is not standing still, and that God is very much at work. This explains why the very difference between religion and the Kingdom of God should be the basis of Barth's socialist decision. Religion tends, even according to Barth's own formulation, to be understood as that human activity in which God, so to speak, becomes practical, but—again according to Barth—without earthly results. By setting up a qualitative difference between religion and the Kingdom of God, Barth questions whether religion is the suitable place for God to become practical. But in the concept of the Kingdom of God—interpreted as the rule of God —God himself is seen to be the doer: God is at work. Religion, understood as pious feeling, verifies that God is at work, but only very ineptly. At that time, Barth thought that he had discovered in socialism, much more than in religion, a worldly praxis which corresponded best to the work of God and the coming Kingdom. He thought so because he was convinced that God is at work in the world in ways quite apart from religion. Barth saw so many signs of this rule and work of God in the very thought and struggle of the Social Democrats that he believed that he would have stood apart from God if he had not stood with them.

It was this insistence on linking praxis with discourse about God that led Barth, after placing religion on the same level with socialism as reflections of the Kingdom of God, to grant socialism a relative, to be sure, but still clear preference. Religion's flaw is that it does not strive toward that precise, earth-shaking praxis in which human work corresponds to God's work. That is why it remains politically ambivalent, while the category of the Kingdom of God demands categorical political activity. Socialism at least strives for this in principle, and to that extent corresponds more closely to the Kingdom of God than religion does. Religion tends to be politically indifferent, while the Kingdom of God tolerates no such indifference. If all that mattered to him was religion,

Barth could probably have found himself as a nonpartisan, or in the liberal-conservative party, as he himself said. But he can find no signs of the Kingdom of God there. Barth acknowledges that the significance of politics and economics for the whole of human life should not be overestimated. But in the arena of political and economic matters, his conscience and Jesus Christ direct him to socialism. Socialism's relative hostility toward religion does not bother him. In fact, he considers it safer and better to stand with God alongside the godless rather than to stand against them without God. One might conclude that Barth says this because he believes that while religion is just as much a reflection of the coming Kingdom of God as socialism, it is only a passing sign, whereas socialism is a sign of the coming of the Kingdom that also belongs to the Kingdom.

To sum up, the beginnings of Barth's new theological position are recognizable in 1915. They await, to be sure, very extensive revision, but they still foreshadow some of the structures of his future theology. (1) His decisive rejection of the one-sidedly anthropological concept of religion leads to the strict differentiation of religion and discourse about God from the Kingdom of God. (2) Anthropologically, the Kingdom of God is the basic fact of life; theologically, it is the rule of the God who is at work. The Kingdom is therefore distinguished from religion; the Kingdom is the essence of the original reality of life, a reality which is to be attained again. (3) This original, and again to be attained, reality of life is reflected in a series of worldly realities. Socialism, in particular, represents the human praxis which corresponds to the work of God. (4) Although Barth distinguishes socialism from the Kingdom of God (in contrast to the view expressed in 1911) as strictly as he distinguishes between religion and the Kingdom, and although religion and socialism rank on the same level before the Kingdom as mere symptoms or signs, he ascribes greater theological significance to socialism because of its basic political aims, because in socialism "God is taken seriously politically."[208] (5) Precisely because both religion and socialism are qualitatively distinct from the Kingdom of God, Barth refuses to be a "political pastor" or a "religious pastor," in the sense that as a pastor he would have to serve the interests of politics and religion. (6) The distinction between religion and the Kingdom of God is drawn more sharply than the equally clear distinction between socialism and the Kingdom. This is because it is particularly easy to identify religion with God, a confusion that immediately threatens to render harmless the praxis which corresponds to the Kingdom of God. Barth understood religion as the expression of merely the relationship of the individual to God. That is not the least of the reasons why he found the concept of religion useless to describe the biblical relation between God and humanity.

Against this background of the development of Barth's thought, we can now assess the significance of Barth's remark to Thurneysen[209] with which we began our discussion of his praxis. At the very moment at which socialism appears politically victorious—revolution in Germany, a general strike in Switzerland—Barth says that there is no "solid ground" under his feet. Brooding alternately over the newspaper and the New Testament, he "actually sees frightfully little" of that which he had proclaimed so energetically (and just now, when what he had proclaimed appears on the horizon): namely, "the organic connection between the two worlds concerning which one should now be able to give a clear and powerful witness," but still cannot. In the midst of this misery, he announces the necessary revision with a sober complaint: "If only we had been converted to the Bible earlier so that we would now have solid ground under our feet." Barth's complaint makes it clear that he expects something from this turn to the Bible—something even for a theology that thinks of itself as a "theory of praxis."

Barth had already learned from Wilhelm Herrmann that theology is eminently concerned with reality, with life—with real life—and that theology is therefore a "theory of praxis." The religious socialists Kutter and Ragaz made it clear to him that theology (or religion) is for the same reason concerned with politics in a special way (insofar as politics means responsibility for the common good). Barth's own particular, unmistakable tones and colors emerge in his development of these two "sources," in the questions which he posed again and again even to these teachers and authorities who he thought were sound. When God is the concern, then real life, living reality, is the concern. But what is life? And this question promptly yields yet another question, a question which calls into question everything previously learned and inherited: Who or what is God?

Barth's own theology develops out of such basic questions, aimed at previously obvious presuppositions, making them not so obvious. A break with what is all too obvious through penetrating, basic questions is the motif which animates and frees Barth's thought. In a sermon on Psalm 42:2–6 [1–5 Eng.], Barth looks into the obvious platitudes that shape discourse about God. God—"merely the great solemn word for the unknown, unsearchable reality . . . *besides* what really stirs us." God —"the ponderous, dark power over our life," with which one "must get right." God—"a beautiful, true thought." God—"the fire . . . next to which we now and then like to warm our feelings."[210] But it is precisely these obvious descriptions of God which are called into question when we are confronted with "real life." "How very pitifully we have to twist and turn in order to understand and organize our real life: the veil of everyday pretense, the yawning chasm of human stupidity, the arduous task of eking out a living, the red flame of passion! How empty, how weak is the God we have set up or have allowed to be set up! If only God were something besides an idea! If only life would now triumph over life, reality over reality, power over power, a divine world over the mocking, sneering human world! Our beautiful, pious, intelligent ideas of God can go to the devil! Indeed, aren't they of the devil?"[211] Barth goes on to say that there is a revolt under way in us, a revolution against all such obvious identifications of God as the unknown, as a power over life that we must postulate, as that which stirs our feelings, as an idea. And this revolution aims to find the living God. But even this formulation, derived from Kutter and Ragaz, is criticized and questioned. "What does 'living' mean? At any rate, it can mean only what 'God' used to mean to us: a God who is really God!"[212] Barth pits the obvious identifications of God against an identification which is even more obvious, a tautology: "a God who is really God." God is God—that is his battle cry for the time being, and it separates him from his teachers.

This tautology, first of all, expresses a theological rejection. Barth rejects the manipulation of God in all these obvious identifications which separate God from "real life." His refusal also implies an affirmation, insofar as the tautology "God is God" means that God is a reality that cannot be eliminated from any other reality. God is no "foreign word on the edge of existence, but existence itself, surging through the nothingness of all that is. No fifth wheel on the wagon, but the wheel that drives all wheels. No distant shrine, but the one who surges mightily into the midst of all that is. No dark power . . . , but the clear power of freedom above all and in all, which seeks to be honored first by human beings. No thought or notion, but the power of life that conquers the powers of death . . . ! No embellishment on the world, but a lever that moves the world! No feeling to be played with, but a fact to be taken seriously. . . . That is what living means! A living God, a God who is really God!"[213]

The proper human response to the tautology "God is God" is, according to Barth, astonishment. "You are astonished that something like this is possible at all? Yes, but we should learn to be astonished by something entirely different, by how alive God really is! What a real miracle this is: a God who is God and not the puny little idol we, in our weakness, have made of God."[214] Barth's criticism of religion also comes through such questioning.[215] From the beginning, that criticism is nothing but the expression of this astonishment before God himself.

And if God is "no foreign word on the edge of existence, but existence itself surging through,"[216] then God, in conformity with the necessity of his essence thus defined, changes life as we know it. Yet life as we know it and live it has always been determined by the human desire to have something else. Greed, the desire for more, dominates the fallen creation. The desire to possess is in particular a basic structure of individual existence. The ego wants to have something. The ego, not the id, wants to possess. In the first edition of *The Epistle to the Romans* Barth again and again identifies the sinner as obsessed with having, with possessing. Barth is primarily thinking in terms of the relationship to God. A true relationship to God does not claim the gifts of God as "private property."[217] Therefore: "If we should ever claim that our faith and hope are our religious-moral possessions and then parade them before others who have fewer or no such possessions—then we too would lose them."[218] Paul's interpreter then launches a polemic against "religious personalities."[219] The infinite value of the "personal life," proclaimed by both liberal theology and liberal politics (and earlier by Goethe as well), is met not only with a theological objection but also with a political objection: " 'Personal life' is no longer the answer to world war and revolution." And again: "Whoever will not join in solidarity with what is happening on the outside, will not save his own soul either."[220] Instead, he will remain in the custody of sin, which is characterized at its deepest level by religious individuality and religious greed. The religious sinner wants to be an I, an ego, and as a religious ego to have a God and to possess a God. But that is just how "a person ruins . . . his original relationship to God's election: God will not be 'owned' by human beings; a person can 'own' only pseudo-gods. Wanting to 'have' God, he misses God and falls victim to the idols."[221]

Barth contrasted this understanding of the reality of sin with the concept of the living God. God lives in contradistinction to the reality of sin, in contradistinction to all possessing and to the cult of individuality, to all greed and self-seeking. This contradistinction, however, is understood as an event, not a mere counterargument. The living God prevails over religious greed and ego-greed. There God manifests himself as living; there God is God. Barth calls this event the "revolution of God." This original expression is a suitable description of the victory of God, not only over self-seeking behavior, but also over the circumstances which condition or even underlie such behavior. This calls for closer examination.

The expression has exercised extraordinary fascination for recent Barth research, reason enough to pay attention to it. But for now we shall stick to our immediate theme, theology as the theory of praxis, recalling that according to the preceding arguments there is, strictly speaking, no such thing as a theory of praxis formed by an ethic. Ethics asks: "What ought we to do?" and then tries to form an answer. But when the sinful reality of humanity is transformed by the revolution of God, ethics comes to an end. Then the theory of praxis must correspond to an event that has already taken place, not to an event that has yet to occur. A theory of praxis stands in need of dogmatics, not ethics. In fact, as Barth dryly declared in the first *Romans:* "From the final point of view that we must take in Christ, there is no ethics. There is only the activity of

God, to which our knowledge of the situation and the action it requires of us must correspond in every moment. . . . For our part, knowledge of God is necessary, . . . but that is the knowledge which grasps the situation in the moment, in God, not a formula which is equally true for today and tomorrow, for here and there."[222]

The judgment that from the final point of view in Christ there is no ethics, but only a knowledge which grasps the situation in the moment, in God, guides us to a proper understanding of the term "revolution of God," which saturates Barth's first interpretation of Romans. It is a political metaphor. Barth could not have been thinking of the scientific meaning of "revolution," which refers to the movements of the heavenly bodies, as in the chief work of Nicolaus Copernicus (1473–1543), *De revolutionibus orbium coelestium.* The description of Christianity as revolutionary was, moreover, not at all restricted to religious socialist circles. It already occurs in Kant[223] (drawing on the French Revolution?), and in Hegel: "This Kingdom of God, the new religion, thus contains within itself the characteristic of negation in reference to all that is actual. This is the revolutionary side of its teaching."[224] In political terminology, "revolution" signifies either (a) the long-lasting process of a basic transformation of, e.g., the social or cultural order; or (b) the political upheaval through which a group or class previously excluded from the political process gains power, or attempts to do so, by breaking down the old order. In the second sense, one speaks of an aristocratic, bourgeois, or proletarian revolution. In the aristocratic revolution, the nobility and the bourgeoisie eliminate the sovereign dynasty; in the bourgeois revolution, the bourgeoisie overthrow the feudal order; and in the proletarian revolution, the working class will end the rule of capitalism and trigger a world revolution.

Barth's employment of the term may well be oriented to socialist usage and thus to the language of the proletarian revolution, including its antidynastic interpretation of revolution (an interpretation which, for example, made Switzerland a republic independent of the Hapsburgs). F.-W. Marquardt's assertion[225] that Barth was "familiar with the first edition" of Lenin's *The State and Revolution* when he was working on Romans 13 may be refuted on chronological grounds.[226] But Barth was close to the content of the socialist manner of speaking about revolution, quite apart from biographical matters, because here a particular event, the "proletarian revolution," is a given a general, universal meaning, insofar as it is to lead to a world revolution. Barth speaks outright of the "divine world revolution."[227]

This language promised to express in a political metaphor what Barth wanted to articulate theologically, namely that the gospel is both "nothing new, but the oldest; nothing particular, but the most universal;

nothing historical, but the presupposition of all history," and still "not an old acquaintance, but a new one; not universal, but particular; not a mere presupposition, but history itself."[228] The unity of these opposites, paradoxical only at first, is summed up in the metaphor "revolution of God." In the second edition of *Romans,* the category of primal history, taken from Overbeck, serves a comparable purpose. Precisely with this metaphorical use of the "revolution of God," Barth leaves the political sphere. Using the categories of the so-called philosophy of origins, Barth is concerned with the theological problem of how the "most particular" can at the same time be or become the "most universal" and, conversely, how the "oldest" can be something "new"; indeed, the absolutely new and renewing. That is the problem Barth is concerned with in his language about God; the concept of God should be "given to us with the immediacy of our own existence,"[229] and thus be the oldest and most universal. And yet it comes to us through a "cosmic eruption into the cosmic context." It is therefore a "revolution which overthrows the dynasty"[230] (as Adam's guilt was overcome through Christ, according to Romans 5). The "revolution of God" is an expression for the particular event in which God, in all concreteness, begins (and has begun) to become all in all. A political metaphor thus depicts the absolutely concrete christological universal, understood as an event.

This expression is at the same time well suited to denote the soteriological aspect of this christological event, this "cosmic eruption into the cosmic context," because the political meaning of revolution always signifies the end of a particular dependence. Barth makes use of this semantic connection (also linking it to Luther's language in *The Freedom of a Christian)* in his interpretation of the "much more" deduction of Romans 5:17 (Barth's translation: "For if it is true that by the fall of one, death achieved royal dominion, then those who accept the fullness of grace and the gift of righteousness will be that much more secure, and may themselves now become kings in life through the one Jesus Christ"). Barth interprets: "We are in captivity, to be sure. . . . *Here* is the kingdom of death, the brutal tyranny of fate which became the fate of nature through the Fall. In virtue of the unity of us all in solidarity[231] with Adam and his spirit, this tyranny stands necessarily and unalterably, always new, over us all. There is no free will . . . , in fact there is no will at all. But what kind of will can meekly come to terms with being no will at all? What conscience, what soul is able to subject itself truly and honestly to the dominion of the fate of death? Do we not all harbor the desire for a revolution against this king . . . ?"[232]

After posing this question, Barth describes the victory of life over death fulfilled in Christ, in such a way that the human "desire for revolution against this king" is not only fulfilled but also surpassed. For "the contradiction between life and death is not the war of one dynasty against another, but the overthrow of all dynasties and the establishment of a republic in which all citizens are called to rule: 'They may themselves become kings in life.' What Christ brings is in fact the revolution, the dissolution of all dependence. For the [new] dependence which Christ gives us is actually the freedom of God." Using Luther's terminology, he continues: "A person should not lie in the chains of the cosmos, but the cosmos should lie at his feet. He should not be a servant, but a lord of all things."[233] Barth is thinking of the "immediate relationship to God," which a person enters anew through Christ. Immediacy means independence from intermediate appeals and is therefore superior to them. It is the person who is "in an immediate relationship to God who replenishes the earth and has dominion over it. . . . The Kingdom of God is a kingdom of the freed and the free, a kingdom of genuine kings!"[234] The "revolution of God" is under way in that it has begun to bring about this kingdom—in analogy to the proletarian revolution—and it will definitely achieve it—in analogy to the world revolution. It will bring not only "the end of all things," but "the return of all things to their source."[235] It must "now" ("now" ever since what Paul says in Romans has been current!) "be near."[236]

To understand Barth's dating of this event as "now" we must recall[237] his programmatic foreword: "The differences between then and now, there and here, must be considered. But the purpose of this consideration can only be the recognition that these differences have no significance for what really matters. . . . Historical understanding is a continuous, more and more honest and penetrating conversation between the wisdom of yesterday and the wisdom of tomorrow, and these are one and the same."[238] That is why Jülicher banished this commentary into the quiet pastures of practical theology. Because the "differences between then and now . . . have no significance for what really matters," Barth can—as in his exegesis of Romans 11:12–15 (where the rejection of the Jews issues in the reconciliation of the world, so that from their later acceptance will issue the resurrection from the dead)—recite an entire list of analogous judgments in the history of the world and the church: "God had to leave the culture of Greece behind, long before all its budding dreams could blossom, in order to make way for the Word which the philosophers always wanted to speak but could not. But what an hour *that* will be, when the spirit of Plato actually does begin to speak in history! God had to leave the Catholic Church and its Gothic architecture and its Thomas Aquinas behind, and the result of this rejection was the liberation of the divine Word from an intolerable bondage. But there will be an even greater result in that hour when the Catholic Church will again find itself whole, in which we will again be able to rejoice in its own inexpressible truth and magnificence, now lying under lock and key."[239] And so the list continues on to the Reformation, back to the Roman Empire, to

Franciscanism, and then again leaps forward in time to the French Revolution, German Idealism, pietism—always with the logic of Paul's "much more" deduction in Romans 11:12–15.

The list concludes with a similar assessment of Marx: "Perhaps God is presently in the process of leaving the now old and uncertain socialism behind. For its historical hour has now perhaps run out, without bringing the world what it was to have brought. . . . But more important than this dissolution will be another hour which fulfills history, when the now dying glow of Marxist dogma will illuminate a new global truth, when the socialist church will be resurrected in a socialist world."[240] Christians anticipate this by anticipating the resurrection of the dead. "You are waiting for the reconciliation of the world—already given as the universal basis of existence—to be proven in an equally universal revelation of life beyond all graves, beyond all the incomplete ideas of God which now lie buried under human guilt."[241]

But this "reconciliation of the world, already given as the universal basis of existence" is certainly no product of any "reformist" tendency in the world's being, no modification of the old, well-known experiences and relationships of the world. If it were, then " 'God' [would be] just another expression for you yourselves!" This is why the "revolutionary" is the right metaphor to use along with the "divine" and the "creative."[242] And because this metaphor is better suited than almost any other to be used against the world as such—even the political world—it is particularly adapted to theology. This is especially clear in Barth's exegesis of Romans 13, where he describes the relationship of a Christian to the state with quotations from liberal theologians, for example: " 'There is no perceptible trace of political thought or even political interest' (Wernle). 'The state is in its essential functions annulled for the faithful' (Weinel). . . . 'The conservative attitude (of Christianity) . . . was founded on a mixture of contempt, submission, and relative recognition. That is why, in spite of all its submissiveness, it did destroy the Roman state by alienating souls from its ideals' . . . (Troeltsch). It is revolutionary in principle in that it calls into question the presupposition of the state—the power of evil—and thus the essence of the state—the evil power, 'and thus an actual revolutionary effect has not been lacking' (Troeltsch)."[243]

Barth agrees, but he departs from Troeltsch's intention. He radicalizes these observations by asserting that Christians can submit ("succumb") to the "ruling powers" because "politics as a whole does not" concern "them as Christians"; the Christian is rather "to concentrate strictly on the war of the spirit against the flesh [Rom. 8:13], on the *absolute* revolution of God, and must give all that is penultimate over to the process of dissolution . . . into which it has already fallen anyway—and obviously without lifting even a finger either to preserve things as they are, or to . . . destroy them."[244] Christianity is therefore not suited to being "one battle cry among others. . . . It cannot enter as power against power, it calls the powers back to their divine source." "This program cannot become the object of an 'ethic,' " not even of any socialist ethic. For it "is more than Leninism."[245] To be sure, it is easy for a Christian "arbitrarily to anticipate the coming revolution in Christ and thereby to disregard it. And this is what I warn you against! The cause of divine renewal must not be confused with the cause of human progress."[246] "And again: submit! Do not anticipate the divine world revolution on your own, but busy yourselves with its presupposition! Do not let your present tension be dissipated in premature explosions."[247]

F.-W. Marquardt claims: "The key term 'world revolution' should be associated with Bolshevism. . . . The 'revolution of God' in Barth takes on precisely the function of the revolutionary dictatorship of the proletariat in Leninism."[248] And he interprets Barth's exclamation, "It is more than Leninism!" thus: "On the one hand he expressly affirms that he has come this far with Lenin up to now, while on the other hand he consciously sets up a theological function in the place of Lenin's dictatorship of the proletariat."[249] When Barth was forced out of Bonn in 1935, he left the students with this advice: "Exegesis, exegesis, and more exegesis!"[250] One would like to give that advice again, this time to the Barthians! How would Marquardt interpret this remark of Barth's, which stands in a similar context: "An individual, conservative or revolutionary, who deals seriously with the state will be overcome by evil"?[251] What Barth means is that Christians, because they "radically" resist the state —namely, by ascribing it a penultimate rank—can deal with it soberly: they "pay their taxes, render unto Caesar what is Caesar's, join a party." They "recognize without hesitation or reservation that the state, within its sphere, has the right to demand . . . that."[252] And while Christians are fulfilling their civic duty, they alienate their souls from the state. That is their revolution! And if the state were "someday to recognize the threat posed by this revolutionary method, then there will be sufficient time to prove ourselves as martyrs."[253]

It is clear that Barth's use of the political metaphor of the "revolution of God" as just a metaphor, was consciously intended to obliterate its political *Sitz im Leben.* This is most clearly expressed in his subsequent use of the metaphor against itself, when he asserts that the revolution of God is "also a revolution against what is today called revolution."[254]

While the first edition of Barth's commentary on Romans is characterized by the language of immediacy taken from the philosophy of origins, the second edition is distinguished by an abrupt distinction between God and humanity, between eternity and time. The rhetoric of political revolution, insofar as it is "real" and not metaphorical, now becomes a direct target for Barth's theological criticism. The Pauline imperative of Romans 13, "Overcome evil with good!" now means simply "the end of human triumph, whether that triumph is celebrated in the existing order or in the revolution. . . . The revolutionary has erred: he should really aim at *the* revolution, which is the impossible possibility, the forgiveness of sins, the resurrection of the dead."[255] The revolutionary, according to Barth, must really aim at this eschatological revolution, because it alone is "the true answer to the injury wrought by the existing order as such. Jesus is Victor!" But what the revolutionary has accomplished, contrary to his intentions, is "another revolution, . . . the possible possibility of discontent and hatred and insubordination, of tumult and destruction. And this choice is not better, but much worse than the opposing possible possibility of contentment and satisfaction, of security and usurpation, for the former thereby understands God far better, but abuses him all the worse. The revolutionary aims at the revolution by which the true order is to be inaugurated; but he launches another revolution which is, in fact, reaction. . . . And so, as always, what men do is the judgment on what they will to do."[256]

Barth demands that the "revolutionary" sacrifice his "revolutionary action" to "the action of God." For "even the most radical revolution can do no more than set what exists against what exists. Even the most radical revolution . . . is in itself simply a justification and confirmation of what already exists."[257] That distinguishes it from the activity of God, which Barth had paraphrased metaphorically as the "revolution of God." This revolution of God brings something really new, something which actually transforms the existing order from the ground up. The political metaphor, precisely as a metaphor, can now express the true meaning of "revolution." In the political sphere, it is precisely the "non-revolution [which] is the best preparation for the true revolution."[258] Barth discredited the word "revolution" politically because he had usurped it theologically. To be sure, the reactionaries—or, as Barth called them, the "supporters of the order"—are given warning. It is for their sakes, and theirs alone, because they might hope to "take encouragement" from such statements, that God has " 'ordained' political revolution as evil" precisely for them, "in order that they may bear witness to the good, . . . that they too many turn and no longer seek to be supporters of the order!"[259]

Barth is no theorist of the "counterrevolution," but goes so far as to assert that those who are not troubled by Paul's statement that the powers that be are ministers of God—and they are!—will find that "revolution is the 'minister of God,' "[260] so that the supporters of the existing order may also know that everything stands under God's judgment. But this warning cannot conceal Barth's thorough depoliticization of the concept of revolution, insofar as he still makes any positive use of it. For "the revolutionary aspect of all ethics" comes to light in love.[261]

It is in love that "the new" truly overthrows "the old."[262] "That is the new, the strangeness of love, that it plays no part in the cycle . . . of reaction and revolution," but instead "radically overturns all givens," insofar as it "radically acknowledges the previously given in all givens" and thereby acknowledges God.[263] Therefore, Barth sees the "true revolution" only where the political alternatives of reaction and revolution are no longer present. This is the love vouchsafed by God. For it is the essence of love simply to accept the beloved and to transform the beloved radically by this acceptance. Whoever wants to change another person first, in order to be able to love that person, does not love. Yet whoever does not in fact change another person through love does not love and is not loved in return. For love unproblematically unites both elements: acceptance of the given for its own sake, and radical change of the given thus loved just by its own acceptance of that love. We can see the change in facial expression alone! That is why love is the true revolution, corresponding to God's action in raising the dead. Love accepts people for their own sake as they are, and thereby transforms them completely, from death to life.

Correspondingly, the metaphor "revolution of God" hermeneutically becomes a theological "proper name,"[264] so that everything which is called "revolution" on earth deserves the name only in a secondary sense —a process which characterizes Barth's hermeneutical construction of theological concepts.[265] Many years later, the old Barth still speaks of the Kingdom of God, revealed in Jesus' call to discipleship, as the revolution of God which breaks with all self-absolutizing powers: "The Kingdom of *God* is revealed in this call; the Kingdom which is among the kingdoms of this world, but which confronts and contradicts and opposes them; the revolution of God proclaimed and accomplished already in the existence of the man Jesus. The one whom Jesus calls to himself has to stand firm by the revelation of this revolution. Indeed, he must correspond to it in his action and inaction."[266] But to "correspond" in this way means to "attest and witness"[267] to the revolution of God; only God can bring about true revolution. "No . . . single individual can make the break with" these self-absolutizing "factors and orders and historical forces. What a person does may take the form of an attempt to repudiate them, but it will always serve to confirm and strengthen them, continually evoking new forms of their authority. The little revolutions and assaults by which they seem to be more shaken than they really are can never succeed in limiting, let alone destroying, their power. It is the Kingdom, the revolution of God which breaks, which has already broken them. Jesus is their conqueror."[268] And if Jesus is already their conqueror, then the one whom Jesus calls to discipleship will, "like Daniel in the lions' den, . . . be careful not to pull the lions' tails! . . . It is better not to describe

him as a 'warrior.' If he is in his right senses, he will not think of himself
as such. He departs from conformity, not against anyone, but for everyone."[269] *If* he is in his right senses . . .

Our study of Barth's terminology of revolution has shown how reflection on what God is doing or has already done urgently impinges on
human action, without establishing a particular ethic. Theology, for the
Barth of *The Epistle to the Romans,* is from the start a theory of God's
deeds *(praxeis)* and thus also of human praxis. It would therefore be a
fundamental mistake to imagine that Barth's theology is a theory about
God which derives from political premises. Barth's theology always had
a strong political component, but never, from the first commentary on
Romans on, did that component function as an overriding political
principle. Simply put, for Barth, the political is surely a predicate of
theology, but theology is never a predicate of the political.

Three

Gospel and Law: The Relationship of Dogmatics to Ethics

According to Barth, the relationship between law and gospel can be properly understood only when "that formula, which has almost come to be taken for granted,"[1] is reversed to read: gospel and law. This reversal of the traditional order has great significance for Barth's doctrine of God, his anthropology, and his doctrine of sin. It is also decisive for his treatment of the relationship of dogmatics to ethics and constitutive of his very understanding of the *Church Dogmatics* as a theology of the Word of God.

The Reformation in the person of Martin Luther inescapably confronts Barth's theology of the Word of God with the question of the correct distinction between law and gospel. For Luther, the difference between law and gospel was essential to any understanding of the "Word of God." This distinction, along with the Pauline-Augustinian distinction between the letter and the spirit, was basic to his theology. One could distinguish good theology from bad, i.e., false theology, on the basis of the distinction between law and gospel. According to Luther, theology is the art of making the right distinctions concerning the Word of God. And in this art of making the right distinctions, the distinction between gospel and law is the most difficult and yet the most elementary of all. An adequate appreciation of Barth's approach to gospel and law requires at least a general understanding of Luther's repeated insistence on making the sharpest possible distinction between these two modes of the Word of God.[2] We will restrict our discussion of Luther to that which is indispensable for understanding Barth's reversal of the traditional sequence law-gospel into the sequence gospel-law.

For Luther, the correct distinction between law and gospel is "the highest art of Christendom that we should know," as he put it in a sermon on Galatians 3:23–29, "Wie das Gesetz und Euangelion recht grundlich zu unterscheiden sind" (How Law and Gospel Are to Be Thoroughly Distinguished), dated January 1, 1532.[3] Whether one is a Christian rather than a heathen or a Jew depends on that recognition.

But that does not mean that the gospel is the Word of God for Christians only, while the law is a human word meant for Jews and the heathen. Identifying the law as a human word would be just as much out of the question for Luther as the opposite error of recognizing only the law, and not the gospel, as the Word of God. The sermon makes this unmistakably clear. "Both are the Word of God: the law or the Ten Commandments, given by God through angels, and the gospel, which is also the Word of God. But this is what counts: that one distinguish the two Words and not mix them together, otherwise, one of them will be lost, if . . . not both."[4] That is why Luther will have nothing to do with subordinating or even eliminating one in favor of the other. Law and gospel are both the Word of God, and neither should be lost. But it is just as dangerous not to distinguish between them. For then one identifies the two modes with each another, distorting the gospel into law, or, conversely, the law into gospel, and one of the modes of the Word of God is lost. In fact, both are lost.

Luther illustrates these two types of confusion of law and gospel with the two heresies he had repudiated: the papacy and the fanatics. For Luther, the Roman Catholic heresy ultimately consisted in a perversion of the gospel into law. What is simply a gift was made a demand. The dispute over the sale of indulgences was itself already a struggle against a perversion of the gospel into law. The same holds true for Luther's rejection of the "juridical" and "philosophical" interpretation of the concept of the righteousness of God in terms of a distributive justice that gives each his own. Such an interpretation fails to see that the righteousness of God does not come through the law but through the gospel (Rom. 1:18f.). Luther sees a similar error in the papacy's perversion of the doctrine of justification from a doctrine of Christian freedom into an exorbitantly demanding ethic. Hence this harsh judgment in the same sermon: "Under the papacy, neither the pope nor any of his learned cardinals, bishops, and exalted schools has ever had any idea of what the gospel or the law is. . . . Their belief is therefore nothing more than the simple belief of a Turk, who only believes: Thou shalt not steal, not kill, etc."[5] According to Rörer's transcript of the sermon, Luther lists the following among the papists' beliefs: "Their faith consists only in what comes from the law—love God, do not kill your neighbor, etc. It sounds lofty, it comes to nothing. That is not yet to speak as a Christian, although it is right and based on God's word, and is not to be condemned. Still the two should be distinguished."[6] Not that what the papists believe should of itself be condemned; but they make the faith into a religion of law and thereby suppress the very thing that makes a Christian in the first place: namely the gospel, the gospel which cannot be identified with any law, not even the new law![7] The gospel is a thing unto itself, not a part of the law, which applies to all people.

In the heresy of the fanatics, Luther sees the opposite mistake, the perversion of the law into gospel. They treat the texts of law from the Bible as though they were gospel, and correspondingly confuse the office of the minister of God's word who preaches the gospel with, for example, the office of the soldier who must wage war. "What led Müntzer to the other [error] was his reading in the books of the Kings how David struck down the godless with the sword, how Joshua slew the Canaanites and other godless peoples, etc. He read that Word and concluded: 'We must . . . therefore do the same, oppose the kings and princes, because here we have an example,' etc. What led Müntzer astray was that he failed to draw the correct distinction from the Word—namely: 'David waged war, but am I David? The Word that called David to war is not addressed to me. He was ordered to wage war, to slay kings, I am ordered to preach.' Müntzer should have preached the gospel from the pulpit, according to the ordinance of Christ."[8] Whoever lacks the ability to make such distinctions has no grasp of the art of theology itself. If David the *king* had not followed his orders to maintain peace by the sword, and if Luther the *theologian* had taken up the sword instead, "that would have been a messy business."[9]

Luther's claim that the Word which commanded David to wage war does not apply to the preacher in the pulpit, who must proclaim the gospel, poses some problems for his identification of the law with the Ten Commandments. The Ten Commandments and the commandment of love which sums them up are addressed to all people (even if not at all times). But there clearly are biblical texts which belong to the category of law and are yet not addressed to all people. In a certain sense, that is true even for the Ten Commandments. For if a person is about to commit a murder, then, e.g., the commandment to keep the Sabbath holy is not at issue, because it is the commandment "Thou shalt not kill" which is at stake. Similarly, no law is of concern to us when we are speaking of the righteousness of God which is revealed in the gospel. Therefore, even when we are dealing with the law, we must distinguish among the various laws. We must ask whether this or that particular command applies at this time, and who is the person to whom this command is addressed. Indeed, we must take care to ascertain whether it is now time to preach the law at all, and whether this particular person should rather be directed to the gospel. "And so I say again that it is a most exalted art to tell what is gospel and what is law and to do it correctly, and even, moreover, to tell what part of the law we must do, to distinguish one law from the other and the peculiar application of each. . . . It is a serious matter to say: This is the Word of God, the Word of God. The Word of God is not all the same, but different. For example [Luther gives an illustration that only half applies today], this word: 'You shall bear children, suckle children,' is addressed only to women;

but on the other hand, women are not told: 'You shall preach, administer the sacraments,' etc. Our fanatics know utterly nothing about these fine points . . . , how one law opposes another, even though each is just as much law as the other. And if it is necessary to distinguish among them and to take account of the person to whom they are directed, how much more important it is to distinguish between law and gospel! Therefore, whoever can perform this art well shall be exalted and called a teacher of the Holy Scriptures, for the difference cannot be understood apart from the Holy Spirit. I know for myself how hard it is, and I see it daily in others as well."[10]

Luther clarifies the difference between law and gospel with an explanation of how each, as the Word of God, speaks to us. As the law, "the Word and command of God . . . bids us what we should do, demanding that we perform works."[11] On the other hand, the Word of God as gospel "does not demand that we do works, does not call us to do them, but rather calls us to take and receive . . . ; that is, God promises and says to you: 'I will give you this and that, [and] you cannot, and do not have to, do a thing about it.' . . . The gospel is nothing but the purest gift, favor, and salvation, and it requires only that we hold fast and receive it. But the law takes us and commands us. Now these two things, taking and giving, must be kept separate."[12] Thus Luther can explain the difference between law and gospel in this way: the person who is commanded by the law and then acts is a doer, but this same person appears in the gospel as a recipient, and is to that extent inactive, a nondoer. God, on the other hand, appears in the gospel precisely as the doer and giver, and appears in the law as the commander (and not inactive). In the law, God acts as the one who commands human beings to act; in the gospel it is God alone who acts, and human beings are only the recipients of this action.

Now this distinction is relatively simple to make in theory, and so it would appear that it is relatively easy to distinguish correctly between law and gospel. But the real problem for Luther is existential, not theoretical: which Word is directed to me now? This question is most pointed when the law exerts its proper influence over me, that is, when it touches my conscience. It is in the conscience alone that the law demands sovereignty. The law declares that it has sole authority in matters of conscience, insisting that there is no other court of appeal: "No, no, says the law, here you must stop, it is commanded . . . . The law accuses me: I have not done this and that, I am unrighteous and a sinner in God's eyes."[13] Thus the law's demand on my conscience is unconditional: not only my action but also my very being is judged (and in my conscience, where I can be comforted or afflicted!). But it thereby interferes with the activity of the Word as gospel. This is precisely what is at stake in Luther's doctrine of law and gospel. This is what makes the right distinction between law and gospel such a difficult matter. The distinction is required precisely because the law acts as though it were the sole authority over my conscience, accusing me of being a sinner and leading me to despair. But then it is time for the gospel, not the law. "When law and gospel clash, . . . when they contend with one another, then I follow the gospel and say: 'Adieu, law; it is better to know nothing of the law than to depart from the gospel. . . .' Therefore I then say: 'Go away, law; I will no longer let my heart be kept in your prison.' "[14]

It is the law, then, that interferes with the correct distinction between law and gospel. The law can even interfere with the gospel to the extent that the Gospel story of Jesus Christ can be preached as law. And a great many preachers do just that, preaching the mere "history"—and that only when they are at their best!—instead of proclaiming righteousness and salvation to the believer and thereby glorifying God.[15] One can even proclaim the benefits of Christ in such a way that the proclamation becomes an accusation of sin: "The preaching of the law makes sin evident. . . . And this can also be done by showing Christ's benefits to us, which are so great for you and for your delight. Thus whether this is done by the preaching of Christ's benefits or by the preaching of the law matters not; that much is law."[16] This passage is surely meant to insist on the necessity of preaching the law, in opposition to the thesis that Christ preached repentance on the basis of the gospel and not the law. Against that thesis, Luther—even the Luther of the third disputation against the Antinomians—maintains that there can and must be also a "preaching of the law through divine goodness."[17] What actually separates law from gospel is the usage that the preacher makes of the biblical text, and the effect that it produces. But the natural inclination is to employ the legal usage, so that the distinction between law and gospel arises only from the gospel, which alone makes the distinction both possible and absolutely necessary. It is the gospel which provides the warrant for the distinction between law and gospel. It is the gospel that makes it possible to reproach the law with this distinction, to challenge its concept of God, to show the law its limits and to push it back within its bounds: "Ah, dear law, is it really so jumbled together? We will not have the same God, and then he can no longer give the law. Know this: I do not mix the two together; here we make a distinction."[18]

This difference between law and gospel, a difference necessitated by the gospel itself, requires us to make a distinction within the law (and a twofold distinction at that): (a) among the various laws which do not apply to everyone at every time; and (b) between, on the one hand, the use of the law which is necessary to rule and restrain the world (the political use of the law) and, on the other hand, the use that arises from the law's demand for complete moral sovereignty over the conscience, when it identifies persons as lawbreakers and brings them to despair (the theological use of the law).[19] The distinction between law and gospel also extends in the same way to the doctrine of God, where one must distinguish between the wrathful God of the law and the gracious God of the gospel. Because the distinction between law and gospel has implications for the doctrine of God, Luther attributes a very great significance to the art of recognizing that distinction.[20] Luther opines: "There is no better method of preserving and handing on pure doctrine than to follow this method, that is, to divide Christian doctrine into two parts: law and gospel."[21] Therefore: "Anyone who knows how to distinguish between gospel and law may give thanks to God and consider himself a theologian."[22]

Turning from Luther's distinction between law and gospel to Barth's *Church Dogmatics,* it is immediately evident that the *Church Dogmatics* is not organized around this division of the Word of God into two opposing and even contradictory Words. Instead, it is structured in terms of the three forms of the Word of God: revelation, Bible, and proclamation. To be sure, Barth does appeal to Luther[23] for his doctrine of the three forms of the Word of God, but not to Luther's doctrine of law and gospel. He appeals instead, somewhat incidentally, to a differentiation of the three ways in which the immediate Word of God can be mediated. Barth's doctrine of the three forms of the Word of God is determined by such a different approach that it should not even be compared to Luther's distinction between law and gospel. For Luther, there are two modes of the Word of God, opposing and antagonizing each other in this world. They can attain unity only in God—and a most dialectical unity at that. For Barth, there are three forms of the Word of God, each corresponding to the others and expressing the same activity of God in a differentiation based on the economy of salvation. And, once he differentiates between them, Barth expressly returns to the theme of their unity once again. Indeed, he concludes that the doctrine of the three forms of the Word of God is the *only* analogy to the doctrine of the triune God, the only *vestigium trinitatis.*[24] One could not truthfully say the same for Luther's distinction between law and gospel in the one Word of God. Luther's theological distinction and Barth's theological differentiation are about different things. Basically they are not comparable.

But if we turn our attention to Barth's treatment of the law of God and of the relationship of dogmatics to ethics, his relationship to Luther's distinction appears in a different light. A comparison is possible here. Indeed, Barth's own doctrine of gospel and law can be thrown into sharper relief against the background of Luther's distinction between law and gospel. It then becomes clear that Barth is not primarily concerned with making the right distinction—which he does think has its place—but rather with seeing the right relationship between them: not the relationship of gospel to law, but of law to gospel.

A survey of the *Church Dogmatics* yields the startling conclusion that there is no specific section devoted to the topic of law and gospel in the entire corpus. There is no heading or subheading with that title. In its place, one finds the several treatments of the Command of God. At the conclusion of the Doctrine of God, following the chapter on the Election of God, stands a chapter entitled "The Command of God" (CD II/2, ch. 8). This chapter deals with the foundation of theological ethics in general, which Barth subsumes under dogmatics. Barth had already said in the prolegomena that ethics and dogmatics cannot be treated separately (CD I/2, §22.3: "Dogmatics as Ethics"). Correspondingly, in the doctrines of creation, reconciliation, and in anticipation, redemption, Barth included a chapter on a particular theme of ethics as a part of dogmatics: "The Command of God the Creator" (CD III/4); "The Command of God the Reconciler" (CD IV/4); and, planned but never written, "The Command of God the Redeemer" (CD V). This partly explains Barth's reversal of the traditional sequence "law and gospel" into "gospel and law." It also partly explains his claim that "anyone who really and earnestly would first say law and only then, presupposing this, say gospel would not, no matter how good his intention, be speaking of the law of God and therefore then certainly not of God's gospel."[25] By subsuming ethics (understood as the command of God) under dogmatics, Barth indicates that the question posed by the law, "What should we do?" presupposes the dogmatic question of God's existence and activity. But we can know God's existence and activity only from the Word of God as gospel. Hence the law or command of God flows from the gospel of God, and that implies the reversal of the traditional sequence "law and gospel," which, "even in the most favorable case," is "enveloped in ambiguities of every sort."[26]

Barth's approach is best understood in terms of his thesis that the very fact that God speaks to us, that there is a Word of God, is grace. It is a gift, free and undeserved, to the human race. And this is equally true of the Word in all three forms (revelation, Bible, and proclamation) and in both modes (gospel and law). "The very fact that God speaks to us, under all circumstances, is in itself grace."[27] But if the very fact that God speaks to us is already grace, then the content of what God speaks must also be grace in all circumstances. This means that the duality of the Word of God as gospel and law is properly expressed only in the context of their unity. "According to scripture, the contrast of gospel and law certainly designates a duality. It can even designate a conflict. But greater still than their duality and their conflict is their peace in the one Word" of the "Father of light in whom there is no variation or alternation of light and darkness."[28] Barth's appeal to James 1:17f. is meant to subordinate "the contrast of gospel and law" to their greater unity in the

peace of the God who speaks, even though their contrast remains inescapable. His appeal to this passage also reflects the extent of his fear that
this inescapable contrast between the two modes of the Word of God
could lead to an opposition within God's own being: an opposition
between the God of grace and the God of wrath, between God revealed
and God hidden, between the God who comes to us in love and the God
of the majestic heights—and thus, finally, to an opposition between God
and God. Barth takes the danger of opposing the revealed God to the
God withdrawn in majesty quite seriously. In this he concurs with the
nineteenth- and twentieth-century Protestant reception of Luther's distinction between law and gospel. Barth sees that Luther had already
opened the door to this danger in various passages in *The Bondage of the
Will* and the disputations against the Antinomians. But even if Luther,
"as an expositor of the Old and New Testaments, . . . often distinguished
between law and gospel, commandment and promise, in a way which was
utterly abstract and schematic, with a Paulinism which was not that of
St. Paul himself," that did not keep him from perceiving and understanding "the original and ultimate unity of the two with an astonishing
clarity" at other times.[29] Barth concludes that Luther can, "in certain
contexts," make it seem as though there is a "hidden God" behind the
revelation of God, "with whose existence and activity we also have to
reckon behind his Word and his Spirit, and whom we also have to fear
and honor behind his revelation."[30] Barth again and again clearly distances himself from such expressions because of Luther's dangerous
tendency to speak of a hidden God.

In a digression on the scholastic distinction between the absolute
(extraordinary) divine power and the ordinary power of God, Barth
observes: "According to Thomas Aquinas (*ST* I.25.5 ad 1) absolute
power is the power of God to do that which he can choose and do, but
does not have to, and does not actually choose and do. Ordinary power,
on the other hand, is the power which God does actually use and exercise
in a definite order."[31] Barth goes on to distinguish the Thomistic interpretation of this distinction from the far more dangerous and problematic
interpretation which arose in the late Middle Ages: "In virtue of his
ordinary power God was indeed able actually to do everything in the way
he chose. But in virtue of his absolute power he could actually have done
everything very differently and can still do so."[32] Turning to Luther, he
continues: "It cannot be denied that Luther sometimes spoke of his
hidden God as if he understood by this concept an absolute power or,
even more, an inordinate power."[33] Barth grants that "Luther clearly saw
. . . that if what the Nominalists understood by absolute power was
correct, there could be no assurance of salvation and therefore no stabil-
ity and confidence in life and death. At bottom there could never be more
than a restless seeking and asking for God's true capacity, while on high

or in the depths it could actually be quite different." Indeed, this was what was finally at stake in his dispute with medieval theology. Nevertheless, Barth concludes that Luther's "advice that we should worry as little as possible about the hidden God and cling wholly to . . . the revealed God, and therefore to the God revealed in Jesus Christ" scarcely constitutes an improvement over the nadir of medieval theology which he sought to overcome. "For how can we do this genuinely and seriously if all the time, as in Luther's teaching about the law, there is not denied but asserted a very different existence of God as the hidden God, a very real inordinate power in the background? Is the correct reference to the revealed God adequate if it is not quite certain that this God as such is also the hidden God, and that in all his possibilities, all his capacity in the regions and dimensions inaccessible to us, the hidden God is none other than the revealed God? In opposition to the thesis of the Nominalists, even in its Lutheran form, it is necessary to maintain that in the choice and action and capacity which he exercised in his freedom God has finally and definitely revealed his absolute power as ordinate power. We are forbidden to reckon on an essentially different omnipotence from that which God has manifested in his actual choice and action."[34]

Therefore, according to Barth, the God we meet in the law is none other than the God of the gospel. That is his chief objection to the dualist peril that he sees, at least as a tendency, in Luther's teaching of law and gospel. He raises a similar objection to Luther's understanding of election by grace.[35] And he also criticizes Luther's anthropological turn, whereby the relationship between God hidden and revealed, between law and gospel, becomes subject to existential verification, so to speak—"to come through fear at length to grace and love," as *The Bondage of the Will* puts it.[36] For Barth, this turn is unworthy of Luther. Barth would prefer to invert the sequence of fear and love in Luther's famous formula from the Small Catechism ("We should fear and love God") because "fear of God" comes from "love of God" and then accompanies it to keep it "in the truth." It is because the fear of God grows out of the love of God, "determining and delimiting" it so that it is "genuine and strong," that Barth wants "to see the two concepts placed in the reverse order from that which Luther followed in the Catechism."[37]

Barth's reason for reversing the traditional order of "gospel and law" becomes particularly clear at the same point where Luther's own interest in distinguishing law and gospel culminates: in confronting a person with his or her sin. A look at the structure of the *Church Dogmatics* will be instructive here also. Barth subsumes the treatment of sin in three forms under the doctrine of reconciliation, and he treats it there only following the Christology. He thereby parts company with "the dogmatics of all ages, churches, and movements," all of which put the doctrine of sin before the Christology, "first stating the problem, then giving the decisive answer to it in the doctrine of the incarnation and atoning death of Jesus Christ, and then . . . developing it in the doctrine of justification, of the church and of faith."[38] Barth develops the reasons for his reversal of the traditional procedure, and for the understanding of gospel and law which it implies, in CD IV/1, §60.1, and IV/2, §65.1. At the corresponding juncture in CD IV/3, §70.1 he defends it against Lutheran objections, declaring that it belongs to the "ironclad substance"[39] of his dogmatics. We shall now turn to these decisive texts for further clarification of Barth's understanding of gospel and law.

Barth justifies his subordination of the doctrine of sin to Christology with the following argument. He presupposes, along with "all serious Christian theology," that the knowledge of sin is a knowledge of God which is mediated by God himself, a "knowledge of revelation and faith. . . . That man is evil . . . is something which he cannot know of himself."[40] Indeed, "man lacks access to the knowledge that he is a sinner because he is a sinner" already.[41]

Barth goes even farther than this, refusing to acknowledge any connection between the theological concept of sin and the ordinary human experience of the ambiguity of human existence. He also denies that this experience of ambiguity could even constitute so much as a preliminary understanding of sin, concluding that "it is better not to consider the insight into the problematical nature of his existence which man can reach of himself apart from the Word of God even as a preparation or a kind of initial understanding in relation to the knowledge of sin."[42] But if this radical reformulation of the issue will not even permit the question of such a preparation to arise, Barth is still left with the question of how he can theologically realize his prior assertion that the knowledge of sin is a knowledge of revelation, especially in light of the fact that all theology, past and present, deals with the doctrine of sin prior to the doctrine of reconciliation. But consider the consequences of dealing with the doctrine of sin prior to the doctrine of reconciliation. Then the claim that the knowledge of sin is a knowledge of revelation would be possible only in the context of a knowledge of God "in his majesty and holiness as Creator and Ruler of the world," i.e., in the majesty and holiness of "the demand with which he confronts man or encounters him in history." This, in turn, would mean that "the knowledge of God" would proceed "from God's law." And this knowledge of God's law would have to be "revealed to man by nature and in general (through the mediation of conscience) or . . . specially revealed in history." The conclusion of this line of reasoning would be that "in the law," apart from the gospel, "we are dealing with that Word of God which has the special function of teaching man that he is a sinner and showing him in what his sin

consists."[43] Barth raises "serious objection"[44] to such a theological conclusion drawn from the otherwise correct insight that sin can be known
only in the presence of God and by the light of divine revelation.

Barth objects first of all to the "division of the knowledge of God and
the Word of God. . . . A division of God into a god in Christ and a god
outside of Christ is quite impossible."[45] A law which is abstracted from
the gospel, apart from Jesus Christ, will necessarily lead to a concept of
God which is abstracted from the revelation of God in Jesus Christ
through the gospel. According to Barth, an opposition between law and
gospel implies "the confrontation of man by the abstract law of an
abstract god." And "this god and his law" are, for Barth, nothing more
than "a product of the free speculation of the human reason and of
arbitrary human imagining,"[46] "a reflection of our own existence"[47] in
which "the real God is dishonored and his real law is emptied of content."[48]

Barth also objects to the biblicism (which even the Reformers shared
in this matter) that builds the concept of the law "wholly or mainly out
of biblical materials" and to that extent does not "lack at least the
severity of the judgment that man is a sinner before God," but nevertheless fails to interpret the law that thus identifies human sin in the overall
context of the orientation of the biblical texts. That is why this sort of
biblicism misses the fact that all biblical pronouncements on sin are
"orientated . . . in the Old Testament by God's covenant of grace with
his people, and in the New by the appearance and person and work of
Jesus Christ himself as the fulfillment of the covenant proclaimed
there."[49] This omission, and the consequent failure to follow a biblical
pattern of thought in dealing with the Bible, results in the loss of a truly
biblical orientation. Barth goes so far as to assert that "the transition
from biblical to biblicist thought does involve the transition to a rationalism, supernaturalistic though it is in content."[50] It leads to precisely the
old orthodox Protestant rationalism which, just like the Enlightenment,
thought that the law of God, apart from the grace and goodness revealed
in Jesus Christ, was a norm by which it could determine what is good
in both in the world and beyond the world, a neutral "normative concept
of the good by which we can measure evil."[51] Barth traces this supernaturalistic variety of rationalism in the older Protestant orthodoxy back to
this: "This theology had failed to follow the Reformers themselves in
learning from Jesus Christ as the substance and center of scripture what
is the will and law of God and therefore what the sin of man is."[52]

The danger posed to theology by this approach stems from its treatment of the concrete command of God as finally nothing more than a
symbolic precept, an illustration of the eternal law to which human
beings are disposed by nature. True human obedience is then a matter
of the law of nature and conscience, and "the concrete commandment

of God" becomes "only a symbolic precept" as a "test" of obedience (as Barth summarizes the position of the Reformed federal theologian F. Burmann.)[53] But what if "the concrete expression of the will of God degenerates into a symbolic precept" which only clarifies what man already knows from nature and "can learn from himself by this immediate self-knowledge?" We would then be on the verge of the catastrophe of rendering the biblical understanding of sin harmless. For the matter of human disobedience of the law (i.e., sin) would be decided "in a discussion in which man not only presents both sides of the case but is also the chairman who can terminate it with a deciding vote."[54] And that would implicitly abandon the affirmation that the knowledge of sin is possible only as a knowledge of God and revelation. To be sure, according to Barth, the Reformers, because they permitted the biblical material to influence them more than their own abstract systematic version of the law, were not themselves guilty of rendering sin harmless in this way. But this was a very present danger, insofar as they sought the knowledge of sin in a law of God that was abstracted from the gospel and from the person of Jesus Christ. Such a knowledge of sin, based on natural law, was what made it impossible to know how serious sin is. In this approach, "sin takes on a most innocuous appearance."[55]

According to Barth, the only thing that can prevent this catastrophe is basing the knowledge of sin on the knowledge of Jesus Christ. He sees indications of such a christologically based doctrine of sin as early as Luther and Melanchthon, and later in Schleiermacher, Lipsius, Ritschl, and Troeltsch, and most clearly in Martin Kähler.[56] But the logical conclusion of these tendencies, to treat sin only after the Christology, is developed first in the *Church Dogmatics.* This is also the first time that anyone seriously pursued the logical implications of the insight that it is not the law "apart from the gospel" but only the law which is interpreted "in the gospel and therefore authentically" that leads to "the knowledge of sin."[57] "Where the Word of God became and is flesh, there it is disclosed that man is flesh, and what it means and involves that this is the case. Where the grace of God encounters him, there his sin is revealed, and the fact that he is a sinner. Where his salvation is achieved, there the perdition from which he is snatched cannot be overlooked or contradicted. The gospel alone, which no man has invented or planned or constructed . . . is the law in the knowledge of which man finds himself accused and judged and condemned."[58]

Law and gospel could not be more closely linked. That is the point of Barth's thesis (despite its most unfortunate logic) that "the law is . . . the necessary form of gospel, whose content is grace."[59] A spatial image appeals to Barth: "The law is in the gospel as the tablets from Sinai were in the Ark of the Covenant, in such a way that the gospel is always in the law . . . as that which concerns man in the crib and in the swaddling clothes of the commandments, of the command and order of God."[60] To sum up: (1) The gospel alone determines what is to be taken as the law of God. (2) There is no gospel which does not also, as law, immediately lay claim to humankind. (3) The gospel is the Word of God addressed to humankind in the grace of God. (4) The law is the Word of God which lays claim to humankind for the grace of God. (5) The grace which is expressed as an indication in the "content" of the gospel is expressed as a gracious imperative in the "form" of the law.

It is only when the proper order of gospel and law has been made clear that we, according to Barth, can accept the reality it implies: that gospel and law "have been put into *our* hands, into the hands of sinners."[61] This is the place, for Barth as for Luther, where the specifically Pauline requirement that gospel and law be properly ordered arises: when "sin deceives us with the law and therefore about the law."[62] It is in the reality of the sinner that the good law of God becomes " 'the law of sin and death' (Rom. 8:2), the executor of divine wrath (Rom. 4:15), the law against which Paul cannot but warn his congregations most urgently— against its service, against its works, against its righteousness, and against its servitude and curse."[63] It is within the horizon formed by this problem that "the traditional order, 'law and gospel,' has a perfect right in its place."[64] But this situation should not be permitted to obscure the fact that the law, though it be "dishonored and emptied" by the sinner, "is and remains the law of God in its every letter," even when the gospel of God first takes effect on the selfsame sinner. If the law is truly part of the gospel, then the gospel works itself out fully "for the first time" in the reality of sin as "the truly glad tidings for real sinners."[65] And if this is the case, then the reality of sin can only obscure the unity of gospel and law, not destroy it. Indeed, this unity, along with the true relationship of gospel and law that comes with it, uses the law to unmask sin's fraud (whereby sin threatens to cheat us out of God's law!). It is precisely in the face of sin that God provides that "the gospel . . . as the good news of human liberation by and for the God who is free, has also the character and form of the true law, of God's law. Thus as the promise of God's grace it contains within itself God's no less gracious demand, just as the Ark of the Old Testament Covenant contained the tablets of the Law."[66]

On the basis of this formulation of the relationship of gospel and law, a relationship informed by the doctrine of sin, we are now in a position to draw out Barth's conclusion about the relationship of dogmatics and ethics. That conclusion is already clearly expressed in the position he assigns to ethics in his dogmatics. We shall pick up just where we left off, turning now to the fundamental relationship between God and humankind that is expressed in gospel and law.

We begin with the divine disposition, which constitutes in the first place this fundamental relationship with humankind as a convenantal relationship. In this relationship, God as Lord of the covenant promises salvation to humankind, but to the sinners that human beings really are, he bestows salvation precisely through his judgment. The gospel is that this judgment is executed on Jesus Christ, the Son of God who became human, instead of on us. But the gospel establishes divine justice—the justice of a gracious God!—and thus has the character of law. Barth's formulation of the relationship—binding the law as closely as possible to the gospel—can be understood only in light of the fact that, for Barth, when the issue is gospel and law, it is primarily a matter of God's own self-attestation. The relation of God to humankind is first and foremost an expression of the divine disposition. Barth's theology follows the direction of God's being and activity, starting with God and speaking to human beings, instead of starting with human beings and coming to God. In this theology, gospel and law are basic predicates of God, which is what makes them anthropologically relevant concepts. Luther frequently gave at least the appearance of making law and gospel into categories which describe human existence before God. But Barth cannot, in accordance with the basic direction of his theological method, speak of humanity in the presence of God before he speaks of God in the presence of humanity. It is God in humanity's presence that first brings a person before God and, as such, constitutes the "primal history" of the existence of humanity in God's presence. That explains why Luther, who is oriented to the dialectic of human existence, is so intent on the proper distinction between law and gospel; it also explains why Barth, referring to the unity of the divine being, will, and activity and the consequent unity of the Word of God, is intent on coordinating the law with the gospel.

But we cannot correctly understand Barth's treatment of gospel and law simply on the basis of the merely formal priority he assigns to God's attitude in the divine-human relationship. We must also attend to the specific nature of God's attitude, to God's loving action in accordance with his being, his gracious action toward the sinner. If we limited ourselves to the merely formal priority of the divine disposition in the divine-human relationship, we could interpret the gospel as a new law, and we could view God as first and foremost a lawgiver. One frequently encounters this interpretation (a grotesque misunderstanding of Barth's position) in Lutheran circles. And it must be conceded that Barth's terminology,[67] insofar as he raises the question of the law in terms of "the question of the goodness of human conduct" and ties it to the doctrine of sanctification, does provide the occasion for such a misinterpretation. That is how he puts it in the opening paragraph of the Münster lectures, where ethics is described "as a special elucidation of the doctrine of sanctification" and "a reflection on how far the Word of God proclaimed and accepted in Christian preaching effects a definite claiming of man."[68] And the superscription to section 36 of the *Church Dogmatics* reads: "As the doctrine of God's command, ethics interprets the law as the form of the gospel, i.e., as the norm of the sanctification which comes to man through God's choice."[69] But traditional dogmatics treated the doctrine of sanctification as a consequence or implication of the doctrine of justification. It is therefore possible to read Barth's treatment of "the law as the form of the gospel" as equating the law with its third use (as it has been known since Melanchthon) or fourth use (as it was known in later orthodoxy). One might even think that for Barth the intention of the gospel is exhausted by the fulfillment of the law which sanctifies the Christian through regeneration. This, at any rate, is the only way in which the Lutherans could make any sense out of the unity of gospel and law in Barth's thought; hence they were bound to reject it as a false and even nonsensical treatment of law and gospel.

But more than two centuries earlier, Lutheran orthodoxy had affirmed the unity of law and gospel in practice, in the life of the penitent sinner and the regenerate. That is how it is described in the *Examen theologicum acroamaticum* of David Hollaz: "Law and gospel are joined as if in a mathematical point. They work together to bring sinners to repentance, to revive those who are justified, . . . and to preserve in piety and perseverance in the faith those who are revived."[70] What Hollaz asserts here concerning human life in practice—that law and gospel are conjoined as in a mathematical point—Barth extends to God's own practice. In God's activity, gospel and law are a single Word. But because God loves from all eternity henceforth and is thus the one who chooses us, not the lawgiver, God's law is first and foremost simply the form taken by his commitment to the good of the human race. And this loving attitude claims and demands a corresponding human attitude toward God. Barth's treatment of gospel and law is supralapsarian, in the same way that he bases the doctrines of God and Creation on the gospel of Jesus Christ. And he expressly calls the doctrine of the election of grace (itself a part of the doctrine of God) the "sum of the gospel."[71] Correspondingly, the expression "the law as the form of the gospel" is clarified by the phrase "as the norm of the sanctification which comes to man through the God who chooses us."[72] Election is prior to justification and regeneration. And if sanctification already belongs to election, then it is for all people, not just the reborn. It is for Barth a matter of the loving and gracious gift that is always being given in God's disposition toward humankind. This is a key distinction in Barth's dogmatics: the God who chooses cannot be conceived apart from his revelation in Jesus Christ; for that reason, the fundamental relationship of God to the human race is not based on changing attitudes, but on one and the same disposition.

And this disposition is the gift of God which is, as such, also a claim, and hence gospel and law.

Whoever attacks Barth here is going for the jugular. Paul Althaus knew that very well when he registered his objection to Barth's treatment of gospel and law: "To be sure, in the primal state . . . it is God's love —his wanting to be for us, so that we may be for him—which is the basis of all his commands. But this original love of God must not be called 'the gospel.' The term 'gospel' must retain its specific meaning as the Word of God's gracious dealing with the sinner. In the beginning there is the grace of the primal state, not the gospel; and from this primal grace there springs not the law, but the divine command—God's loving call, his wooing claim upon our hearts. Barth rides roughshod over these important distinctions between primal grace and the gospel, between command and law—not only in his terminology but also in the substance of what he says. It is this failure to distinguish between the several epochs of God's dealings with humankind that also governs Barth's doctrine of revelation, and that is the real theological root of his disregard for God's basal or primal revelation."[73]

This is just what Barth does. And it is not a careless or inadvertent error that he can correct when someone reproaches him for it. On the contrary, Barth's theology is specifically about God, and it derives its logic from the action of God; furthermore, it cannot arrange and classify the action of God according to the several epochs of the sinner's disposition. And it is in just this way that theology truly honors the human, according to Barth. For the action of God, the deed which precedes all human disposition, is really the eternal election of humankind, in which he establishes his claim to the human race. Therefore, discourse about the human—the human in correspondence to God—is an inseparable part of that specifically theological discourse which takes God as its point of departure. For that reason, Barth subsumes the concept of the covenant under the doctrine of God, expounding the doctrine of the election of grace (which is the basis of the covenant) and the doctrine of the command of God (which is the foundation of theological ethics) as parts of the doctrine of God. Therefore, as a rejoinder to Althaus (and despite his assertion that "in terms of what we both really want to say, our positions are not far from each other"[74]), I submit the opening lines of Barth's general theological ethics, in which he makes it crystal clear that he is taking a different path: "In the true Christian concept of the covenant of God with man, the doctrine of the divine election of grace is the first element, and the doctrine of the divine command is the second. It is only in this concept of the covenant that the concept of God can itself find completion. For God is not known and is not knowable except in Jesus Christ. He does not exist in his divine being and perfections without Jesus Christ, in whom he is both very God and very man.

... The Christian doctrine of God cannot have 'only' God for its content, but since its object is *this* God it must also have man, to the extent that in Jesus Christ man is made a partner in the covenant decreed and established by God.''[75] If "election" is what determines human beings as human (insofar as they are to be God's covenant partners), then "sanctification" cannot be limited to the regenerate alone, but "comes on man from all eternity and therefore once and for all.''[76] And if "election" is the inclusive concept, the sum of the gospel, then the essence of humanity is determined in the gospel, and sanctification is nothing but a demand to realize our essence. The law requires people to live according to their election. It is in this sense that "the gospel itself has the form and fashion of the law.''[77]

Barth's formulation of gospel and law is the basis of his exposition of theological ethics as a part of dogmatics. We shall now examine the basic content (which we have already encountered) of his understanding. According to Barth, the Lord of the covenant encounters the human now, and does so as the God of the gospel from all eternity. And even as God turns to humankind in this way, so too he immediately claims humanity for himself. As God surrenders himself to humanity—finally giving himself for humankind—he demands the same surrender in return. The priority of the gospel is material but not temporal. This clarifies his description of the law as the form of the gospel: the form cannot be preceded by its content.

That also implies a significant anthropological conclusion which can clarify Barth's dispute with Luther's distinction between law and gospel. Barth understands human being in the same way that he understands divine being: as a "being in action," as active being, as activity. Again and again in the *Church Dogmatics* we read passages like the following: "For it is as man acts that he exists as a person.''[78] "To exist as a man means to act. And action means choosing, deciding.''[79] Barth can also describe human being in this way: "This being . . . does not subsist of itself, but only in a specific activity on the part of the subject.''[80] Human activity, however, is for its part basically understood as the act in which one chooses oneself. Correspondingly, when Barth refers to the being or essence of the human, he speaks of the "self-determination without which the human being would not be human,''[81] or of "that act of self-determination which we call our human existence.''[82] A human being is regularly defined as "that essence which is constantly realizing its existence in acts of free determination and decision.''[83]

A polemic against Barth could take the form of a charge that this constitutes Barth's own unacknowledged philosophical preconception of humanity. And a critic who wished to fan the flames could also charge that this unacknowledged philosophical preconception rather closely resembles that philosophy which was one of his more or less favorite targets, namely, so-called existentialism. "I am my deed" is, e.g., Jean-Paul Sartre's basic insight, to be found throughout his theoretical and literary work. One is what one does with oneself. It is in choosing and deciding that one determines oneself. Therefore a person is the essence of freedom, or, so to speak, doomed to freedom. At first glance, it seems that Barth's description differs from such "existentialist" ideas only in that he views persons as created for self-determination by God and therefore not doomed to freedom but chosen for freedom.

Over against the objection that Barth falls into an uncritical, untheological preconception of human natures it should be noted that his understanding is in fact not the result of anything but his concept of God, which is his real presupposition. His understanding of humanity attains its fullest development in the doctrine of God and in the corresponding discussion of the gospel as the one Word of God and of the law as the form of the gospel. Anthropologically speaking, Barth links the gospel to human being and the law to human activity, an activity of self-determination. Thus far he is in agreement with Luther. He also seems to agree with Luther in anthropologically tying the gospel to the "determinateness of the inward . . . aspects of human life," while anthropologically tying the law to the "determinateness of the . . . outward aspects."[84] (This corresponds to Luther's distinction between the "inner" and the "outer man" in *The Freedom of a Christian*.) And he is also one with Luther in insisting that the inner must be expressed in the outer and in asserting that the Word of God "demands that we leave the sanctuary of an abstract 'inwardness' and give ourselves to the decision." "It does not demand individual works from us. It demands us as doers ourselves,"[85] namely as doers of this very Word of God. It is just as necessary to be a doer of the Word as it is to be a hearer of the Word in the first place.

Barth first parts company with Luther when, in accordance with his description of the Word of God as gospel in the form of the law, he affirms the unity of the human person. The "inner" is already apparent in the "outer"; human being is apparent in human doing; human existence is apparent in self-determination; the essence of the human is apparent in human "acts of free determination and decision";[86] one's person is apparent in one's activity. And so Barth can concur with Calvin's conclusion on James 1:21–25: "Blessedness is to be found in doing." Barth continues: It is "in the doing of the Word, which is true [sic] hearing," that "we are saved and blessed."[87] Luther could not have said that. For him, a person is saved and blessed by hearing and believing, not by doing anything; indeed, one refrains from activity. Luther took seriously Paul's description in Romans 4:5 of "believing" as "not doing works." For Luther, one is first a recipient of God's activity, i.e., one who is justified, before one becomes a doer of works. And Barth did not, of course, describe the justified as actively cooperating in salvation. Barth can join the Formula of Concord[88] in describing the human person, with respect to obtaining salvation, as "similar to a block of wood and a stone." For Barth there can be "no 'cooperation on the part of our will in our conversion.' "[89] But Barth sets great store by the fact that the Formula of Concord expressly describes the human person, even after the Fall, as "a rational creature," capable both of doing and not doing. "Moreover," Barth continues in his reference to the Formula, "man is in this respect 'witty, intelligent, and accomplished.' But in 'spiritual and divine things' he is 'similar to a block or stone.' "[90] He is *similar* to wood or stone—for it is not stones or blocks of wood that are created for the regeneration brought about by the Spirit of God, but people. " 'Indeed, no stone or block, but man alone was created to be renewed by the Holy Spirit.' As man and therefore as a 'rational creature' man becomes the object of the divine action."[91] The work of the Holy Spirit is therefore not coercion, but rather something to which human activity spontaneously corresponds. "But this means that 'the impulse of the Holy Spirit is not coercion or compulsion, because the converted man spontaneously does that which is good.' "[92] Barth takes a great deal of interest in this "spontaneously," a concept which the Formula of Concord appropriated from Luther.[93] He understands it not only as the result of divine action, but also as based on an ontological characteristic of the person who is transformed by God into a rational, self-determining, acting creature: "In his very self-determination, without which he would not be human, man becomes an object of the divine predetermination."[94] We are not really coerced into self-determination when we encounter the grace of God; it is rather a matter of "being determined in our self-determination."[95] God's "miracle . . . is performed upon a man who is really identical with himself. It does not take place in one who is outside of himself. . . . It takes place in the man who is himself and with himself."[96] That is why Barth rejects the view that "a passive, receptive attitude" on the human side "necessarily corresponds to the divine possibility. In certain circumstances an active, spontaneous attitude may correspond much better."[97]

Here is where the Reformation's distinction between law and gospel and Barth's subordination of the law to the gospel come to the real parting of their ways. It is a question of anthropology. On the one side, Luther's understanding of the gospel requires human passivity and receptivity—a highly intensive and creative passivity, to be sure—which can then issue spontaneously in human activity and good works. But these good works can never arise apart from that prior passivity. And so, according to Luther, the gospel "snatches us away from ourselves and places us outside ourselves."[98] To be "away from ourselves" and "outside ourselves" is the basic pattern for the hearer of the Word and thus the basic pattern of human existence. On the other side, Barth's anthropology has an entirely different orientation. The human is understood by definition to be constituted by action and self-determination. Barth's anthropology therefore permits the gospel to be transformed immediately into the form of the law which demands human action. And that is why Barth cannot agree with Luther's trenchant judgment that the "gospel . . . does not demand our works, but means to seize us and make us yield."[99] And he certainly cannot join Luther in saying, "I put myself beyond all active righteousness," or, "Therefore the highest art and wisdom of Christians is not to know the law [and] to ignore works and all active righteousness," or, "If you do not ignore the law and thus direct your thoughts to grace as though there were no law, but as though there were nothing but grace, you cannot be saved."[100] And Barth could absolutely never concur with Luther that "Therefore the law slays us because it is impossible to keep," i.e., to obtain justification,[101] or that the true office of Christ is therefore to free us from the law.[102]

Barth agrees with Luther that the gospel unambiguously brings life and salvation. He does not agree with Luther about how the gospel does so. According to Luther, the gospel is unambiguous in contrast to the ambiguous law. The gospel then clarifies the law as only for the "old man." The law henceforth "stays within its limits."[103] "For the old man and the law are joined together. But the law is not joined to the spirit."[104] This is precisely what Barth rejects, for the unambiguous gospel that brings life and salvation also brings with it an already unambiguous law. And this law has the function of leading us to a decision which corresponds to God's primal decision of election.

Barth's anthropology, therefore, in distinction to Luther's teaching, understands human beings as, so to speak, an image of God's being, while Luther describes the image of God in human beings as a convex-concave relationship: God acts, and we receive (and only then can begin to act). For Barth, where God acts, there we are seen to act—precisely in receiving. Therefore, as Barth puts it in a particularly trenchant phrase, God himself, "as Lord of the covenant . . . necessarily becomes the judge of man, the law of his existence. Man is judged as he is measured against God. And as he measures himself against God he necessarily judges himself." The indicative of the gospel creates a (new) being for a person only by permitting him to act, so that he may come to a "human decision which corresponds to the divine decision."[105] Barth's version of the relationship of gospel and law is, in the final analysis, concerned with this correspondence, this analogy between God and humanity, an *already* ontological correspondence between the existence of God as pure act and the existence of the human person who is self-defined in action. "As the one Word of God which is the revelation and work of his grace reaches us" (gospel), "its aim is that our being and action should be conformed to his" (law). " 'Be (literally, you shall be) therefore perfect (literally, directed to your objective), even as (i.e., corresponding to it in creaturely-human fashion as) your Father which is in heaven is perfect (directed to his objective)' (Matt. 5:48). The truth of the evangelical indicative means that the full stop with which it concludes becomes an exclamation mark. It becomes itself an imperative."[106]

Now if the law is concerned with the human fulfillment of the correspondence, or analogy, of God and humanity which is based on the gospel, then the doctrine of the law or command of God cannot be kept separate from dogmatics. If it is precisely as a doer that a person corresponds to God, then the question of the goodness of human conduct, as well as its answer—the doctrine of the command of God—is part of dogmatics. Thus theological ethics is a part of dogmatics. That is why Barth sharply disputed the possibility of "theological ethics as an independent discipline," a development which can be traced back to Calixtus.[107] The entire approach derives from a false premise, i.e., "that the goodness" of the human activity which God commands, "the holiness of the Christian character, unlike the other objective content of Christian proclamation, is not hidden with Christ in God (in spite of Col. 3:3), but can be directly perceived and therefore demonstrated, described, and set up as a norm."[108] Wherever theological ethics has gained independence from dogmatics on the basis of this false presupposition, this "independent ethics has always shown at once a tendency . . . to replace dogmatics as the basic theological discipline, absorbing dogmatics into itself, transforming it into an ethical system."[109] Discourse about God becomes a predicate in discourse about the human. "This . . . means that dogmatics itself and theology as a whole simply becomes applied anthropology"[110] —something that has also happened in philosophy: "The turn to anthropology has been the ruin of philosophy" (Martin Heidegger).[111] It would then be all too easy to suspect real dogmatics "of being no more than an idle intellectual frivolity."[112] Indeed, Barth takes "the whole idea of a distinction between 'theoretical' and 'practical,' " which is the basis of such an independent ethics, to be "from the very first a primal lie, which has to be resisted in principle."[113] For if it is "through the Word of God that human existence acquires theological relevance," and if a person "exists in that he acts," then it is precisely dogmatics, which deals with the Word of God, that "raises the ethical question or rather recognizes and treats it as its most characteristic problem."[114] And that is why "dogmatics itself must be ethics" and "ethics can be only dogmatics."[115]

Barth therefore dealt with ethics, as already pointed out, as part of dogmatics, the doctrine of the command of God, expounded at the conclusion of each volume of the *Church Dogmatics.* The doctrine of God includes both the foundation and the content of theological ethics.

The divine disposition, seen in the law, is described as a "claim on humankind." Concretely, this foundation for ethics signifies that God, in his election to grace, has made himself responsible to humankind. This is the essence of the divine attitude and the sum of the gospel. And it is also precisely how God lays claim to humankind with the law, fulfilled in Christ, as the form of the gospel. The command of God is correspondingly interpreted as demand, decision, and judgment.

Thus, Barth develops his ethics under the doctrines of creation, reconciliation, and redemption, in the doctrines of the command of the Creator, the Reconciler, and the Redeemer. His emphasis moves from the commanding position of God to the commanded position of humankind, from the unquestionable goodness of the divine action itself to the problematic goodness of human activity.[116] And so, first, the doctrine of creation moves in the direction of the demand made on humanity through the command of God, insofar as "we exist and live."[117] That is, we live and exist before God in (commanded) freedom: freedom in community, freedom for life, freedom in limitation. Next, the doctrine of reconciliation develops the ethics of the doctrine of the Christian life: the reconciled God lays claim to humanity through his command, insofar as we are judged and uplifted, justified and sanctified in the gospel. This claim is made when God commands us to call upon him. We obey this command by (a) asking for the Baptism of the Holy Spirit and thereby grounding the Christian life, (b) fulfilling the Christian life in praying and living the Lord's Prayer, and (c) renewing the Christian life through thanksgiving to God in the Lord's Supper. The conclusion of Barth's ethics was to have come with the doctrine of redemption: the command of the Redeemer lays claim to humanity by calling us "not merely to live and bow before the Word, but, living and bowing before his Word, to advance toward a genuine, qualitatively and indeed infinitely better future."[118]

Barth's subordination of ethics to dogmatics was based on his understanding of gospel and law. It is surely clear that this is the basic theological reason why his theology, precisely as dogmatics, had a political impact such as has scarcely been the case since the Reformation. Its impact came because of its dogmatic character, not in spite of it. That was because its doctrine of the law honored the God of the gospel, the God of grace.

Four

The Royal Man: A Christological Reflection on Human Dignity in Barth's Theology

A proper theology makes no compromises. That is what distinguishes it from church administration and leadership. And to the extent that it makes no compromises, theology performs a critical function in church leadership. As a theologian, Karl Barth performed this function in many ways. The whole of the *Church Dogmatics* is to be read as a textbook of church leadership. It is therefore an eminently critical text, for it measures the reality of the church against the criterion of evangelical truth, namely, the person of Jesus Christ. Dogmatics is thus an aggressive science, but not in the sense of a fractious, querulous, pseudoacademic or obscurantist attachment to the status quo. The *Church Dogmatics* assails the church (and not only the church) with the gospel. That is what makes it of service to the church. Barth's theology is a deliberate assault with the gospel. Hence it is not only an *uncompromising* theology, but also an uncompromising *theology*.

Therefore, when we consider the topic of "the royal man" in Barth's theology, we should not expect to find a compromise between a theology whose overriding interest is in the deity of God and an anthropology whose overriding interest is the humanity of humankind. Such a compromise would only reproduce the hopeless logical confusion that characterizes the contemporary theological discussion. Instead, we will find that Barth's doctrine of the royal man marks the beginning of a new development in Protestant theology, even though it is undertaken in the context of an intensive dialogue with tradition. Barth's doctrine is free of any compromise, yet it is also free of any unfortunate dichotomy between the deity of God and the humanity of humankind; it is freed by the event of the revelation of God, and henceforth it can think of deity and humanity together and still give each its due. A resolute refusal to compromise in theology does not at all mean a forced choice between two abstract alternatives.

The Christology of Karl Barth was the topic chosen for the seminar in systematics at the seminary of the Evangelical Church of Berlin-Brandenburg during the winter semester of 1965–66. On the occasion of his eightieth birthday, we present to this most instructive, uncompromising theologian, who throughout his life has summoned both theology and the church "to the heart of the matter," a glimpse into the work of that seminar. It can only be a glimpse, and at that, nothing more than a glimpse, of a portion of Barth's *Church Dogmatics:* his doctrine of the royal man, which gives humanity its due.

Who Is the Royal Man?

According to Barth, humankind can never receive its due as long as it seeks it within itself. The same holds true for our reflections on the topic. We can conceive what God intends for humankind only by reflecting on the one human being that God himself has uniquely intended and directed, and in whom his own divine being is taken up: Jesus Christ. He is the royal man. And his royalty does not exclude, but includes, us. All humankind is reflected in him.

The subject of Barth's Christology, then, is the royal man. At the same time, however, humanity is the implicit subject of Barth's Christology, for it is a reflection on every human being. Christology is the carefully considered foundation of anthropology in Barth's characteristically christological thought. There can be no question of a "Christomonism," precisely because this christological concentration is not a principle from which a system can be deduced. The only important thing is to concentrate on the concrete existence of Jesus Christ. But this concrete existence constitutes a history in which we cannot speak of God apart from the man Jesus, nor about the man Jesus apart from God. At the same time, we cannot speak of the history of Jesus Christ without speaking of all human beings, for the royal man was there in such a way precisely because he was there for humankind. And insofar as that was the case, God was there for all persons.

Therefore Christology cannot tolerate any sort of "respectful isolation."[1] Everything must be seen in the light of Christology: the human person, the church, the world, and even the devil (though only with a brief, sideways glance–but, nevertheless, the devil). For when "dogmatics cannot regard itself and cause itself to be regarded as fundamentally Christology, it has assuredly succumbed to some alien sway and is already on the verge of losing its character as church dogmatics."[2] A dogmatics that did not understand itself as Christology would be an apologetic, self-justifying discipline, not an active discipline, inspired by the gospel. It would have to seek to satisfy objections based on criteria alien to the subject. But then it would fail its own subject matter and would be theologically discredited as an assimilative science. For the subject matter of theology is Christology. And to think christologically means to reflect only on the revelation of God. "The pertinence of theology consists in making the exposition of revelation its exclusive task."[3] Revelation is just that event in the world which meets objections that rest on worldly criteria by raising its own objections to those criteria. "God's revelation has its reality and truth wholly and in every respect —i.e., ontically and noetically—within itself."[4]

We can think about the royal man, therefore, only in the dimension of revelation. That means in a quite specific connection with God, a connection which comes from God to us. Not a connection in which God and a man have been united! Rather, it is a connection in which God unites with a man. The royal man *becomes.* His becoming arises neither from himself nor from human presuppositions. His becoming depends exclusively on God's becoming—God's becoming human.

Where Is the Royal Man?

But if it is the case that God, in becoming man, unites with the man Jesus, have we not fallen into a contradiction? We say that the man Jesus, as this union is formed, first becomes what he is, that is, the royal (and therefore the real) man. But how can God unite with a man, if it is only in this union that the man first becomes what he is?

If it is truly the case that the reality and truth of God's revelation is comprehensive and self-contained in all respects, then it must also be the case that this revelation brings its own historical location, its own reality in space and time. Note that the revelation establishes its location as a historical location, its reality as an earthly reality. There is nothing ghostly or ethereal about the revelation. History becomes an authentic predicate of revelation. But the revelation brings its own history, seeking to be historically real and effective for us. This is what Karl Barth calls election.

The history of Jesus Christ is the history elected by God. God has bound himself to this history from all eternity. The implications of this are twofold.

1. God's own eternal being is moved by the man Jesus. God's eternal being is therefore a moved being. God's being is moved by the history of the man Jesus because God moves from eternity to this history. God's eternal being is therefore both a history that he moves and a history full of movement. It is the moving history of the love of God for humankind, in which the love of God himself is expressed in the movement of history. God's being is the moving—and moved—history of an eternal love which did not will to be eternal without also becoming temporal. The history of the eternal self-movement of God was intended to be a history affected by a human being in time. For that reason, the eternal triune God chose the man Jesus, in order to be truly divine *and* truly human in him. Thus the eternal being of the Son of God cannot be conceived

apart from his incarnation. And all talk about an eternal, "fleshless" Word of God is an impermissible theological abstraction. Theology is forbidden "to imagine a 'Logos in itself' "[5] and thereby to ignore the eternal decision of God to be true God as a human being, in the mode of the Son's being.

2. The elect man Jesus is moved in his human history by the eternal being of God and is, from the beginning, with God in all the works and ways of God. That means that the man Jesus, before he is real in himself, is already truly with God. And the eternal Son of God holds a place for the earthly Son of Man. That is, God's gracious election holds a place for the man Jesus in the being of God from all eternity. The true man Jesus is chosen for this exaltation, even as God chooses himself for the loneliness of human existence. In this choice, the elect man Jesus is already with the God who chooses him. We can therefore no more describe God's being in and for himself than we can conceive of the being of humankind in and for itself. Instead, God, by his eternal election of the temporal being of Jesus of Nazareth, has created space within himself for another being, alien to himself. There is a realm of grace within God himself. Here, in this space, created for the man Jesus from all eternity in the being of God, the essence of humanity finds God before it finds itself. This is what graces our existence.

Thus it becomes theologically comprehensible that the revelation of God in our history brings its own history along with it. The man Jesus owes his historical reality to the being and becoming of God alone. All human existence is enlightened by the truth that the true man is at home with God. But if this is so, then the person who is at home with himself or herself can be only a false human being, one who falls short of true humanity.

From Whence Does the Royal Man Come?

If the true man is at home with God, then the humanity of humankind cannot be known apart from the deity of God. and if the actual human being is at home with himself or herself—and, as such, a sinner—there can be no question of the humanity of humankind unless the deity of God is revealed in the midst of an evil society whose essence is "not God and indeed opposed to God."[6] Christology relates the history of this revelation of God in the midst of the evil society of sinners. It tells of the restoration of that society and of the reconciliation that takes place in the true man and true God Jesus Christ. In the history of Jesus Christ, "It comes to pass that God is the reconciling God and man is the reconciled man."[7]

The history of Jesus Christ is the history of reconciliation, in which the Son of God, as a man, takes up the evil company of sinners: "The

Way of the Son of God Into the Far Country."[8] We must look at the way of the Son of God into the country that is far from God in order to learn what is divine. The essential thrust of the divine majesty is unreservedly directed toward the depths. At the same time, the way of the Son of God into the far country also determines what is human. For it is only by the way of the Son into the far country that humankind finds its home, that humankind is brought home. "The Homecoming of the Son of Man"[9] coincides with the way of the Son of God into the far country. The way of the Son of God into the depths leads the Son of Man into the heights. And humanity as a whole is bound to his truth.

We must therefore inquire after the ways of God if we would learn the truth about our being. We must ask where God goes if we wish to know from whence the royal man comes.

God reveals himself in that God the Father, in an act of the divine spirit, sends the Son of God into the far country. God also reveals himself in that God the Son obediently goes into the far country. The Son obediently endures the far country into which he goes. God reveals himself in this obedience: God is the Lord as Servant. Thus he reveals himself as a God who suffers for his creation. God suffers! And just in this way he shows that he is God. We must make three observations about this suffering.

1. This suffering is necessary: The Word of God did not "simply become any 'flesh.' . . . It became Jewish flesh."[10] The Son of God who goes into the far country participates in the history of the chosen people, who must suffer the wrath of God because of their debasement. This history of the suffering of the chosen people Israel is a sign that "the history of salvation is essentially the history of the passion."[11] And this suffering history reflects how passionately God is moved by the history of his creation. According to Barth, this is the import of the Old Testament. The Son's "history must be a history of suffering."[12] The Son of God obediently submits to this requirement. His obedience shows him to be the true God.

2. This suffering is real. If the deity of God is revealed in the suffering of Jesus Christ, then we must base our concept of God on this suffering. The pious person will resist, protesting that a God who suffers ceases to be God and that the specifically human experience of death contradicts the deity of God. The history of theology is saturated with these objections, but they ignore the self-revelation of God in Jesus Christ—that God in Jesus Christ suffered and died—and thus they prove to be "quite untenable, corrupt, and pagan."[13]

3. This suffering is possible. If God does not cease to be God in the suffering of his Son, but rather manifests the greatest humility, then this great humility cannot be foreign to the essence of God. It is therefore impossible to refer to a ruling contradiction in the being of God on the

grounds of the Son's suffering, as Lutheran theologians in particular have done and still do. On the contrary: "By doing this God proves that he *can* do it, that to do it is within his nature."[14] The fact that the Son of God manifested his deity in obedient suffering demands the conclusion that it is not only the deity of the Son that can and will perform this obedience. The deity of God, as such, discerns and makes possible obedience in himself; indeed, it belongs in the same way to all three "Persons" of the one God. So it is that "in one equal Godhead the one God is in fact the One and also Another, that he is indeed a First and a Second, One who rules and commands in majesty and One who obeys in humility."[15] That is not a contradiction in God; it is how the Father and the Son are one in the Spirit. They affirm one another. In this way God corresponds to himself. In this way he is the living God.

This possibility of God's earthly life is grounded in God himself. Thus we understand that God is not overcome even in suffering. What God does and is as he turns toward humankind can be understood only as something "unnecessary and extravagant."[16] "God gives himself to the world in that he, as its reconciler, becomes worldly," and so "his inner being as God . . . take[s] outward form."[17] God's outgoingness and worldliness issue from his loving, eternal gift to the human race. This gift is the "whence" from which the royal man comes and lives.

What Is the Royal Man?

The event of reconciliation does not involve only a God who reconciles humanity to himself, but also the human being who is reconciled. By no means is this human being unimportant or incidental, a figure who could be mentioned only in passing or even not at all. The slogan "God is everything, humanity nothing" (not coined by Barth, but attributed to him—not without cause—during the heyday of his commentary on Romans[18]) fails to give God his due precisely because it denies humanity its due. If anyone thinks that this renewed attention to the humanity which is reconciled to God will necessarily revive "the fatal theology of the pious man," Barth must reply that the other alternative, merely to exchange one abstraction for another, "is a poor and in the true sense 'reactionary' procedure" (CD IV/2, p. 10).[19] Instead of becoming agitated over the errors of the abstract, anthropocentric theologians, it is much better "to look calmly at the problem they raised, not dropping and leaving it, but taking it up again in a new and better way" (10R).

We can formulate our question more clearly and pertinently if we see it anew in its concrete context. The human being who is reconciled to God is named Jesus of Nazareth. In him, humanity became the new humanity, the humanity that is reconciled to God. Anyone who asks the question of what humanity is in the abstract, disregarding its concrete context, will soon be "wandering in a fog, thinking that which is only trivial or nonsensical, telling us and others an attractive fairy story, presenting an inspiring piece of poetry, proclaiming a myth or merely spinning pious sayings" (282–283R).

The history of the royal man Jesus includes implicitly the history of all humanity. There is an ontological connection between the being of the human Jesus and all other human being, because God, in Jesus, transforms history into history for all humanity. It is precisely for this reason that the history of Jesus Christ is both God's history and humanity's history. In order for justice to be done to both aspects of this history, it must be told twice. First we hear of how God humbled himself and journeyed into the far country. This movement from above to below simultaneously causes a vigorous movement from below to above. Hence we also hear of the exaltation and homecoming of humanity. "In its . . . original sense . . . , 'to reconcile' means 'to exchange.' " Reconciliation is "the *exinanitio,* the abasement, of God, and the *exaltatio,* the exaltation, of humanity. It was God who went into the far country, and it is man who returns home" (21). Thus in him we recognize the true man, chosen and affirmed by God. But who is the true man?

Jesus manifests his humanity as the true man in such a way as to be entirely like us and entirely unlike us in equal measure. He is completely "like us in our creaturely form, but also in its determination by sin and death. . . . He is not, then, an angel, a middle being, a demigod," but rather "totally and unreservedly" human (27). He is completely unlike us in that "this same 'human nature' in which he and we both share . . . became and must become" something different (27R). Since he suffered and acted as a human being, "there took place an exaltation of the humanity which we both share." In him the servant becomes Lord. "This is the secret of the humanity of Jesus Christ which has no parallel in our own" (28). It is only in him that the God who is Lord becomes a servant, and that is why the servant was exalted to the dignity of Lord. What is unique about the humanity of Jesus is that his exaltation is based on his humiliation. Sinful humanity is too slothful, too stupid, too inhuman, too dissipated, too cautious, according to Barth, for such exaltation. The history of the man Jesus on earth actualizes the being of the man Jesus, which was in the beginning with God. It also actualizes the exaltation of humanity to God implied in Jesus' being. The history of the man Jesus concerns not only the downward movement of the eternal being of God, but also a movement upward to God. Since this history entails both downward and upward movement, we can "at no level or time . . . have to do with God without having also to do with this man" (33). God chooses to be God by being with us in this man. And humanity will be human by being raised to God in this man.

The true humanity of Jesus Christ consists, then, in the history of its elevation through God. Accordingly, what makes the man Jesus truly human can only be Jesus Christ as true God. If the history of Jesus were not moved by God, it could not also be the history of a man moved by God's eternal being.

But is it not a deficiency in Jesus' humanity, that it can exist only in union with his divinity and is therefore not independent? All other human beings certainly exist independently without needing to be divine. Yes, but look at how they exist! An "independent" human existence is an existence as a prisoner of sin. When we exist independently, we lose our humanity and ensure our own death. The humanity "of the lineage of Adam" (45R) does not constitute true human existence, but rather its mendacity and lostness. In contrast to that existence, the surplus of true humanity in the existence of the human Jesus derives from the being of the Son of God. The apparent deficiency in Jesus' humanity turns out to be the achievement of a true humanity in the coexistence of the God-man.

This true humanity is achieved in a history, the history of the elevation and exaltation of human nature. It concerns "a being which does not cease as such to be a becoming" (46). The exaltation of human nature achieved in the history of Jesus cannot, therefore, be understood as a passive state. That would be an abstraction, opening the door to an "anthropology 'in a higher key,' " to a doctrine "of a humanity which is not only capable of deification, but perhaps already deified, or at any rate on the point of . . . deification" (82R).

The exaltation of human being to God is not the deification of human- ity. It was just this danger that Barth saw in the Lutheran doctrine of the *genus majestaticum,* that is, the communication of the particular characteristics of the divine essence to the human essence of Jesus Christ. For this reason he set himself against this particular Lutheran teaching, while at the same time he preserved its true significance. According to Barth, the true humanity of Jesus Christ actually consists in the exalta- tion of human being to the honor, dignity, and majesty of the divine being. Insofar as God abases himself in the godforsaken far country of the human race, humanity can actually return to God as "the spoils of the divine mercy." But this does not deify humanity. In the man Jesus, God chooses to take the human essence into himself. "It is a clothing which he does not put off. It is his temple which he does not leave. . . . It is an organ the use of which he does not renounce" (101). And thus he reveals himself as God in this man. That is why "we cannot have to do with God without at once having to do also with his human essence (our own), with the flesh of his Son (and in him with our own flesh)" (101R). But the human essence of Jesus is not itself to be honored and adored. Indeed, this human essence of Jesus does not exist in itself. The true man Jesus is present only in the concrete coexistence of God and man in one and the same history. He is the royal man in this coexistence. The royal man is precisely what God does with him and what he, with God, does with himself.

It now becomes clear why Barth must conceive of the humiliation and the exaltation of Jesus Christ not as two separate, sequential movements, but rather as one event with two corresponding movements. Dividing the humiliation and the exaltation of Jesus Christ into two distinct historical periods will assuredly result in abstracting the true man as separate from the true God. But if we understand the humiliation and the exaltation together as two simultaneous movements in one history, then the earthly existence of Jesus Christ is "perfect and complete in itself. . . . It does not need to be transcended or augmented by new qualities or further developments" (132). Everything is fulfilled in the death of Jesus Christ.

The resurrection of Jesus Christ is not the fulfillment of Jesus' being, but rather the revelation of Jesus' fulfilled being. The resurrection of Jesus Christ (along with his ascension) constitutes the revelation of the complete being of Jesus Christ, a revelation which demands faith. But this revelation adds nothing to the being of Jesus Christ. How could it be otherwise? Jesus Christ's pre-Easter existence, including his death, belongs to the dimension of revelation. The community, looking back from Jesus' resurrection, discovered that his pre-Easter existence already had "the character of revelation, and was actually revelation" (135). Thus Barth has no place for an abstract theology of the cross. Both the cross of Jesus and the way that led to it already shine with the light of revelation. The truth of the royal man was present from the start, beginning with his birth. But it was present as this man's secret, completed in his life and death, so that its completion correspondingly can be seen as the truth in his resurrection. In this way, the completed revelation of Jesus Christ occurs in his resurrection, corresponding to the existence of Jesus, which was completed in his death (cf. 141f.).

The Gospels relate the history of the life, suffering, and death of Jesus as the history of the royal man. The royal man "belongs to the very substance of Christology" (156), and hence dogmatics must relate the concrete history of his existence. Barth does this by attending to the particularly striking characteristics of Jesus' historical existence.

How Did the Royal Man Exist?

The royal man existed in such a way that he was unmistakably and unavoidably present to each and every person, without forcing himself on anyone. His presence was unforgettable and irrevocable—summoning, leading, and bringing people to decision. This distinctive presence is what led the evangelists to describe his earthly reality as "the concrete limit and measure and criterion of all other earthly reality" (166). They spoke not only of him, but of his presence and its significance.

The peculiar manner of Jesus' presence arises from the fact that "as a man he exist[ed] analogously to the mode of existence of God." The royal man is "a parallel in the creaturely world to the plan and purpose and work and attitude of God" (166). It is consistent with God's self-abasement that the one who is exalted to God "is not as such a great man." His kingship has no worldly luster, his power is powerlessness compared to the strength of others. "He who alone is rich is . . . the poorest of the poor" (167). In word and deed he turns especially toward the poor; their poverty corresponds to his. The royal man's activity shows a marked affinity for the shadowy side of human existence. This, in turn, is closely linked to the "revolutionary character of his relationship to the orders of life and value current in the world around him" (171). Precisely because Jesus proclaimed no program of his own, he called all human programs and principles into question. Living under the ruling order of his day, he nevertheless had the royal freedom to testify to the Kingdom of God, which is the limit to all human activity. No human system is fully valid for God, nor is any fully applicable to the human Jesus. God is the one who shatters all human conventions, the judge of all human constructions. And Jesus manifests this in his existence "as this (if we may risk the dangerous word) partisan of the poor, and finally as this revolutionary" (180). But in all this he is not opposed to the human race, but for it—as the Savior of the world, whose assault on the world is spearheaded by the gospel. God judges the human race only in order to restore it.

The life of the royal man was his deed. The person and work of Jesus are identical, his one momentous history. It is the history of a word, for Jesus' life-act "was his word" (194). This was, moreover, a human word, separated from other human words only by its content. It was a royal word, the word of the sovereignty of God. It sought to address the entire universe in sovereignty and reconciliation.

Jesus' concrete activity constituted a commentary on his word. The utterly "particular character of his activity" (210) was a commentary on the gospel; indeed, it was gospel itself. In the power of the gospel, which flows from the sovereignty of God, the royal man struggled against the evil in the world. He did miracles through which "a new and completely astonishing light . . . was thrown on the human situation" (220). The superabundance of the grace of God became manifest in the world through the activity of Jesus. The faith which his deeds evoked thus has something of the character of a "surplus," a "luxury" over and above the rule of faith (245). "The normal Christian of the West is all for the norm and does not understand or trust the luxury, even if it is of God himself." But "can we really understand even the rule of faith if we refuse to know anything of this surplus?" (247).

Everything we have said about the royal man Jesus must now be placed under the sign of the decisive feature of his existence, the cross. The New Testament knows nothing of "the risen and living and exalted man Jesus except as the man . . . whose story is finally the story of his passion" (249–250). The passion "is not an alien element" in Jesus' life-act. It has neither "the character of a tragic entanglement" nor the mark of a "misfortune" sent by fate or chance (251). His sufferings are rather the fulfillment of the royal man's being. The man who affirms God and his grace is crowned king on the cross. "What we have said finds its true climax and glory in the fact that . . . he finally hung on the gallows as a criminal between two other criminals, and died there, with that last despairing question on his lips, as one who was condemned and scorned and maltreated by men and abandoned by God" (252).

Jesus' death is the consummation of his entire existence: it is the hallowing of God's name, the doing of God's will, the coming of the Kingdom, all "in a form and as a power to which as a man he can only give a terrified but determined assent" (252R). And so his sufferings showed and his dying confirmed that he is "the one he is—the Son of God who is also the Son of Man. In the deepest darkness of Golgotha he enters supremely into the glory of the unity of the Son with the Father. In that abandonment by God he is the one who is directly loved by God" (252).

The fact that the royal man has this form, that the one exalted by God appears in this way, should not be made an occasion for "false seriousness" (355). The death of the royal man does not require theology to indulge in its own "foolish paradoxes" (359). For the human Jesus on the cross does not cease to exist in unity with the Son of God. It is precisely here that the unique divine-human coexistence is affirmed, for the God who in this man hangs upon the cross and there takes to himself "the alien suffering" (357) of his creature (so that humankind need not suffer it) does not cease to be God even in death. In dying, God abandons himself to death but does not surrender to death. The Son of God really dies the death of a sinner. But in dying, God plucks out the sting of death. And so in death he overcomes death. And so in death he remains highest God. And so Jesus Christ is the death of death.

The royal man Jesus shares in God's sovereign victory over death. This human being's existence is consummated not only in conforming to God's humiliation but also in sharing God's victory. Jesus is Victor! The lofty majesty of the divine mortification, the majesty of the Son of God, "works itself out in the fact that he became man, and that, fulfilling as the elect man Jesus the humiliation of God, he is the new and true and

royal man, who is triumphantly alive, even—yes, especially—in death"
(357–358). That is the mystery of the royal man. It is determined by the
mercy of God the Father and based on the majesty of God the Son. The
dignity of the royal man is constituted by the life-act of God and consummated in the life and death of the human Jesus. And not only is this
life-act free of contradiction, it triumphs over the contradiction posed by
sin and death. This human being becomes the hope of the world through
the life-act of God, which manifests the divine love in the royal man. And
so the world that returns to God as the Christian community believes
"in the grounding of the life of all men in the dying of this One, in the
fulfillment of their election in the fulfillment of his rejection, in their
glory in his shame, in their peace in his chastisement" (356).

Thus faith confesses the royal man Jesus as Victor in the light of death,
"believing that we also are victorious in him" (356). And not only can
one live a life of hope with this certainty, one can also die in it.

Notes

Introduction

1. Karl Barth, "Vorwort zum Nachdruck dieses Buches," in *Der Römerbrief*, unaltered reprint of the 1st ed. of 1919 (1963), p. [4].

2. Karl Barth, Foreword to the First Edition (1919), in *The Epistle to the Romans*, trans. by Edwyn C. Hoskyns from the sixth German edition (London: Oxford University Press, 1933), p. 2.

3. G. W. F. Hegel, *Phenomenology of Spirit*, trans. by A. V. Miller (Oxford: Clarendon Press, 1977), pp. 6–7 [translation revised].

4. Foreword to the First Edition (1919), in *The Epistle to the Romans*, p. 2.

5. Adolf von Harnack, "Postscript to My Open Letter to Professor Karl Barth," in James M. Robinson, ed., *The Beginnings of Dialectic Theology*, p. 196.

6. Barth, "Vorwort zum Nachdruck dieses Buches," p. [1].

7. Hegel, op. cit., p. 7 [revised].

8. Now the doctrine of election in the *Church Dogmatics* can be analyzed "as a historically-dialectically accurate expression of the current phase of monopoly capitalism." (Quoted from F.-W. Marquardt, *Theologie und Sozialismus. Das Beispiel Karl Barths* [1972], p. 343, where reference is made to two French analyses of the *Church Dogmatics:* A. Casanova, "Religion et Révélation dans la doctrine de Karl Barth," *Christianisme sociale* 74 [1966], pp. 199–215, and G. Mury, "L'évangile de Judas. Note sur l'élection dans le 2e tome de la dogmatique de Karl Barth," ibid., pp. 217–247.) But at the same time we are supposed to "see that the structure and content of Barth's theology is related, not only to socialism, but also to fascism and the making of fascist theory." (F. Wagner, "Theologische Gleichschaltung. Zur Christologie bei Karl Barth," in T. Rendtorff, ed., *Die Realisierung der Freiheit. Beiträge zur Kritik der Theologie Karl Barths* [1975], p. 41. For a critical rejoinder see the review by W. Krötke, *Theologische Literaturzeitung* 105 [1980], cols. 300–303.)

9. In this, as in many other respects, I am happily in agreement with W. Kreck, *Grundentscheidungen in Karl Barths Dogmatik* (1978).

10. CD IV/1, p. 765.

Karl Barth: A Tribute at His Death

1. A lecture given at the theological college of the University of Zurich on December 11, 1968.

2. See CD III/3, p. 519.

3. Karl Barth, "Gottes Gnadenwahl," *Theologische Existenz heute* 47 (1936), p. 56.

4. J. W. Goethe, *Goethes Werke,* in the edition commissioned by the Grossherzogin Sophie von Sachsen, part I, vol. 41, 2 (1903), p. 201.

5. Karl Barth, *Evangelical Theology: An Introduction,* p. 165.

6. Ibid., p. 46 [revised].

7. Ibid. [revised].

8. See CD IV/4, p. 28.

One: Barth's Life and Work

1. Cf. Karl Barth, "Nachwort," in H. Bolli, ed., *Schleiermacher-Auswahl* (Siebenstern-Taschenbuch, 1968), pp. 290–312.

2. Karl Barth, *Theological Existence Today!* trans. by R. Birch Hoyle (London: Hodder & Stoughton, 1933), p. 11.

3. Cf. Karl Barth, *Die protestantische Theologie im 19. Jahrhundert,* 3rd ed. (1960), p. 124; *Fürchte Dich nicht!* (1949), pp. 300f.; letter to W. Kaegi dated Jan. 2, 1944, cited in Eberhard Busch, *Karl Barth: His Life from Letters and Autobiographical Texts,* trans. by John Bowden (Philadelphia: Fortress Press, 1976), p. 6.

4. Karl Barth, *Church Dogmatics* (hereafter CD) IV/2, pp. 112–113.

5. Letter to G. Lindt, dated Dec. 30, 1939, and July 17, 1940, cited in Busch, *Karl Barth,* p. 12 [revised].

6. Interview with H. Fisher-Barnicol, 1964, cited in ibid., p. 12.

7. W. Härle, "Der Aufruf der 93 Intellektuellen und Karl Barths Bruch mit der liberalen Theologie," *Zeitschrift für Theologie und Kirche* 72 (1975), pp. 223f.

8. "Anfang der 1966 begonnenen Memoiren," cited in Busch, *Karl Barth,* 8.

9. Letter to J. Jaggi, dated Aug. 1, 1951, cited in ibid., p. 30.

10. Karl Barth, "Systematische Theologie," in *Lehre und Forschung an der Universität Basel zur Zeit der Feier ihres fünfhundertjährigen Bestehens* (Basel, 1960), pp. 35f.

11. Ibid., p. 36.

12. "Nachwort," in Bolli, *Schleiermacher-Auswahl,* p. 291.

13. "Selbstdarstellung" (1964), cited in Busch, *Karl Barth,* p. 40.

14. "Autobiographische Skizze" (Münster), p. 304.

15. Ibid., p. 306.

16. Ibid.

17. Cf. *Karl Barth–Martin Rade. Ein Briefwechsel,* ed. and with an introduction by C. Schwöbel (1981). See especially the Introduction, pp. 9–56.

18. Cf. Karl Barth, *The Epistle to the Romans,* pp. 8–9; "The Need and Promise of Christian Preaching," in *The Word of God and the Word of Man,* pp. 98f.

19. Karl Barth, "Music for a Guest," in *Final Testimonies,* p. 23.

20. Cf. W. Groll, *Ernst Troeltsch und Karl Barth—Kontinuität in Widerspruch* (1976), pp. 65–68, in opposition to F.-W. Marquardt, *Theologie und Sozialismus. Das Beispiel Karl Barths,* p. 127.

21. Karl Barth, *Die christliche Dogmatik im Entwurf,* 1927. (See Bibliography.)

22. CD IV/4, p. viii. (See Bibliography.)

23. *Theological Existence Today!* p. 10.

24. Karl Barth, "No! Answer to Emil Brunner," in *Natural Theology,* pp. 65–128.

25. H. Prolingheuer, *Der Fall Karl Barth. 1934–1935* (1977), pp. 198f.

26. Karl Barth, "Church and State," in *Community, State, and Church,* pp. 101–148.

27. In Karl Barth, *Eine Schweizer Stimme 1938–1945,* 2nd ed. (1948), pp. 58f.

28. "Foreword," ibid., p. 6.

29. CD IV/1, p. 312. Cf. E. Wolf, "Hinweise," *Evangelische Theologie* 22 (1962), p. 224

30. Cf. Karl Barth, " 'Conciliorum Tridentini et Vaticani I inhaerens vestigiis'?" [" 'Continuing in the Footsteps of Trent and Vatican I'?"], in idem, *Ad Limina Apostolorum* (ET 1967), p. 43.

31. Karl Barth, "Account of the Trip to Rome," in ibid., p. 17.

32. "Nachwort," in Bolli, *Schleiermacher-Auswahl.*

33. Cf. "Colleges over Schleiermacher," in A. Dekker and G. Puchinger, *De oude Barth* (Kampen, 1969), pp. 95–121.

34. "Music for a Guest," in *Final Testimonies,* pp. 20–21.

35. Ibid., p. 24 [revised].

36. Cf. CD IV/3, pp. 477–478.

37. Karl Barth, *Evangelical Theology: An Introduction,* p. 165.

38. Karl Barth, "The Principles of Dogmatics According to Wilhelm Herrmann," in *Theology and Church,* p. 258. Cf. also pp. 256–257.

39. Interview with H. Fischer-Barnicol, cited in Busch, *Karl Barth,* p. 45.

40. Karl Barth, "Moderne Theologie und Reichsgottesarbeit," *Zeitschrift für Theologie und Kirche* 19 (1909), p. 319.

41. Letter to J. Rathje, dated April 27, 1947, cited in Busch, *Karl Barth,* p. 51 [my translation].

42. Ibid.

43. "Nachwort," in Bolli, *Schleiermacher-Auswahl,* p. 291.

44. "Moderne Theologie und Reichsgottesarbeit," p. 319.

45. P. Drews, "Zum dritten Mal: Moderne Theologie und Reichsgottesarbeit," *Zeitschrift für Theologie und Kirche* 19 (1909), p. 478.

46. "Moderne Theologie und Reichsgottesarbeit," p. 320.

47. Sermon on Phil. 3:12–15, dated Sept. 26, 1909, cited in Busch, *Karl Barth,* p. 52.

48. Karl Barth, "Der christliche Glaube und die Geschichte," *Schweizerische theologische Zeitschrift* 29 (1912), p. 1.

49. Ibid.

50. Ibid., p. 2n.

51. Ibid., p. 3.

52. Ibid., p. 68n.

53. Adolf von Harnack, "Postscript to My Open Letter to Professor Karl Barth," in Robinson, *The Beginnings of Dialectic Theology,* p. 186.

54. "Der christliche Glaube und die Geschichte," p. 4.

55. Ibid., p. 5.

56. Ibid., p. 7.

57. Ibid., p. 53.

58. Ibid., p. 55.

59. Ibid., p. 58.

60. Ibid., p. 61.

61. Ibid., p. 68.

62. Ibid., p. 71.

63. Ibid., p. 72.

64. Ibid., p. 70.

65. "Autobiographische Skizze" (Münster), p. 306.

66. Cf. "Der christliche Glaube und die Geschichte," pp. 71f.

67. Karl Barth, "Rückblick," in H. Dürr, A. Fankhauser, and W. Michaelis, eds., *Das Wort sie sollen lassen stahn. Festschrift für Professor D. Albert Schädelin* (Bern, 1950), pp. 3f.

68. "Nachwort," in Bolli, *Schleiermacher-Auswahl*, p. 293.

69. CD I/1, p. 82.

70. Ibid.

71. H. Kutter, *Sie müssen. Ein offenes Wort an die christliche Gesellschaft* (1904), pp. 185f.

72. Karl Barth, "Jesus Christus und die Soziale Bewegung," *Der Freie Aargauer* 6 (1911), Nos. 153 (second section), 154, 155, and 156 (second section), dated Dec. 23, 26, 28, and 30, respectively.

73. "Nachwort," in Bolli, *Schleiermacher-Auswahl*, p. 294.

74. Karl Barth, "Religion und Sozialismus," an unpublished lecture delivered in Baden on Dec. 7, 1915 (in the Karl Barth-Archiv, Basel).

75. Karl Barth, "Kriegszeit und Gottesreich," a lecture delivered in Basel on Nov. 15, 1915, cited in Busch, *Karl Barth*, p. 87.

76. Karl Barth, "Das Eine Notwendige," *Die XX. Christliche Studenten-Konferenz* (Aarau, 1916), March 13–15, pp. 10f.

77. Cf. "Autobiographische Skizze" (Münster), p. 307, and "Autobiographische Skizze" (Bonn), p. 312.

78. Karl Barth, "Auf das Reich Gottes warten," *Der freie Schweizer Arbeiter* 9 (1916), nos. 49 and 50 (Sept. 15 and 22), reprinted in Karl Barth and Eduard Thurneysen, *Suchet Gott, so werdet ihr leben!*" p. 175.

79. Ibid., p. 177.

80. Ibid., p. 178.

81. Ibid., p. 189.

82. Karl Barth, "Past and Future," in Robinson, *The Beginnings of Dialectic Theology*, p. 41.

83. R. Lejeune, ed., *Christoph Blumhardt, Eine Auswahl aus seinen Predigten, Andachten und Schriften*, vol. 2 (1925), p. 513.

84. "Past and Future," in Robinson, *The Beginnings of Dialectic Theology*, p. 42 [my translation].

85. Karl Barth, *Das christliche Leben* (1979), p. 144.

86. Karl Barth, *Der Römerbrief* (1st ed.), p. 175.

87. CD IV/3, pp. 168–173.

88. "Autobiographische Skizze" (Bonn), p. 312.

89. Letter to Thurneysen, dated Nov. 11, 1918, in *Revolutionary Theology in the Making*, p. 45 [my translation].

90. "Nachwort," in Bolli, *Schleiermacher Auswahl*, p. 294.

91. "Autobiographische Skizze" (Münster), p. 307.

92. *Der Römerbrief* (1st ed.), p. 1.

93. Ibid., p. 7.

94. Ibid., p. 344.

95. Ibid., p. 14.

96. Ibid., pp. 7f.

97. Ibid., p. 135.

98. Ibid., p. 141.

99. Ibid., p. 303.

100. Ibid., p. 332.

101. Ibid., p. 303.

102. Ibid., p. 387.

103. Ibid., p. 234 (revised). Cf. also "The Christian's Place in Society," in *The Word of God and the Word of Man*, p. 299: "The revolution which is before all revolutions."

104. *Der Römerbrief* (1st ed.), pp. 241, 246, and 250.

105. Ibid., p. 392.

106. Ibid., p. 170.

107. Ibid., p. 344.

108. J. Fangmeier, *Erziehung in Zeugenschaft* (1964), p. 46.

109. Karl Barth, "Abschied," *Zwischen den Zeiten* 11 (1933), p. 536.

110. "The Christian's Place in Society," in *The Word of God and the Word of Man*, p. 323.

111. Ibid., p. 273.

112. Ibid., p. 325 [revised].

113. Ibid., pp. 276–277 [revised].

114. Ibid., p. 280.

115. Ibid., p. 285 [revised].

116. Ibid., p. 289 [revised].

117. Ibid., p. 283.

118. Ibid., pp. 285–286 [revised].

119. Ibid., p. 287

120. Ibid., p. 286 [revised].

121. Ibid., p. 294.

122. Ibid., p. 305.

123. Ibid., p. 303.

124. Ibid., p. 321.

125. Ibid., p. 322.

126. "Autobiographische Skizze" (Münster), p. 308.

127. Karl Barth, "Biblical Questions, Insights, and Vistas," in *The Word of God and the Word of Man*, pp. 51–52 [revised].

128. Ibid., p. 55 [revised].

129. "The Christian's Place in Society," p. 274; "The Need and Promise of Christian Preaching," p. 116; "The Word of God and the Task of the Ministry," pp. 208 and 211, in *The Word of God and the Word of Man*.

130. "Biblical Questions," in *The Word of God and the Word of Man*, p. 55 [revised].

131. "Preface to the Second Edition," *The Epistle to the Romans*, pp. 10–11.

132. Letter to Thurneysen, dated Oct. 27, 1920, in *Revolutionary Theology in the Making*, p. 53.

133. "Foreword to the Second Edition," in Robinson, *The Beginnings of Dialectic Theology*, p. 94.

134. *The Epistle to the Romans*, pp. 141–142 [my translation].

135. Hans Urs von Balthasar, *Karl Barth*, p. 77. (ET *The Theology of Karl Barth*, New York: Holt, Rinehart & Winston, 1971.)

136. E. Przywara, *Gott. Fünf Vorträge über das religionsphilosophische Problem*, in idem, *Schriften*, vol. 2 (1962), p. 286.

137. *The Epistle to the Romans*, p. 2.

138. *Der Römerbrief*, 2nd ed., p. 118. [This clause, as far as I can tell, is not translated in *The Epistle to the Romans.*—TRANS.]

139. *The Epistle to the Romans*, p. 29 [my translation].

140. Ibid., p. 137.

141. Plato, *Parmenides* 156d6–e3.

142. CD II/1, p. 636; cf. pp. 631–638.

143. *The Epistle to the Romans*, p. 314 [my translation].

144. "Foreword to the Second Edition," in Robinson, *The Beginnings of Dialectic Theology*, p. 94.

145. Ibid., p. 93 [revised].

146. Ibid., [revised].

147. "Foreword to the First Edition," in ibid., p. 61 [revised].

148. "Foreword to the Second Edition," in ibid., p. 96 [revised].

149. "Foreword to the Third Edition," in ibid., p. 128.

150. Ibid., p. 127.

151. "Foreword to the Second Edition," in ibid., p. 91.

152. Ibid., p. 96.

153. "Foreword to the Third Edition," in ibid., p. 127.

154. T. Rendtorff, "Radikale Autonomie Gottes," in *Theorie des Christentums* (1972), p. 164.

155. In this connection cf. H. J. Adriaanse, *Zu den Sachen selbst* (The Hague, 1974).

156. Letter to Thurneysen, dated Dec. 19, 1922, in *Revolutionary Theology in the Making*, p. 123.

157. "The Need and Promise of Christian Preaching," in *The Word of God and the Word of Man*, pp. 98, 101.

158. "The Word of God and the Task of the Ministry," in ibid., pp. 198–212.

159. Ibid., p. 207 [revised].

160. Ibid., p. 186 [revised].

161. T. Stadtland, *Eschatologie und Geschichte in der Theologie des jungen Karl Barth* (1966), p. 11.

162. "The Need and Promise of Christian Preaching," in *The Word of God and the Word of Man*, p. 98.

163. Friedrich Gogarten, "The Holy Egoism of the Christian," in Robinson, *The Beginnings of Dialectic Theology*, pp. 82–87.

164. Adolf Jülicher, "A Modern Interpreter of Paul," in ibid., pp. 72–81.

165. Emil Brunner, "*The Epistle to the Romans* by Karl Barth," in ibid., pp. 63–71.

166. Rudolf Bultmann, "Karl Barth's *Epistle to the Romans* in Its Second Edition," in ibid., pp. 100–120.

167. Paul Tillich, "Die Überwindung des Religionsbegriffs in der Religionsphilosophie," in idem, *Gesammelte Aufsätze,* ed. by R. Albrecht, vol. 1 (7th ed., 1972), pp. 3f.

168. Rudolf Bultmann, "Liberal Theology and the Latest Theological Movement," in idem, *Faith and Understanding,* vol. 1, trans. by Louise Pettibone Smith (New York: Harper & Row, 1969), pp. 30f.

169. Karl Barth, "Fifteen Answers to Professor von Harnack," in Robinson, *The Beginnings of Dialectic Theology,* pp. 167–170.

170. Adolf von Harnack, "Fifteen Questions," in ibid., pp. 165–166.

171. Ibid., p. 166.

172. Barth, "Fifteen Answers," in ibid., p. 170.

173. Ibid., p. 167.

174. Cf. *The Epistle to the Romans,* pp. 45f., 78f., 113f., and 140f.

175. "Biblical Questions," pp. 67f., 70f., and "The Need and Promise of Christian Preaching," pp. 116f., in *The Word of God and the Word of Man;* "Church and Theology," in *Theology and Church,* pp. 297f.

176. Ludwig Feuerbach, *Lectures on the Essence of Religion,* trans. by Ralph Manheim (New York: Harper & Row, 1967), p. 17; Karl Barth, "Ludwig Feuerbach," in *Theology and Church,* p. 223.

177. Barth, "Ludwig Feuerbach," in *Theology and Church,* p. 226.

178. Ibid., p. 230.

179. Cf. also CD IV/2, pp. 81–83.

180. Karl Barth, "The Word in Theology from Schleiermacher to Ritschl," in *Theology and Church,* pp. 215–216.

181. Hans Urs von Balthasar, *Karl Barth,* p. 78.

182. Karl Barth, "The Doctrinal Task of the Reformed Churches," in *The Word of God and the Word of Man,* p. 253.

183. "The Word in Theology," in *Theology and Church,* p. 216.

184. Karl Barth, "Roman Catholicism: A Question to the Protestant Church," in *Theology and Church,* p. 314 [revised].

185. Karl Barth, "Zum Geleit," in H. Heppe and E. Bizer, *Die Dogmatik der evangelisch-reformierten Kirche,* 2nd ed. (1958), pp. viif.

186. Circular letter to Thurneysen, dated May 18, 1924, in *Revolutionary Theology in the Making,* p. 185.

187. E. Peterson, "Was ist Theologie?" in G. Sauter, ed., *Theologie als Wissenschaft* (1971), pp. 136, 151, and 134.

188. Karl Barth, "Möglichkeiten liberaler Theologie heute," *Schweizerische Theologische Umschau* 30 (1960), p. 101; but this already appeared in a letter to Thurneysen, dated April 20 [sic; actually April 8—TRANS.], 1924, in *Revolutionary Theology in the Making,* p. 177; and also in Karl Barth, "Unsettled Questions for Theology Today," in *Theology and Church,* p. 72. In this connection, cf. F. Overbeck, *Christentum und Kultur,* ed. by C. A. Bernoulli (1919; reprint, 1963), p. 16.

189. *Die christliche Dogmatik im Entwurf,* p. ix.

190. Ibid., p. 16.

191. "The Word of God and the Task of the Ministry," in *The Word of God and the Word of Man,* p. 217.

192. Werner Elert, *Karl Barths Index der verbotenen Bücher* (Leipzig: A. Deichert, 1935).

193. *Die christliche Dogmatik im Entwurf,* p. 230.

194. Ibid., p. 231.

195. Ibid., p. 232.

196. Ibid., p. 237.

197. Ibid., p. 188.

198. Ibid., p. 189.

199. Ibid., pp. 239f.

200. Ibid., pp. 436 and 437.

201. Karl Barth, *Ethics,* trans. by Geoffrey W. Bromiley (New York: Seabury Press, 1981), p. 1.

202. Ibid., p. 14.

203. Ibid., p. 16 [revised].

204. Karl Barth, "Church and Culture," in *Theology and Church,* pp. 334–354, and esp. pp. 344–347.

205. Karl Barth, "Schicksal und Idee in der Theologie," in idem, *Gesammelte Vorträge,* vol. 3 (1957), pp. 54–92.

206. Ibid., p. 85.

207. Karl Barth, "Das erste Gebot als theologisches Axiom," in idem, *Gesammelte Vorträge,* vol. 3, pp. 127–143; Barth had already, in 1927, insisted that "the reality of the Word of God must be reckoned as a theological axiom" (*Die christliche Dogmatik im Entwurf,* p. 105).

208. "Das erste Gebot," in *Gesammelte Vorträge,* vol. 3, p. 141.

209. "Abschied," *Zwischen den Zeiten* 11 (1933), p. 536.

210. Karl Barth, "Das Evangelium in der Gegenwart," *Theologische Existenz heute* 25 (1935), p. 17.

211. Ibid.

212. "Abschied," *Zwischen den Zeiten* 11 (1933), p. 542.

213. H. Gollwitzer, "Reich Gottes und Sozialismus bei Karl Barth," *Theologische Existenz heute* 169 (1972), p. 10n, in support of F.-W. Marquardt, *Theologie und Sozialismus. Das Beispiel Karl Barths.*

214. Cf. also CD I/1, p. xi.

215. *Theological Existence Today!* p. 9.

216. Gollwitzer, "Reich Gottes," p. 59.

217. K. Scholder, *Die Kirchen und das Dritte Reich,* vol. 1, *Vorgeschichte und Zeit der Illusionen 1918–1934* (1977), p. 553 and p. 834 n. 83; H. Stoevesandt, " 'Von der Kirchenpolitik zur Kirche!' Zur Entstehungs geschichte von Karl Barths Schrift 'Theologische Existenz heute!' im Juni 1933," *Zeitschrift für Theologie und Kirche* 76 (1979), pp. 118–138.

218. "Music for a Guest," in *Final Testimonies,* p. 24; For evidence against the misinterpretation of Barth as apolitical, cf. Karl Barth, "Reply" to Emil Brunner in "The Christian Community in the Midst of Political Change," in *Against the Stream,* p. 118.

219. Cf. CD I/1, p. 80.

220. Karl Barth, *How I Changed My Mind*, p. 44.

221. Cf. CD III/4, p. xii.

222. CD I/1, p. 17. Cf. "Foreword to the Second Edition," in Robinson, *The Beginnings of Dialectic Theology*, p. 93, where Barth writes that the biblical author "can speak in my name, and I myself can speak in his name." [See pp. 75–76 above.]

223. CD I/1, p. 501; II/2, p. 13.

224. CD I/2, p. 27.

225. "No!" in *Natural Theology*, p. 73 [my translation].

226. CD I/1, p. ix.

227. Karl Barth, *Anselm: Fides Quaerens Intellectum* (ET 1962).

228. *How I Changed My Mind*, p. 43.

229. *Anselm: Fides Quaerens Intellectum*, p. 11.

230. Ibid., p. 27.

231. Ibid., p. 28 [revised].

232. Ibid., p. 51.

233. Ibid., p. 117 [revised].

234. Ibid., p. 52.

235. Ibid., p. 53.

236. Ibid., pp. 41–42.

237. Cf. H. U. von Balthasar, *Karl Barth*, pp. 93–181.

238. CD I/1, p. x.

239. From the literature on the problem of analogy cf. especially the following: H. U. von Balthasar, *Karl Barth;* E. Jüngel, "Die Möglichkeit theologischer Anthropologie auf dem Grunde der Analogie," *Evangelische Theologie* 22 (1962), pp. 535–557; idem, *God as the Mystery of the World*, trans. by Darrell L. Guder (Grand Rapids: Wm. B. Eerdmans Publishing Co., 1983); G. Söhngen, "Analogia fidei: Gottähnlichkeit allein aus Glauben?" *Catholica* (Münster) 3 (1934), pp. 113–136; idem, "Analogia fidei: Die Einheit in der Glaubenswissenschaft," *Catholica* 3 (1934), pp. 176–208; idem, Review of Hermann Diem, *Kritischer Idealismus in theologischer Sicht*, in *Catholica* 4 (1935), pp. 38–42; idem, "Bonaventura als Klassiker der analogia fidei," *Wissenschaft und Weisheit* 2 (1935), pp. 97–111; idem, "Analogia entis in analogia fidei," in E. Wolf, C. von Kirschbaum, and R. Frey, eds., *Antwort. Karl Barth zum siebzigsten Geburtstag* (1956), pp. 266–271; idem, *Analogie und Metapher* (1962); idem, "Die Weisheit der Theologie durch den Weg der Wissenschaft," *Mysterium Salutis* 1 (1965), pp. 905–977.

240. Cf. CD II/1, pp. 260–261, and E. Jüngel, *Gottes Sein ist im Werden*, 3rd ed. (1976); cf. also C. E. Gunton, *Becoming and Being: The Doctrine of God in Charles Hartshorne and Karl Barth* (Oxford, 1978), esp. pp. 115–185.

241. CD II/1, p. 261; cf. W. Härle, *Sein und Gnade* (Berlin: Walter de Gruyter, 1975).

242. Cf. "The Christian's Place in Society," in *The Word of God and the Word of Man*, p. 278.

243. *How I Changed My Mind*, p. 43.

244. Cf. CD II/2, pp. 7–8; III/2, p. 403.

245. CD II/1, p. 5.

246. CD I/1 and I/2.
247. CD II/1 and II/2.
248. CD II/1.
249. CD II/2, ch. 7.
250. CD II/2, ch. 8.
251. CD II/2, p. 557.
252. Cf. W. Sparn, " *'Extra Internum.'* Die christologische Revision der Prädestinationslehre in Karl Barths Erwählungslehre," in T. Rendtorff, ed., *Die Realisierung der Freiheit* (1975), pp. 44–75.
253. CD II/2, p. 96 [my translation].
254. CD II/2, p. 103 [revised].
255. Ibid., pp. 162–175.
256. CD II/1, p. 350.
257. Ibid.
258. CD I/1, p. 440.
259. CD II/2, pp. 133–145.
260. Ibid., pp. 103 and 54.
261. Ibid., p. 54.
262. CD II/1, pp. 639–640; III/2, pp. 463f.; related to the Parousia of Jesus Christ, CD IV/3, pp. 295–296.
263. CD I/1, pp. 425f.
264. Cf. CD IV/3, pp. 477–478.
265. CD II/2, p. 539.
266. CD III/1, §41.2, 3
267. CD III/2.
268. CD III/3.
269. CD III/4.
270. CD III/1, p. 44.
271. Ibid., p. 234.
272. Ibid., p. 232.
273. Ibid., pp. 99f., 189f., and 302f.
274. Ibid., p. 185.
275. CD III/2, p. 40 [revised].
276. Ibid., p. 319.
277. Ibid., p. 344.
278. Ibid., p. 349.
279. Ibid., p. 424 [revised].
280. Ibid., p. 632.
281. Ibid., p. 321.
282. Ibid.
283. CD III/3, p. 351. In this way, Barth puts his earlier positive expression to a negative use. Cf. W. Krötke, *Sünde und Nichtiges bei Karl Barth* (1970).
284. CD III/3, p. 58 [revised].
285. CD IV/1, p. ix.
286. CD IV/4 and *Das christliche Leben.*
287. CD IV/1, p. ix [revised].
288. CD IV/2, p. ix.
289. Cf., e.g., CD IV/1, p. 304.

290. Karl Barth, "Evangelical Theology in the 19th Century," in *The Humanity of God*, p. 11; also *Evangelical Theology: An Introduction*, p. 12.

291. CD IV/2, p. 10.

292. *The Humanity of God*, p. 46.

293. Ibid., p. 52.

294. CD IV/1, ch. 14.

295. CD IV/2, ch. 15.

296. CD IV/3, ch. 16.

297. Cf. CD IV/3, §72.2.

298. CD IV/4 *(Baptism as the Foundation of the Christian Life)*.

299. *Das christliche Leben*, p. 443. [ET *The Christian Life: Church Dogmatics IV/4: Lecture Fragments.*]

300. Karl Barth, *The Teaching of the Church Regarding Baptism*, trans. by Ernest A. Payne (London: SCM Press, 1948).

301. CD IV/3, p. 136.

302. *Das christliche Leben*, p. 254.

303. Karl Barth, *Christ and Adam: Man and Humanity in Romans 5*, trans. by T. A. Smail (1952; ET 1956, New York: Macmillan & Co., 1968), pp. 113–114 [revised].

304. Karl Barth, "Gospel and Law," in *Community, State, and Church*, p. 72 [my translation].

305. CD IV/1, p. 501; cf. pp. 499–501 [revised].

306. CD IV/2, p. 275.

307. CD IV/3, p. 538.

308. Cf. CD I/2, §17; "No!" in *Natural Theology;* CD I/2, pp. 263–265; II/1, §26; III/4, pp. 263–265.

309. CD I/2, §17.3.

310. CD IV/3, pp. 110–153.

311. Ibid., p. 110.

312. Ibid., pp. 136f.

313. Ibid., p. 114.

314. [IV/3, §69—TRANS.]

315. Cf. O. Herlyn, *Religion oder Gebet* (1979).

316. CD IV/1, pp. 94f. and 576.

317. Hans Küng, *Justification: The Doctrine of Karl Barth and a Catholic Reflection*, trans. by Thomas Collins, Edmund E. Tolk, and David Granskou (Philadelphia: Westminster Press, 1981), p. 278 [revised].

318. Cf. E. Jüngel, *Karl Barths Lehre von der Taufe* (Zurich, 1968).

319. CD IV/4, p. 210.

320. H. Stirnimann, "Barths Tauf-Fragment, CD IV/4," *Freiburger Zeitschrift für Philosophie und Theologie* 15 (1968), p. 23.

321. R. Schlüter, *Karl Barths Tauflehre* (1973).

322. CD IV/1, p. 661.

323. CD IV/2, p. 621.

324. Ibid., p. 620.

325. Ibid., p. 621 [revised].

326. "Church and State," in *Community, State, and Church*, p. 101. [The German title of this essay is *Rechtfertigung und Recht*, "Justification and Justice."]

327. Karl Barth, "The Christian Community and the Civil Community," in *Against the Stream.*

328. "Church and State," in *Community, State, and Church,* p. 102 [revised].

329. "The Christian Community and the Civil Community," in *Against the Stream,* p. 25.

330. Ibid., p. 32 [revised].

331. Ibid., p. 34 [revised].

332. CD IV/3, p. 119.

333. Cf., e.g., the reception of Barth in the English-speaking world: S. W. Sykes, ed., *Karl Barth: Studies of His Theological Method* (Oxford University Press, 1979).

334. H. Bouillard, *Karl Barth,* vol. I: *Genèse et évolution de la théologie dialectique;* vol. II, 1.2: *Parole de Dieu et existence humaine* (Paris, 1957); cf. also idem, "Logik des Glaubens," *Quaestones disputatae* 29 (1966), pp. 73–96.

335. The Catholic discussion also includes E. Riverso, *Intorno al pensiero di Karl Barth* (Padua, 1951); idem, *La teologia esistenzialistica di Karl Barth* (Naples, 1955); J. Hamer, *Karl Barth: L'occasionalisme théologique de Karl Barth* (Paris, 1949).

336. G. Gloege, "Barth, Karl," in *Die Religion in Geschichte und Gegenwart,* 3rd ed., vol. 1, col. 897.

337. Cf. CD IV/3, §69.3.

338. *Die protestantische Theologie im 19. Jahrhundert,* 3rd ed., 1960 (see Bibliography for ET).

339. G. Gloege, "Barth, Karl," col. 897.

340. Karl Barth, "Gottes Gnadenwahl," *Theologische Existenz heute* 47 (1936), p. 56.

Two: Barth's Theological Beginnings

1. Karl Barth, "Möglichkeiten liberaler Theologie heute," *Schweizerische theologische Umschau* 30 (1960), p. 101.

2. Ibid., p. 95.

3. Ibid.

4. Ibid., p. 101.

5. Franz Overbeck, *Christentum und Kultur. Gedanken und Anmerkungen zur modernen Theologie,* ed. by C. A. Bernoulli from Overbeck's literary estate, 1919. Cf. the critical description of Overbeck's literary estate and of Bernoulli's editing in M. Tetz, *Overbeckiana,* part II: *Der wissenschaftliche Nachlass Franz Overbecks* (Basel, 1962).

6. Overbeck, *Christentum und Kultur,* p. 16.

7. Karl Barth, "Unsettled Questions for Theology Today," in *Theology and Church,* p. 72 [revised].

8. Barth recalled it in a sharper form: "*through* audacity." Note also the other changes made in his citation!

9. Cf. H. Schindler, *Barth und Overbeck* (1936; reprint, 1974).

10. Letter from Barth to Thurneysen, dated Jan. 5, 1920, in *Karl Barth-Eduard*

Thurneysen. Briefwechsel, Bd. I: 1913–1921, ed. by E. Thurneysen, *Karl Barth-Gesamtausgabe,* vol. 5 (1973), p. 364.

11. Franz Overbeck, *Über die Christlichkeit unserer heutigen Theologie,* 2nd ed. (1903; reprint, 1963).

12. They can be found in R. Wehrli, *Alter und Tod des Christentums bei Franz Overbeck* (Dissertation submitted to the University of Zurich, 1977).

13. From Overbeck's estate; also in Wehrli, *Alter und Tod,* pp. 114f.

14. Overbeck, *Über die Christlichkeit unserer heutigen Theologie,* p. 25.

15. Ibid., p. 27.

16. Ibid., p. 34.

17. From Overbeck's estate; also in Wehrli, *Alter und Tod,* p. 141.

18. Overbeck, *Über die Christlichkeit unserer heutigen Theologie,* p. 35.

19. Ibid.

20. Ibid., p. 36.

21. Ibid.

22. Cf. Hegel's famous thesis that "the thought of the world . . . appears only when actuality is already there cut and dried after its process of formation has been completed. . . . When philosophy paints its grey in grey it cannot be rejuvenated but only understood. The owl of Minerva spreads its wings only with the falling of dusk" (*Philosophy of Right,* trans. by T. M. Knox [London: Oxford University Press, 1942]).

23. From Overbeck's estate; also in Wehrli, *Alter und Tod,* pp. 140f.

24. Ibid., also in Wehrli, *Alter und Tod,* p. 137.

25. Overbeck, *Christentum und Kultur,* p. 199.

26. Ibid., p. 204.

27. Ibid., p. 206.

28. Note the epochal consciousness!

29. "Unsettled Questions," in *Theology and Church,* p. 57.

30. Ibid.

31. Ibid., p. 55.

32. "Biblical Questions, Insights, and Vistas," in *The Word of God and the Word of Man,* p. 53 [revised].

33. Cf. also ibid., p. 55.

34. Ibid., p. 66 [revised].

35. Ibid. [revised].

36. Ibid., p. 88.

37. Letter from Barth to Agnes von Zahn, dated Dec. 23, 1935, cited in Eberhard Busch, *Karl Barth,* p. 115.

38. Letter from Barth to Thurneysen, dated April 20, 1920, in *Revolutionary Theology in the Making,* p. 50 [revised].

39. Ibid.

40. [The reference is to Harnack's famous lectures published in German as *Das Wesen des Christentums* (The Essence of Christianity); ET *What Is Christianity?* trans. by Thomas Bailey Saunders (New York: Harper & Row, 1957).] Overbeck's comment is from *Christentum und Kultur,* p. 68.

41. Overbeck, *Christentum und Kultur,* p. 68.

42. Ibid.

43. Ibid., p. 66, cited in Barth, "Unsettled Questions," in *Theology and Church*, p. 63.

44. Barth, "Unsettled Questions," p. 63, in reference to *Christentum und Kultur*, p. 64.

45. Overbeck, *Christentum und Kultur*, p. 64.

46. Karl Barth, *The Epistle to the Romans*, p. 314 [my translation].

47. Karl Barth, "The Word of God and the Task of the Ministry," in *The Word of God and the Word of Man*, p. 186 [revised].

48. CD III/3, p. 351 and passim.

49. W. Krötke, *Sünde und Nichtiges bei Karl Barth* (Berlin, 1970), p. 16.

50. *The Epistle to the Romans*, p. 137.

51. Ibid., p. 113.

52. Ibid., p. 79.

53. Ibid., p. 113 [revised].

54. Unlike his younger friend Friedrich Nietzsche, Overbeck was free of any "bristling hostility to Christianity and religion" in his life and thought. But he found himself "entirely unsuited to be an advocate for Christianity" and recognized his duty to "demonstrate the *finis Christianismi* to modern Christianity" (Overbeck, *Christentum und Kultur*, pp. 288f.).

55. "Unsettled Questions," in *Theology and Church*, p. 73.

56. Ibid.

57. Ibid. [revised].

58. Ibid.

59. Ibid. [revised].

60. Ibid. [revised].

61. Karl Barth, *Das christliche Leben*, p. 443.

62. Ibid., pp. 445–447.

63. Ibid., pp. 447f.

64. Christoph Blumhardt, *Haus-Andachten nach Losungen und Lehrtexten der Brüdergemeine*, 1916, p. 101. See also Barth, *Das christliche Leben*, p. 449 n. 120.

65. *Das christliche Leben*, pp. 449f.

66. Karl Barth, "Auf das Reich Gottes warten," *Der freie Schweizer Arbeiter* 9 (1916), nos. 49 and 50 (Sept. 15 and 22), reprinted in Karl Barth and Eduard Thurneysen, *Suchet Gott, so werdet ihr leben!* p. 175.

67. In his review of the Blumhardts' devotions, Barth said that "for me, this is the most immediate and incisive Word of God in the midst of the world's need that has yet come to light in this time of war. I am left with the impression that *this* is just what we would like to say now—if we could!" (*Suchet Gott*, p. 175). And he observes, not without approval, that Blumhardt, who knows "nothing, absolutely nothing of the theology of the war" also "amicably but impartially bypasses the dogmatic, the liberal, the 'religious-moral,' and us socialist theologians" (p. 176). "He wishes to say nothing clever, to launch no fireworks, to score no points, but simply to tell us of the divine-worldly truth as it has encountered him" (ibid.). This book of devotions appealed to Barth because he was convinced "that our cause— our hope— is now better served by household devotions than by treatises. Our dialectic has come to a dead end, and if we are to be healthy and strong we must

start over and become as children" (p. 177). Blumhardt's book is a means to that end, because in it "God's cause is advocated to the world and not against the world" (ibid.). It seems noteworthy to Barth that Blumhardt, in opposition to traditional Pietism, can "love the world and stay true to God" (ibid.). "Blumhardt always proceeds from God's existence, power, and design; he starts with God" (p. 178). The human response to this is to wait for the God who makes all things new —a response which is "at first introspective, but essentially revolutionary" (p. 189). "Divine and human action are, for Blumhardt, closely intermeshed . . . , not dialectically, but materially" (p. 190). Barth therefore hoped that many would read this book of meditations "through neither dark nor rose-colored glasses," and be enticed to "think its thoughts after it" (p. 191).

Three years later, on the occasion of the deaths of Friedrich Naumann and Christoph Blumhardt, Barth, writing for the newspaper *Neuer Freier Aargauer* [The New Free Aargauer], tried to honor both men by siding with one of them: by saying no to Naumann and yes to Blumhardt. "The future" for which Naumann strove "was past before it could become present. . . . If anything has been exposed as a lie, abolished, and annihilated through the present world catastrophe, then it is the religious and political thought-world of Friedrich Naumann. One cannot pass so close to truth and escape unpunished" ("Past and Future," in Robinson, *The Beginnings of Dialectic Theology,* p. 40 [revised]. Blumhardt, on the contrary, did not need any such religious thought-world. "That unhappy word 'religion,' . . . with which man, tired of life, turns to the distant unknown, was no longer used in Möttlingen and Boll" (p. 41). Instead of that, both Blumhardts inquired after the living God. "What appeared again in Boll that was new and in accord with the New Testament can be comprehended in a single word: *hope,*" indeed "hope for all, for humankind . . . , hope for the physical side of life" (pp. 41–42). In Barth's judgment, Blumhardt's lifelong concern— entirely different from Naumann's—was nothing less than "the victory of the future over the past" (p. 45).

68. *Das christliche Leben,* p. 444.
69. "Unsettled Questions," in *Theology and Church,* p. 56.
70. Ibid.
71. Karl Barth, *Der Römerbrief* (1st ed.), p. 241.
72. Ibid., p. 246.
73. Ibid., p. 250.
74. Ibid., p. 252.
75. *The Epistle to the Romans* (2nd ed.), p. 10 [revised].
76. Ibid.
77. Ibid., p. 75.
78. Ibid. [my translation].
79. Ibid., p. 113 [revised].
80. Ibid., pp. 137–138 [revised].
81. Ibid., p. 137.
82. Ibid., pp. 3–4.
83. Friedrich Schleiermacher, *On Religion: Speeches to Its Cultured Despisers,* trans. by John Oman (New York: Harper & Brothers, 1958), p. 101 [revised].
84. Plato, *Parmenides,* trans. by Francis MacDonald Cornford (New York: Humanities Press, 1951), 156d6–7 [revised].

85. Ibid., 156d7–e1 [revised].

86. "The Word of God and the Task of the Ministry," in *The Word of God and the Word of Man,* p. 186 [revised].

87. "Foreword to the Second Edition," in Robinson, *The Beginnings of Dialectic Theology,* p. 93.

88. Ibid., p. 94.

89. Adolf Jülicher, "A Modern Interpreter of Paul," in Robinson, *The Beginnings of Dialectic Theology,* pp. 72–81. This review was first published in *Die christliche Welt* [The Christian World] in 1920. Later that year in the same journal, Rudolf Bultmann, who later expressly welcomed the second edition of *The Epistle to the Romans,* made several very critical remarks about the first edition. Barth recalled this in his old age, not without a certain satisfaction: he thought it "not uninteresting that Rudolf Bultmann, who later on came to share an important theological common ground with me for a while, put off this first edition with unmistakable annoyance, . . ." calling it " 'an enthusiastic renewal' —and even more sharply, an 'arbitrary adaption of the Pauline Christ-myth' " ("Vorwort zum Nachdruck dieses Buches," in *Der Römerbrief,* unaltered reprint of the 1st ed. of 1919 [1963], p. [3].

90. Jülicher, "A Modern Interpreter of Paul," in Robinson, *The Beginnings of Dialectic Theology,* p. 72.

91. "Foreword to the First Edition," in ibid., p. 62.

92. Jülicher, "A Modern Interpreter of Paul," in ibid., p. 81 [revised].

93. "Foreword to the First Edition," in ibid., p. 61 [revised].

94. Ibid.

95. Ibid., pp. 62 and 61.

96. Letter from Barth to Thurneysen, dated Jan. 1, 1916, in *Revolutionary Theology in the Making,* p. 36 [revised].

97. Cf. Adolf von Harnack, "Postscript to My Open Letter to Professor Karl Barth," in Robinson, *The Beginnings of Dialectic Theology,* p. 186.

98. Jülicher, "A Modern Interpreter of Paul," in ibid., p. 81.

99. Ibid., p. 80 [revised].

100. "Foreword to the First Edition," in ibid., p. 61.

101. Jülicher, "A Modern Interpreter of Paul," in ibid., p. 81.

.102. Ibid., p. 79.

103. Ibid.

104. Friedrich Gogarten, "The Holy Egoism of the Christian: An Answer to Jülicher's Essay, 'A Modern Interpreter of Paul,' " in Robinson, *The Beginnings of Dialectic Theology,* p. 83 [revised].

105. Jülicher, "A Modern Interpreter of Paul," in ibid., p. 81 [revised].

106. Ibid., p. 80 [revised].

107. Gogarten had already published an essay under the title "Between the Times" (Robinson, *The Beginnings of Dialectic Theology,* pp. 277–282). This title was later given to the soon-to-be famous journal.

108. Jülicher, "A Modern Interpreter of Paul," in Robinson, *The Beginnings of Dialectic Theology,* pp. 78–79 [revised].

109. Ibid., p. 73 [revised].

110. Ibid., p. 72.

111. Ibid., p. 73.

112. "Foreword to the Second Edition," in ibid., p. 98.

113. Graf Yorck had identified the maxim "to admit of practice" as the "legal basis of argument in science" (*Briefwechsel Wilhelm Dilthey und Graf Paul Yorck* [1923], p. 42).

114. "Foreword to the Second Edition," in Robinson, *The Beginnings of Dialectic Theology,* p. 94.

115. Ibid., p. 96.

116. Ibid. [revised].

117. Ibid. [revised].

118. *The Epistle to the Romans,* p. 12.

119. "Foreword to the First Edition," in Robinson, *The Beginnings of Dialectic Theology,* p. 62 [revised].

120. "Foreword to the Second Edition," in ibid., p. 95 [revised].

121. Ibid., p. 94.

122. Ibid., p. 93 [revised].

123. Ibid. [revised].

124. Ibid.

125. Ibid., pp. 95–96 [revised].

126. Ibid., p. 96 [revised].

127. Ibid., p. 89.

128. Ibid., p. 92.

129. Ibid., p. 91.

130. Ibid., p. 95.

131. Ibid. [revised].

132. Ibid.

133. Ibid. [revised].

134. E. Thurneysen, "Wo Liebe ist, da ist Gott" (sermon on Luke 10:25–37), in Karl Barth and Eduard Thurneysen, *Suchet Gott, so werdet ihr leben!* pp. 109f.

135. CD I/1, pp. 4–5 [revised].

136. "Foreword to the Second Edition," in Robinson, *The Beginnings of Dialectic Theology,* p. 95 [revised].

137. Ernst Troeltsch, "Über historische und dogmatische Methode in der Theologie," in idem, *Gesammelte Schriften,* vol. 2 (Tübingen: J. C. B. Mohr, 1922; reprint, Aalen: Scientia, 1962), pp. 729–734.

138. "Foreword to the Second Edition," in Robinson, *The Beginnings of Dialectic Theology,* p. 94.

139. Ibid.

140. "Foreword to the Third Edition," in ibid., pp. 126–129.

141. Ibid., p. 126 [revised].

142. Rudolf Bultmann, "Karl Barth's *Epistle to the Romans* in Its Second Edition," in ibid., p. 120.

143. "Foreword to the Third Edition," in ibid., p. 127.

144. Ibid.

145. Ibid. [revised].

146. Ibid., p. 128.

147. Ibid.

148. Ibid.

149. Ibid., p. 127.

150. Ibid., p. 128.

151. Cf. Martin Kähler, *The So-called Historical Jesus and the Historic, Biblical Christ,* trans. by Carl E. Braaten (Philadelphia: Fortress Press, 1964), Introduction, p.10. [For the (untranslated) essays containing the expression *sturmfreies Gebiet,* see Martin Kähler, *Der sogenannte historische Jesus und der geschichtliche, biblische Christus,* 2nd ed. (1896), pp. 147, 200f.]

152. Letter from Barth to Thurneysen, dated Nov. 11, 1918, in *Revolutionary Theology in the Making,* p. 45.

153. *The Epistle to the Romans,* pp. 426–427 [my translation]. Cf. also CD II/2, p. 548.

154. Compare the following with M. E. Brinkman, *Karl Barths socialistische stellingname* (Baarn, 1981).

155. Letter from Barth to Thurneysen, dated Nov. 11, 1918, in *Revolutionary Theology in the Making,* p. 46.

156. Ibid., pp. 45–46 [revised].

157. Letter from Barth to Thurneysen, dated Sept. 9, 1917, in *Revolutionary Theology in the Making,* p. 42 [revised: the last sentence in this citation is lacking in the translation].

158. Karl Barth, "Nachwort," in Bolli, *Schleiermacher-Auswahl,* p. 292.

159. Cf. Karl Barth, "Der Pfarrer, der es den Leuten recht macht. Eine religiös-soziale Predigt" (sermon on Ezek. 13:1–16), in *Die christliche Welt* 30 (1916), cols. 262–267.

160. "Autobiographische Skizze" (Münster), p. 306.

161. In *Der Freie Aargauer. Offizielles Organ der Arbeiterpartei des Kantons Aargau* 6 (1911), nos. 153 (second section), 154, 155, and 156 (second section), Dec. 23, 26, 28, and 30.

162. L. Ragaz, "Was ist uns Jesus Christus?" in idem, *Weltreich, Religion, und Gottesherrschaft,* vol. 1 (1922), pp. 77–109.

163. H. Kutter, *Sie müssen. Ein offenes Wort an die christliche Gesellschaft* (1904), passim, esp. pp. 185f. and 188f.

164. In this thesis, Barth was expressing the viewpoint of a well-known contemporary theologian and writer. For a demonstration of the influence of Kutter on Barth, see H.-A. Drewes, *Das Unmittelbare bei Hermann Kutter. Eine Untersuchung im Hinblick auf die Theologie des jungen Karl Barth* (Dissertation submitted to the University of Tübingen, 1979).

165. "Jesus Christus und die soziale Bewegung," *Der freie Aargauer* 6, no. 153 (Dec. 23, 1911), second section, p. 1, col. 1.

166. Ibid.

167. Ibid.

168. Ibid., col. 2.

169. Ibid.

170. Ibid.; Barth cites the materialist philosopher J. Dietzgen, "Die Religion der Sozialdemokratie," in idem, *Schriften,* vol. 1 (Berlin, 1961), p. 216.

171. "Jesus Christus und die soziale Bewegung" (Dec. 23, 1911), p. 1, col. 2.

172. Ibid.

173. Ibid., cols. 2f.

174. Ibid., col. 3.

175. Ibid.

176. Ibid., p. 2, col. 1.

177. Ibid.

178. "Jesus Christus und die soziale Bewegung," in *Der Freie Aargauer,* 6, no. 154 (Dec. 26, 1911), p. 1, col. 1.

179. Ibid., col. 2. In an unpublished lecture titled "Christus und die Sozial-democraten" (Christ and the Social Democrats), given at the district meeting of the Social Democratic Party of the district *(Bezirk)* of Lenzburg on April 25, 1915 (Karl Barth-Archiv, Basel), Barth develops a variation of the same theme: Jesus was no politician, social reformer, preacher of morals, or founder of a religion, but a man whose life was solely directed to bringing the authentic this-worldly reality, which alone deserves to be called reality, to light—and not some other-worldly thing. Barth would remain true to this understanding of reality for the rest of his life, even if he expounded it in an entirely different manner: what really deserves to be called reality in this world must be determined on the basis of God, that is, the Kingdom of God.

180. "Jesus Christus und die soziale Bewegung" (Dec. 26, 1911), p. 1, col. 2.

181. Ibid.

182. Ibid., col. 3.

183. Ibid.

184. Ibid.

185. Ibid., p. 2, col. 1. Cf. F. C. Oetinger, "Leib, Soma," in idem., *Biblisches und Emblematisches Wörterbuch, dem Tellerischen Wörterbuch und Anderer falschen Schrifterklärungen entgegen gesetzt* (1776), p. 407.

186. "Jesus Christus und die soziale Bewegung," *Der Freie Aargauer* 6, no. 155 (Dec. 28, 1911), p. 2, col. 2.

187. Ibid., col. 3.

188. Ibid.

189. W. Hüssy, "Offener Brief an Herrn Karl Barth, Pfarrer in Safenwil," in *Zofinger Tagblatt. Täglicher Anzeiger fur den Bezirk Zofingen und die Mittelschweiz,* 40, no. 29 (Feb. 3, 1912), p. 1, cols. 3–5.

190. Ibid., col. 4.

191. Karl Barth, "Antwort auf den offenen Brief des Herrn W. Hüssy in Aarburg," in *Zofinger Tagblatt* 40, no. 34 (Feb. 9, 1911), p. 4, cols. 1f.

192. "Jesus Christus und die soziale Bewegung," in *Der Freie Aargauer,* 6, no. 156 (Dec. 30, 1911), second section, p. 1, col. 1.

193. Ibid., col. 2.

194. Ibid., col. 1. Sweeping criticism of the theology of the Reformers is frequent in the early Barth. Particularly noteworthy is his reference to how Calvin's concept of the godly state on earth led him—despite the fact that Calvin, having learned of the poverty in Geneva, immediately held that it was a "natural, necessary fact of life"—to Jesus' description of the Kingdom of God as a circumstance of complete love for God and one another. ("Evangelium und Sozialismus," unpublished lecture given before the Worker's Union of Küngoldingen, Feb. 1, 1914 [Karl Barth-Archiv, Basel].)

195. "Jesus Christus und die soziale Bewegung" (Dec. 30, 1911), second section, p. 1, col. 2.

196. Ibid.

197. Ibid.

198. Ibid.

199. Letter from Barth to Thurneysen, dated Feb. 5, 1915, in *Revolutionary Theology in the Making,* p. 28.

200. "Autobiographische Skizze" (Münster), pp. 306f.

201. Karl Barth, "Die innere Zukunft der Sozialdemokratie," unpublished sketch dated Aug. 12, 1915 (Karl Barth-Archiv, Basel).

202. Cited in T. Heuss, *Friedrich Naumann. Der Mann, das Werk, die Zeit,* 2nd ed. (1949), pp. 325f.

203. Barth had already previously rejected Naumann's hopes, charging that Naumann had no real understanding of what is crucial to social democracy. In a review of Naumann's newspaper *Die Hilfe* [Aid] and its contents during the year 1913, Barth wrote: "What distinguishes the aspirations of social democracy is above all that it is politically serious about the absolute, about God. . . . But for this inmost essence of social democracy, for its revolutionary unrest, for its radicalism, for its enthusiasm—*Die Hilfe* has *no,* I repeat, *no* understanding. It has a good understanding for the industrial-democratic element, for the whole apparatus of reform . . . ; but for what gives social democracy its uncanny greatness, it has nothing but . . . a disapproving shake of the head over its 'unrealistic ideals.' " In place of those ideals it invites social democracy "to make 'common cause' arm in arm with a decisive liberalism" (*Die christliche Welt* 17 [1914], cols. 777f.).

204. Karl Barth, "Religion und Sozialismus," an unpublished lecture given in Baden on Dec. 7, 1915 (Karl Barth-Archiv, Basel).

205. This expression is used by U. Dannemann, *Theologie und Politik im Denken Karl Barths* (1977), p. 21, inter alia.

206. Barth apparently first found a description of this opposition between the Kingdom of God and religion in Christoph Blumhardt. "The Kingdom of God is something different from what the religions are"; indeed, "nothing is more inimical to the progress of the Kingdom of God than a religion, which will turn us back into pagans." *Christoph Blumhardt. Eine Auswahl aus seinen Predigten, Andachten und Schriften,* ed. by R. Lejeune, vol. 4 (1932), p. 247, and vol. 2 (1925), p. 513.

207. "Jesus Christus und die soziale Bewegung" (Dec. 23, 1911), second section, p. 1, col. 1.

208. Review of *Die Hilfe,* in *Die christliche Welt* 17 (1914), loc. cit. col. 777.

209. Letter from Barth to Thurneysen, dated Nov. 11, 1918, in *Revolutionary Theology in the Making,* p. 45.

210. Karl Barth, "Wo ist nun Dein Gott?" in Karl Barth and Eduard Thurneysen, *Suchet Gott, so werdet ihr leben!* pp. 97f.

211. Ibid., p. 100.

212. Ibid., p. 102.

213. Ibid., pp. 102f. In the first edition of 1917, it is put this (probably better) way: "who *comes* with power into the midst of everything that is," and: "seeks *to be* honored" (p. 99).

214. *Suchet Gott, so werdet ihr leben!* p. 103.

215. Cf. p. 97: "If . . . there were no supposed 'religious need,' then, put plainly, we would have no need of God!"

216. Ibid., p. 102.

217. *Der Römerbrief* (1st ed.), p. 72.

218. Ibid., p. 260.

219. Ibid.

220. Ibid., p. 366.

221. U. Dannemann, *Theologie und Politik im Denken Karl Barths,* p. 60; cf. n. 138.

222. *Der Römerbrief* (1st ed.), p. 392.

223. Immanuel Kant, *Religion Within the Limits of Reason Alone,* trans. by Theodore M. Greene and Hoyt M. Hudson (New York: Harper & Row, 1960), pp. 118 and 120.

224. G. W. F. Hegel, *Lectures on the Philosophy of Religion,* ed. by E. B. Speirs (London: Kegan Paul, 1895), p. 79.

225. F.-W. Marquardt, *Theologie und Sozialismus. Das Beispiel Karl Barths* (Munich: Chr. Kaiser Verlag, 1972), p. 127; cf. also B. Wielenga, *Lenins Weg zur Revolution* (1971), p. 433.

226. Cf. W. Groll, *Ernst Troeltsch und Karl Barth—Kontinuität im Widerspruch* (1976), pp. 65f. One notes that the first edition of the *Römerbrief,* though dated 1919, was already delivered to the publisher in December 1918, while Lenin's article first appeared in German translation on November 20, 1918 (cf. Lenin's letter to J. A. Berun; W. W. Worowski and A. A. Joffe, cited in Groll, pp. 65f.)

227. *Der Römerbrief* (1st ed.), p. 387.

228. Ibid., pp. 7f., cf. p. 307.

229. Ibid., p. 14.

230. Ibid., p. 135.

231. Also a political metaphor of socialist origins!

232. Ibid., pp. 140f.

233. Ibid., p. 141. [Cf. Martin Luther, "The Freedom of a Christian," trans. by. W. A. Lambert, in *Luther's Works,* vol. 31 (Philadelphia: Fortress Press, 1957), p. 354; also reprinted as *Christian Liberty* (Philadelphia: Fortress Press, 1957), p. 17.—TRANS.]

234. *Der Römerbrief* (1st ed.), p. 141.

235. Ibid., p. 332.

236. Ibid.

237. Cf. W. Groll, *Ernst Troeltsch und Karl Barth,* p. 67.

238. "Foreword to the First Edition," in Robinson, *The Beginnings of Dialectic Theology,* p. 61.

239. *Der Römerbrief* (1st ed.), p. 331.

240. Ibid., pp. 331f.

241. Ibid., p. 332.

242. Ibid., p. 303.

243. Ibid., p. 378. [Translations of Barth's citations from Troeltsch are taken from Ernst Troeltsch, *The Social Teaching of the Christian Churches* (1912), trans. by Olive Wyon (New York: Harper & Brothers, 1931), p. 82 (revised).]

244. *Der Römerbrief* (1st ed.), pp. 378f.

245. Ibid., p. 379.

246. Ibid., p. 381.

247. Ibid., p. 387.

248. F.-W. Marquardt, *Theologie und Sozialismus. Das Beispiel Karl Barths,* pp. 135f.

249. Ibid., p. 132.

250. Karl Barth, "Das Evangelium in der Gegenwart" [The Gospel Today], *Theologische Existenz heute* 25 (1935), p. 17.

251. *Der Römerbrief* (1st ed.), p. 380.

252. Ibid., p. 390.

253. Ibid., p. 391.

254. Ibid., p. 234; cf. pp. 331f. Cf. also Karl Barth, "The Christian's Place in Society," in *The Word of God and the Word of Man,* p. 299.

255. *The Epistle to the Romans* (2nd ed.), p. 481 [revised].

256. Ibid. [revised].

257. Ibid., pp. 481–482 [revised].

258. Ibid., p. 483.

259. Ibid., p. 485 [revised].

260. Ibid., p. 488 [revised].

261. Ibid., p. 493 [revised].

262. Ibid. [revised].

263. Ibid., p. 496 [revised].

264. Cf. Aristotle, *Poetics* 1457b1–4.

265. Luther is somewhat similar in this respect. Cf. Eberhard Jüngel, "Metaphorische Wahrheit," in idem, *Entsprechungen: Gott—Wahrheit—Mensch* (Munich: Chr. Kaiser Verlag, 1980), p. 100, and idem, *Zur Freiheit eines Christenmenschen. Eine Erinnerung an Luthers Schrift,* 2nd ed. (Munich: Chr. Kaiser Verlag, 1981), pp. 40–49.

266. CD IV/2, p. 543 [revised].

267. Ibid. [revised].

268. Ibid., p. 544 [revised]. Cf. CD III/4, p. 545, where, analogously, it is said that "the Christian community both can and should also espouse the cause of this or that branch of social progress or even socialism—in the form most helpful at a specific time and place and in a specific situation. But its decisive word cannot consist in the proclamation of social progress or socialism. It can consist only in the proclamation of the revolution of *God* against 'all human ungodliness and unrighteousness' (Rom. 1:18), that is, in the proclamation of his Kingdom as it has already come and still comes."

269. CD IV/2, p. 546 [revised].

Three: Gospel and Law

1. Karl Barth, "Gospel and Law," in *Community, State, and Church,* p. 71.

2. Reference may be made to two brief discussions which are more appropriate than the glut of literature because they are concerned with the problem posed by the fact that the Word of God comes in two ways: as gospel and as law. The best introduction to Luther's teaching about the difference between them is in Gerhard Ebeling, *Luther: An Introduction to His Thought* (Philadelphia: Fortress Press, 1972), pp. 110–158. A helpful introduction to Barth's relationship to Luther's teaching of law and gospel is H. J. Iwand, "Zwischen Karl Barth und

Luther," a series of propositions for debate that he directed to Gustaf Wingren in 1950 (see his *Nachgelassene Werke,* vol. 2, ed. by D. Schellong and K. G. Steck [1966], pp. 401–405). Along with these, one may consult W. Joest, "Karl Barth und das lutherische Verständnis von Gesetz und Evangelium," *Kerygma und Dogma* 24 (1978), pp. 86–103. B. Klappert's *Promissio und Bund. Gesetz und Evangelium bei Luther und Barth* (1976) is a rather heavily schematic treatment of the issue.

3. WA 36, p. 9. [References to this and other untranslated works of Luther which Jüngel cites are given for the Weimar edition (WA) of Luther's works, *D. Martin Luthers Werke. Kritische Gesamtausgabe* (Weimar: Hermann Böhlau, 1883–). References to translated works are given for the American Edition (LW), *Luther's Works* (St. Louis: Concordia Publishing House, and Philadelphia: Fortress Press, 1955–1976).—TRANS.]

4. WA 36, pp. 9–10.

5. Ibid., p. 10.

6. Ibid.

7. Cf. ibid., p. 18: "St. Jerome has also written much about this, but like one who is color-blind: They speak of the law, which tells one to circumcise, to make offerings, not to eat this and that, etc. Thereby they make the gospel into a new law, which teaches how one should pray and fast, how you should become a monk or nun or go to church, etc. That is what they call making a distinction, but is really more of a jumble, for they do not even know themselves what they are chattering about."

8. Ibid., p. 11.

9. Ibid., p. 12.

10. Ibid., pp. 12–13.

11. Ibid., p. 13.

12. Ibid., pp. 14–15.

13. Ibid., p. 17.

14. Ibid., pp. 19–21.

15. *Operationes in Psalmos* (1519–1521), WA 5, p. 543.

16. *Die dritte Disputation gegen die Antinomer* (1538), WA 39/1, pp. 535–536.

17. Ibid., p. 536.

18. Sermon on Gal. 3:23–29, WA 36, p. 17.

19. Cf. *Lectures on Galatians* (1535), LW 26, pp. 336f.

20. *Enarrationes epistolarum et euangeliorum, quas postillas vocant* (1521), WA 7, p. 502.

21. *Die erste Disputation gegen die Antinomer* (1537), WA 39/1, p. 361.

22. WA 40/1, p. 207.

23. CD I/1, pp. 137–139.

24. Cf. ibid., pp. 136f. and 366f.

25. "Gospel and Law," in *Community, State, and Church,* p. 71.

26. Ibid. Barth planned to deliver the lecture in Barmen on Oct. 7, 1935, but was barred from doing so. A Pastor Immer read the lecture for Barth while Barth was escorted to the border adjacent to Basel the same evening.

27. Ibid., p. 72 [revised].

28. Ibid. [revised].

29. CD I/2, p. 311.

30. CD II/1, p. 210 [revised].
31. Ibid., p. 539.
32. Ibid., p. 541.
33. Ibid.
34. Ibid., p. 542.
35. CD II/2, pp. 65f.
36. *The Bondage of the Will,* LW 33, p. 61.
37. CD II/1, pp. 35–36 [revised].
38. CD IV/1, p. 359.
39. CD IV/3, p. 370 [my translation].
40. CD IV/1, pp. 359–360.
41. Ibid., pp. 360–361.
42. Ibid., p. 361.
43. Ibid., p. 362 [revised].
44. Ibid., p. 363.
45. Ibid. [revised].
46. Ibid., pp. 363–364 [revised].
47. Ibid., pp. 364–365.
48. Ibid., p. 365.
49. Ibid., pp. 365–366.
50. Ibid., p. 368.
51. Ibid., p. 370.
52. Ibid., p. 371.
53. Ibid.
54. Ibid., p. 372 [revised].
55. Ibid., p. 373 [revised].
56. Cf. ibid., pp. 391–397.
57. Ibid., p. 396.
58. CD IV/2, p. 381.
59. "Gospel and Law," in *Community, State, and Church,* p. 80. Cf. the criticism of Barth's formula in, among others, Gerhard Ebeling, "Reflections on the Doctrine of the Law," in Ebeling, *Word and Faith,* trans. by James W. Leitch (Philadelphia: Fortress Press, 1963), pp. 247–281, esp. pp. 262–270 (and particularly p. 267n and 268 n. 1). Also cf. Rudolf Bultmann, *The Second Letter to the Corinthians,* trans. by Roy A. Harrisville (Minneapolis: Augsburg Publishing House, 1985), p. 87, where he characterizes Barth's thesis as "largely the opposite of what Paul says." B. Klappert, *Promissio und Bund,* offers an apologetic. It should be noted that Barth, for his part, when he describes the law as the form of the gospel, here too gives a content to the gospel: grace. But it is poor logic.
60. "Gospel and Law," in *Community, State, and Church,* p. 80.
61. Ibid., p. 84.
62. Ibid., p. 89 [revised].
63. Ibid., p. 94.
64. Ibid., p. 71.
65. Ibid., p. 95.
66. CD IV/3, p. 370. Cf. also pp. 370–371, where Barth writes: "With the conception of the gospel and the law which supports and integrates them (cf. my work *Evangelium und Gesetz* [Gospel and Law], 1935, and CD II/2, §36–39),

these statements belong to the ironclad substance of my dogmatics as hitherto presented. This does not prove that they are right. But I must declare in passing that I have not been convinced that they are wrong by what has been urged against them by theologians of Lutheran background and upbringing to whom they are particularly repugnant (e.g., W. Elert, P. Althaus, E. Sommerlath, H. Thielicke, W. Joest, and, in the *Antwort* of 1956 [see note 239 of chapter 1 above], G. Wingren, and with particular circumspection Edmund Schlink). There are still far too many things which I cannot understand in the counterthesis, advanced with varying degrees of sharpness and consistency by these authors, that the gospel and the law differ and are even antithetical in significance and function.

"I do not understand (1) with what biblical or inherent right, on the basis of what conception of God, his work and his revelation, and above all in the light of what Christology, they can speak, not of *one* intrinsically true and clear Word of God, but of *two* Words in which he speaks alternately and in different ways to man according to some unknown rule.

"I do not understand (2) the meaning of a supposed *gospel* the content of which is exhausted by the proclamation of the forgiveness of sins and which is to be received by man in a purely inward and receptive faith; nor of a supposed *law* which as an abstract demand can only be an external ordinance on the one side but on the other is ordained to accuse man and therefore to indicate and prepare the way for the gospel.

"I do not understand (3) how there can be ascribed to the apostle Paul a conception of the law of God in which he admittedly does not agree with the self-understanding of the Old Testament, or in plain terms contradicts it, the more so when this conception is so obviously false in the light of the Old Testament itself, and especially of what we know (M. Noth, G. von Rad, J. H. Kraus) of the Old Testament concept of law in its positive relationship to the covenant of Yahweh. I am surprised how lightly this very disturbing problem of exegetical presupposition is taken.

"I do not understand (4) how the concept of a supposed law can be attained or exploited except (as in the 16th century, and with very serious consequences in the 17th, 18th and 19th) by appealing to the idea of a 'natural law' and therefore of a general natural revelation, or by falling back on a most primitive form of biblicism; and I am surprised that this dilemma has not been accepted as a warning.

"I do not understand (5) how there can be achieved in this way what is at issue in the present context, namely, how the confrontation of man by this supposed law can give him a serious, precise and inescapable knowledge of human transgression and therefore of human sin, or how far such a law can have the divine authority and power to bring man into subjection to its judgment. Nor do I understand how or to what degree man is to find himself on the way to the gospel by falling short of this law.

"Do I not understand Martin Luther if I do not understand these things? I certainly do not understand the Luther of the conflict against the Antinomians, whom I also encounter with something of a shock in not a few of his earlier and later writings. Nor do I understand that which subsequently developed as classical Lutheran teaching on this subject. But when we consider the varied wealth of the secrets enclosed in the Weimar edition, do we not have to admit that there is perhaps more than one Luther in this respect, and that there is one Luther to whom appeal cannot be made by the classical teaching or its modern expositors and exponents who oppose me in his name? For my part, I might set alongside the critical contributions of Wingren and Schlink the essay of H. Gollwitzer which appears along with theirs in the *Antwort,* or more recently the book of Gerhard Heintze, *Luthers Predigt von Gesetz und Evangelium* (1958), from which I learn that, especially on the fairly broad lines of his exposition and application of the Decalogue, and specifically of the first commandment, Luther in his sermons on the Sermon on the Mount and the passion story could *also* follow a program (*Nihil nisi Christus praedicandus* [Nothing but Christ must be preached]) in relation to which it might well be asked whether I am not quite a good Lutheran after all. But to maintain this, or at least to be able to appeal on my behalf to an authentic Luther, I should have to be as well versed in the intricacies of the Weimar edition as those who, equipped and claimed for this task both by nature and grace, attack me with 'their' Luther. Hence my only option is, either with Luther or against him, to stand by the insight which I have previously attained and proved." [Revised.]

67. Cf. the criticisms of Werner Elert, *Law and Gospel,* trans. by Edward H. Schroeder (Philadelphia: Fortress Press, 1967); Helmut Thielicke, *Theologische Ethik,* vol. 1 (Tübingen: J. C. B. Mohr [Paul Siebeck], 1951), pp. 188–214. [The material Jüngel cites is not included in the English translation of Thielicke edited by William Lazareth.—TRANS.]. And cf. Paul Althaus, *The Divine Command,* trans. by Franklin Sherman (Philadelphia: Fortress Press, 1966).

68. Karl Barth, *Ethics,* p. 3.

69. CD II/2, p. 509. In the first two editions of II/2, this sentence reads: "As the doctrine of God's command, ethics interprets the law as the form of the gospel, i.e., as the sanctification which comes to man through the electing God." In the third edition of 1959, Barth revised this sentence through the addition of the words "norm of the," apparently because of the logical confusion present in the original. In so doing, however, he introduced a grammatical confusion ("Norm *des*") which I have rectified in my citation ("Norm *der*"). [Barth's revision is not included in the English translation of CD II/2; I have added it, following Jüngel's reading of *der* for Barth's *des.*—TRANS.]

70. D. Hollaz, *Examen theologicum acroamaticum* (1706; reprint 1971), Partis Tertiae Theologiae Sectio II, Caput II, Quaestio 13 (p. 76).

71. CD II/2, p. 3.

72. Ibid., p. 509 [revised].

73. P. Althaus, *The Divine Command,* p. 28 [revised]. [A literal translation of Althaus' complaint about Barth's "failure to distinguish between the several epochs of God's dealings" would be: "the epochlessness (*or* timelessness) of Barth's understanding of God's activity."—TRANS.]

74. Ibid., p. 28 n. 23.

75. CD II/2, p. 509.

76. Ibid., p. 512.

77. Ibid., p. 511.

78. Ibid., p. 516.

79. Ibid., p. 535.

80. CD I/2, p. 369 [revised].

81. Ibid., p. 364.

82. Ibid., p. 266.

83. Ibid., p. 364 [revised].

84. Ibid., p. 369.

85. Ibid., p. 365.

86. Ibid., p. 364.

87. Ibid., p. 367. [For the reference to Calvin, see note 100 below.—TRANS.]

88. *Formula Concordiae,* Solida Declaratio II, 19ff. [Cf. *The Book of Concord,* ed. by Theodore G. Tappert (Philadelphia: Fortress Press, 1959), p. 524. Barth's citations from the *Formula* are in Latin; we will use the English translation of this edition in subsequent citations.—TRANS.]

89. CD I/2, p. 364; cf. *Formula Concordiae,* Solida Declaratio II, 44 (*Book of Concord,* p. 529) [revised].

90. Ibid. [revised]; cf. *Formula Concordiae,* Solida Declaratio II, 20 (*Book of Concord,* p. 525) [revised].

91. Ibid. Cf. *Formula Concordiae,* Solida Declaratio II, 22 (*Book of Concord,* p. 525) [revised].

92. Ibid. Cf. *Formula Concordiae,* Solida Declaratio II, 64 (*Book of Concord,* p. 533).

93. Cf., e.g., Martin Luther, *The Freedom of a Christian (Christian Liberty),* LW 31, p. 365 (reprinted in *Christian Liberty,* Philadelphia: Fortress Press, 1957, p. 28): "This is a truly Christian life. Here faith is truly active through love, that is, it finds expression in works of the freest service, cheerfully and lovingly done, with which a man willingly serves another without hope of reward; and for himself he is satisfied with the fullness and wealth of his faith." The German version puts it even better: "With zest and love faith goes about its work" (WA 7, p. 34).

94. CD I/2, p. 364 [revised].

95. Ibid., p. 266 [revised].

96. Ibid.

97. Ibid., p. 267.

98. LW 26, p. 387.

99. WA 36, p. 14.

100. LW 26, p. 6. Compare this against Calvin's dictum on James 1:25, which Barth cites approvingly: "Blessedness is to be found in doing" (*Commentaries on the Catholic Epistles,* trans. by John Owen, Grand Rapids: Wm. B. Eerdmans Publishing Co., 1948, p. 298), as well as with Barth's own commentary: "In this doing of the Word, which is true hearing, we are saved and blessed" (CD 1/2, p. 366).

101. WA 39/I, p. 383.

102. WA 40/I, p. 561.

103. LW 16, p. 6.

104. Ibid., p. 7 [my translation].

105. CD II/2, p. 511 [revised].

106. Ibid., p. 512.

107. Georg Calixtus, *Epitomes theologiae moralis pars prima,* in idem., *Ethische Schriften, Werke in Auswahl,* vol. 3, ed. by I. Mager (1970), pp. 25–242; cf. p. 90.

108. CD I/2, p. 782.

109. Ibid., pp. 782–783 [revised].

110. Ibid., p. 783.

111. Martin Heidegger, "Overcoming Metaphysics," in idem, *The End of Philosophy,* trans. by Joan Stambaugh (New York: Harper & Row, 1973), p. 99.

112. CD I/2, p. 787.

113. Ibid.

114. Ibid., p. 783 [revised].

115. Ibid., p. 795.

116. Cf. Karl Barth, *Das christliche Leben,* p. 2.

117. CD I/2, p. 881 [revised].

118. Ibid., p. 883.

Four: The Royal Man: A Christological Reflection on Human Dignity

1. CD IV/1, p. 125.

2. CD I/2, p. 123.

3. CD II/1, p. 203.

4. CD I/1, p. 350.

5. CD IV/1, p. 52.

6. Ibid., p. 158 [revised].

7. Ibid.

8. CD IV/1, §59.1.

9. CD IV/2, §64.2.

10. CD IV/1, p. 166.

11. Ibid., p. 167 [revised].

12. Ibid., p. 175.

13. Ibid., p. 186.

14. Ibid.

15. Ibid., p. 202.

16. Ibid., p. 158.

17. Ibid., p. 204 [revised].

18. Cf. *The Humanity of God,* p. 43.

19. CD IV/2, p. 10. For the remainder of this chapter, references to CD IV/2 will be in the text, enclosed in parentheses. [Where a translation has been revised, this is indicated by the letter R.]

Bibliography

The works of Karl Barth listed below are those cited most frequently in the Notes.

Ad Limina Apostolorum: An Appraisal of Vatican II (1967). Trans. from the German by Keith R. Crim. Richmond: John Knox Press, 1968.

Against the Stream: Shorter Post-War Writings 1946–52. Ed. by Ronald Gregor Smith. New York: Philosophical Library, 1954.

Anselm: Fides Quaerens Intellectum (1931). Trans. of 2nd ed. (1958) by Ian W. Robertson. Cleveland: World Publishing Co., Meridian Books, 1962.

"Autobiographische Skizze" (Bonn). In *Fakultätsalbum der Evangelisch-Theologischen Fakultät in Bonn* (1946). Reprinted in *Karl Barth-Gesamtausgabe*, vol. 5 (1971). (See next entry.)

"Autobiographische Skizze" (Münster). In *Fakultätsalbum der Evangelisch-Theologischen Fakultät in Münster* (1927). Reprinted in *Karl Barth–Rudolf Bultmann. Briefwechsel 1922–1966*. Ed. by B. Jaspert. Zurich: Theologischer Verlag, 1971. *Karl Barth-Gesamtausgabe*, vol. 5, *Briefe*. [ET *Karl Barth–Rudolf Bultmann: Letters, 1922–1966*, ed. by Bernd Jaspert, tr. and ed. by Geoffrey W. Bromiley (Grand Rapids: Wm. B. Eerdmans Publishing Co., 1981).]

Die christliche Dogmatik im Entwurf. Erster Band: Die Lehre vom Worte Gottes. Prolegomena zur christlichen Dogmatik. Munich: Chr. Kaiser Verlag, 1927. [This untranslated volume should be distinguished from the later *Dogmatik im Grundriss*, 1947 (ET *Dogmatics in Outline*, 1949).]

Das christliche Leben. Die Kirchliche Dogmatik IV/4, Fragmente aus dem Nachlass. Vorlesungen 1959–1961. Ed. by H.-A. Drewes and E. Jüngel, in *Karl Barth-Gesamtausgabe*, vol. 2. 2nd ed. Zurich: Theologischer Verlag, 1979. [ET *The Christian Life: Church Dogmatics IV/4: Lecture Fragments*. Trans. by Geoffrey W. Bromiley. Edinburgh: T. & T. Clark; Grand Rapids: Wm. B. Eerdmans Publishing Co., 1981.]

Church Dogmatics (abbreviated CD). (English translation of *Die Kirchliche Dogmatik*.) Ed. by G. W. Bromiley and T. F. Torrance. Edinburgh: T. & T. Clark, 1936–1969, 1975.

Church Dogmatics IV/4. The Christian Life (Fragment): Baptism as the Founda-

tion of the Christian Life. Trans. by Geoffrey W. Bromiley. Edinburgh: T. & T. Clark; Grand Rapids: Wm. B. Eerdmans Publishing Co., 1969.

Community, State, and Church: Three Essays. Trans. by A. M. Hall, G. Ronald Hower, and Stanley Godman. Intro. by Will Herberg. Garden City, N.Y.: Doubleday & Co., Anchor Books, 1960.

The Epistle to the Romans. Trans. by Edwyn C. Hoskyns (from the 6th German edition of *Der Römerbrief*). London: Oxford University Press, 1933. [Quotations from the 2nd edition (1922) have—unless otherwise stated—been taken from this English edition and revised where necessary.]

Ethics. Trans. by Geoffrey W. Bromiley. New York: Seabury Press, 1981.

Evangelical Theology: An Introduction (1962). Trans. by Grover Foley. New York: Holt, Rinehart & Winston, 1963.

Final Testimonies. Trans. by Geoffrey W. Bromiley. Grand Rapids: Wm. B. Eerdmans Publishing Co., 1977.

How I Changed My Mind. Richmond: John Knox Press, 1966.

The Humanity of God. Trans. by John Newton Thomas and Thomas Wieser. Richmond: John Knox Press, 1960.

"Nachwort," in H. Bolli, ed., *Schleiermacher-Auswahl.* Siebenstern-Taschenbuch, 1968.

Natural Theology: "Nature and Grace" by Emil Brunner and the Reply "No!" by Karl Barth (1934). Trans. by Peter Fraenkel. London: Geoffrey Bles, 1946.

Die protestantische Theologie im 19. Jahrhundert. 3rd ed., 1960. [ET *Protestant Theology in the Nineteenth Century: Its Background and History.* Trans. by Brian Cozens and John Bowden. London: SCM Press, 1972; Valley Forge: Judson Press, 1973.]

Revolutionary Theology in the Making: Barth–Thurneysen Correspondence, 1914–1925. Trans. by James D. Smart. Richmond: John Knox Press, 1964.

James M. Robinson, ed. *The Beginnings of Dialectic Theology.* Trans. by Keith R. Crim and Louis De Grazia. Richmond: John Knox Press, 1968. [Trans. from Jürgen Moltmann, ed., *Anfänge der dialektischen Theologie*, 2 vols., Munich: Chr. Kaiser Verlag, 1962–63. Includes many essays and occasional writings of Barth and others. The forewords to the several editions of Barth's commentary on Romans have generally been quoted from this volume.]

Der Römerbrief. Unaltered reprint of the 1st ed. of 1919. 1963.

Suchet Gott, so werdet ihr leben! by Karl Barth and Eduard Thurneysen. 2nd ed. Munich: Chr. Kaiser Verlag, 1928.

Theological Existence Today! (ET of *Theologische Existenz heute!* 1933.) Trans. by R. Birch Hoyle. London: Hodder & Stoughton, 1933. [This pamphlet was followed by a series of pamphlets, written by Barth and others, bearing the general title *Theologische Existenz heute.*]

Theology and Church: Shorter Writings 1920–1928. Trans. by Louise Pettibone Smith. New York: Harper & Row, 1962.

The Word of God and the Word of Man (1924). Trans. by Douglas Horton, 1928. Reprint, Gloucester, Mass.: Peter Smith, 1978.